There are a few critical basic criteria to achieve for growth and success in the Infrastructure business. Refresh your understanding of the industry, where your business fits and what it offers before setting your vision for development and growth. All too often there is an urge to charge on forgetting there is a need to recognize what are the key elements to achieve success.

Whilst technology has developed in giant leaps it is essential to keep our feet on the ground as real success is driven by competent people working in a disciplined and professionally led team.

Peter fits all the pieces of this puzzle together.

Robert J (Bob) Evans, MD Evans Project Management Services BE(Hons) FIE Aust CPEng EngExec NER APEC Engineer IntPE(Aus)

The Steel Ceiling is necessary reading for anyone in the engineering and construction industry. Australia is in need of strong businesses in this sector who are able to compete on a global stage and remain sustainable in uncertain times. Peter provides the framework to do this, explains the coveted tipping point of growth and provides the tools for navigating this volatile industry.

Kim McGuinness, Business Consultant, Mentor and Founder of co-created.biz

Starting up and scaling a new business in the infrastructure sector is challenging, confusing and stressful. Better understanding what lies ahead, before you reach each stage, will lead to a more successful outcome. *The Steel Ceiling* will not only help you to identify what will influence the outcome you strive for, but provide you with the easily understood and implemented tools. These will enable you to plan for, and navigate the road to success. The strategies discussed in this book, have been instrumental in our journey and I am confident that everyone who reads this, will recognise its value.

Logan Mullaney, Managing Director of InQuik Australia & President of InQuik USA

T03326773

Many people who start businesses in the construction industry do so on the back of holding key positions as an employee in project delivery. Whilst the passion, vision and knowledge of how to construct a project is typically very strong, often the external challenges of the industry, business stages and strategy are overlooked by a belief and genuine intent that delivering a good job for the client, will be enough to succeed. Hence many find themselves at the Tipping Point, when the excitement of owning a business starts to fade and turns to the reality of its challenges. This book 'nails' these very common trends and I highly recommend its features to anyone who is truly serious about building a sustainable business in the construction industry. A MUST READ.

Derek Mullally, Managing Director, Quickway

The Steel Ceiling is a timely prompt to principals, contractors and technical advisors to review their interaction in a market that is increasingly unbalanced. The author expertly draws out the risks to all players if alternative approaches to scope development and project procurement are not examined with objective vigor.

Jock Murray AO, consultant, Company Director

Energy use in building is about 27 per cent of global CO_2 emissions. So those in the engineering and construction industries will need to balance the rising demands of external climate stakeholders with the changing economics of new business models and technologies. Peter Wilkinson guides the reader on how to juggle these forces in a practical way, honed by a career consulting to Australia's engineering leaders.

Geoff Waring, Managing Partner, Stoic Venture Capital

The Steel Ceiling empowers business owners to become advocates of 'beginning with the End in Mind'. In the engineering and construction industry, there is generally no shortage of technical talent and expertise. The shortage is in business acumen. Peter fills this gap by introducing the simple model of the '4 Key Pillars' which may be used systematically to sustainably grow one's business in this sector. A must-read for all who want their business to withstand the test of time.

William Zhang, Founding Director, Palantir Consulting

The
Steel
Ceiling

The
Steel
Ceiling

Achieving Sustainable Growth
in Engineering and Construction

Peter Wilkinson

WILEY

First published in 2023 by John Wiley & Sons Australia, Ltd

Level 1, 155 Cremorne St, Richmond Vic 3121

Typeset in Chaparral Pro 11.5pt/15pt

© John Wiley & Sons Australia, Ltd 2023

The moral rights of the author have been asserted

ISBN: 978-1-119-91044-2

 A catalogue record for this book is available from the National Library of Australia

Cover design by Wiley
Cover Image: © Fair.ksd/Shutterstock

Disclaimer

*To my loving and supportive wife and partner Dianne, who placed
her trust in me when I began this phase of my journey
over a decade ago.*

'Love does not consist in gazing at each other, but in looking outward
together in the same direction'
*Antoine de Saint-Exupéry (French writer, poet, aristocrat, journalist
and — interestingly — pioneering aviator)*

Contents

A note to the reader

Writing is not a natural process for me. I'm someone who, when faced with spare time to fill, typically seeks a new outdoor pursuit. Book writing undoubtedly fits squarely into the category of 'indoor time'.

Nevertheless, once the idea of writing this book took hold, research on the writing game led me to one of my favourite authors. Po Bronson's *What Should I Do with My Life?* and *Why Do I Love these People?* profoundly moved and inspired me. As it turned out, not only was Po's birthdate within two years of mine, but he had also pursued a 'real' career in finance before abandoning it in favour of writing. This seemed to me to be the perfect case study upon which to model my own journey. Imagine my horror when I discovered that Po's writing method consisted of locking himself away in a space literally the size of a small cupboard to create the necessary silence and focus to pursue his craft!

The next and more fundamental challenge concerned natural talent. They say that there is a book in everyone. I'm still not fully convinced of the truth of this statement. However, I am now sure that some books are buried more deeply within than others, as mine was certainly well internalised. I was comforted to learn that Elizabeth

Gilbert, acclaimed author of *Eat, Pray, Love,* characterises her creative process as 'mule-like'. An apt description of my own efforts.

The final challenge concerned the practicalities of taking myself offline from my business for what I anticipated to be some months — as was suggested by those I approached with previous experience in this field — to focus on completing the task at hand. I dwelt for quite some time on the attractiveness of the project, and the various advantages and disadvantages, before realising that I was falling back into a long-standing habit of procrastination by looking for an excuse not to get started on the project in the first place. This did not change the reality of needing to earn a living; however, the awareness did shift me towards finding the time to devote to the book.

The most productive phases of my life have occurred when I have overcome the inertia borne of having lots to do and not being sure what to concentrate on first. My method, not unique but tried and tested for me, comprises breaking down large challenges into progressively smaller, more doable, pieces. In this case, my approach commenced a few years prior by writing blog articles (you might like to refer to these at www.samwilkoadvisory.com). Initially, the subject didn't particularly matter — I simply wrote about what was of importance and/or interest to me at the time. Or put another way: I wrote about subjects I most needed to learn more about.

Once I'd written a few articles, I was encouraged by Doyle Buehler of Digital Delusion — the builder of my first business website — to have a go at an e-book. This seemed to be a really good way to synthesise the business lessons I was exploring with my early business clients, and the themes that were emerging in my articles.

I wrote my first e-book in 2014 during the most welcome spare time on the plane to and from Berlin, where I attended the week-long 10th anniversary InnoTrans International Rail Trade Fair held at the massive Messe Exhibition Grounds in the Charlottenburg-Wilmersdorf precinct, now known as Berlin ExpoCenter City. Glancing back at the document, it's rather salesy and quite cringe-worthy for that. It was a huge step for me at the time though, and I'm still quite proud of the effort that went into it.

My more recent e-book was developed in collaboration with One Rabbit, a Geelong-based organisation specialising in marketing for professional services firms. Founder Jim Thompson and Technician Conal McLure taught me a great deal regarding the principles and application of digital marketing. The process I worked through with Conal and Jim in compiling my material for small- and medium-sized enterprises was very similar to the 'co-design' approach I apply today with clients in developing business strategy. What the process felt like at the time was a huge amount of work for me during a period where I was particularly time-poor. The proud feeling I experience, even now, when I look back on this time was borne of an ability to keep my end of the bargain in completing a significant body of work. I'm pleased that the results at www.tippingpointadvisory.com.au have enhanced my business enormously over the years.

Since I founded SamWilko Advisory, many readers (as well as the occasional business adviser) have urged me to publish articles on a regular basis. I have come to understand that this need is, in part, driven by the Google 'reward' system that drives so much of our online behaviour. Regular writing, however, definitely results in better writing, and I particularly credit James Clear (author of *Atomic Habits*) for this valuable lesson.

I believe this book demonstrates the value that good-quality coaches and advisers have created for my business, aligned with my belief that every competent business owner needs to be open to coaching and advice.

I encourage anyone considering starting a business to take up writing as a craft. The value created through writing for and about my enterprise has been immense. If nothing else, it is a means of creating content for marketing purposes — in my view, the most effective form of marketing in this modern age of saturated sales messaging.

You will find several themes in this book in previously published articles at www.samwilkoadvisory.com. My overriding intention with this book is to create a consistent, integrated narrative whilst exploring these and other themes in depth. I trust you will find my articles and book add value to each other.

Peter Wilkinson

Preface

My story

Every author, whether explicitly acknowledged or not, brings their personal experience to the story they tell. I've certainly found that learning about a business owner's story is an extremely effective — and enjoyable — way to start a conversation that leads to a better understanding of why business is showing up for the owner in the way it does. How business owners interact with their enterprises, and what they do in reaction to the situations they face, is a source of endless fascination for me. Accordingly, I've interspersed relevant elements of my story throughout the book in the interest of hopefully providing you, the reader, with a deeper understanding of what lies behind my approach.

I certainly have had a great deal of luck over the course of my working life. Not the least of which was the influence of my father, who took the time and interest to encourage a reasonably good (but not particularly well-motivated) higher school certificate holder in the direction of what was then known as the NSW State Rail Authority. I successfully applied for a cadetship, which, like other government sector programs around at that time, comprised sponsored education semesters interspersed with paid work experience. This set me on a career path in an industry that has been very good to me over 30-plus years.

The value of practical education

The terms of my cadetship required simultaneous enrolment in the NSW Institute of Technology (later to become the University of Technology Sydney) as an undergraduate mechanical engineer. The highlight of my university years was the final year project, culminating in submission of the UTS equivalent of an undergraduate thesis. In my case, I collaborated with three colleagues on an inherited project that had been taken on by UTS student teams in previous years. The Shell Mileage Marathon event was held annually at Amaroo Park Raceway in Annangrove (eventually closed in 1998 to make way for a housing development). The race involved vehicles powered by 50cc internal combustion engines specifically designed to travel the maximum possible distance on as little fuel as possible. Our team inherited a vehicle that had been constructed and entered by past UTS student teams, and we set about improving upon previous years' performance. In our case, this consisted of:

- casting aside the previous spine-based vehicle chassis — which appeared to be old and broken — and replacing it with a new aluminium vehicle manufactured with the assistance of an Australian Defence Industries (ADI) colleague in their Rosebery workshops

- optimising rolling resistance for the bicycle wheels used for the new vehicle

- improving on engine performance by optimising the set-up via bench dynamometer testing.

What we didn't know at the time was (a) the 'old and broken' spine chassis had just the right degree of flexibility, enabling it to ride the bumps and undulations of the Amaroo Park track in an efficient manner, and (b) the engine needed to be carefully managed during bench testing to ensure it didn't overheat and seize (which it did).

We co-opted a driver (the girlfriend of a fellow student) whose size enabled her to squeeze into the small cockpit of the vehicle. Her driving skills and ability to withstand the heat generated within the vehicle (essentially a plastic-wrapped shell sat out in the hot sun) were most admirably up to the task. We turned up at Amaroo Park on race day, decked out in white UTS and ADI badged overalls, and placed third. First place went to a Nulon Australia–sponsored vehicle with a larger budget than ours, with second place taken by a vehicle by regular competitor and privateer racing driver Moss Angliss.

I'm, even now, acutely reminded of the seemingly relentless stress associated with the entire experience. The UTS team had won the event the two prior years, and expectations were high. The idea of co-opting students for a group project was extra work that no-one was keen to own. If I recall correctly, our team took on a significant mission in replacing the old, successful chassis without much university advice or support. The engine overheating debacle referred to earlier also did not go down well with UTS staff. Ultimately, getting to the line on competition day was a close-run thing.

At the time, I managed the situation by concentrating on my part of the project — rolling resistance optimisation — and achieved a distinction for my undergraduate thesis (my first published book!). Hindsight eventually dawned upon me as I realised that my reluctance to take on more responsibility for the overall health and direction of the project was a major failing on my part. I resolved, going forward, to either take full responsibility for the outcome of a project I'm involved in or not participate at all. It's a lesson I've only forgotten on rare occasions.

From engineering to business

Overall, though, the combination of education, project work and industry experience provided a great starting point for a career. This went some way towards making up for the fact that engineering was at that time (and, to a rather disappointing extent, still is) an overwhelmingly male-dominated profession. This is despite concerted efforts by the profession to encourage more diversity in the field. Where

I believe this lack of diversity and balance shows up most acutely is in the typical engineering-based approach to problem-solving. Well-trained engineers are excellent at solving 'bounded' problems, but can struggle to deal with the less structured, humanistic environment, in which more complex problems exist. I suspect this bias aligns with the 'thinker' orientation of many engineers, manifesting itself in the need to solve the problem at hand. A more 'feeler' and 'knower' oriented, contextual approach that could be introduced with a broader demographic typically results in greater insight into the nature of the problem faced, thereby improving the odds of solving the right problem. The linear mindset-based approach to problem-solving creates business risks, which can be effectively mitigated via greater diversity of thought. Refer to the Conclusion for further information regarding our differing preferences for processing and communicating information.

After graduating from UTS in 1990, I was appointed to State Rail's Flemington Maintenance Centre in Sydney's western suburbs as a passenger railcar maintenance engineer. I learnt a great deal over these four years, working with a more experienced (if a little eccentric) electrical engineer with a real talent for fault diagnosis. Eventually though, I realised I was not heading in the right direction career-wise. This, allied with my aforementioned lack of skill and interest in design, resulted in me being drawn in a managerial direction. Flemington's operational management were very supportive of my interests; for example, they allowed me to relieve the depot manager whilst he was on annual leave and experience the weight of responsibility. I was also supported in my eventual decision to leave the public sector for a role with Goninan (now UGL) at Maintrain, where I learnt several valuable business lessons that will be explored in chapter 6.

In 1996, I resolved to take on an MBA with the NSW University's Australian Graduate School of Management. I signed up to the part-time course to reduce the risk of the experience living up to its unofficial label as the 'divorce course'. I recall the initial thrill of the induction session, where we were informed that our investment in the 'elite' $40 000 course would guarantee our future success!

Those who have undertaken an MBA would be familiar with the more mundane reality of dabbling in a range of business-related subjects just enough to be potentially dangerous in a number of specialist areas, such as finance, marketing and law. I found the business strategy elements of the course of great interest: the contextual anchor that brought together the various threads into a relatively coherent whole. I was also lucky enough to be able to apply the strategy theory to the corporate roles I held with Serco Asia Pacific, as a management consultant with GHD and later with Transfield Services.

Of course, the networking opportunities are what makes these courses so valuable — a reality that persists today with a great many Australian institutions offering MBA programs. My most valuable learnings arose from working with a small cohort of colleagues with diverse backgrounds and experience, where I was forced to explain myself to people, including one dear friend with drama and jazz singing in her past! Imagine my surprise when I discovered there is more than one right way — not just the linear method — of getting to a correct answer.

The experiences I've outlined stand out as being particularly influential in shaping my approach to what I now do as a business adviser and coach. It would be remiss of me, however, not to acknowledge a much broader context in which I exist. In the greater scheme of things, being a healthy, white male born in one of the richest countries on the planet, and experiencing the buoyant journey that Australia has experienced over the last 30 years, confers great privilege. And with privilege comes a responsibility to give back to the infrastructure engineering and construction industry from which I've benefited in so many ways.

Notwithstanding the huge slice of luck I've been afforded in life, I cannot recall experiencing immediate or easy success in business. Outcomes, arising from improvements made in how I've gone about my business, have typically felt hard won. This certainly gives rise to my preferred approach to implementing a plan, which basically consists of formulating a strategy and sticking with it unless and until it becomes evident that the original strategy is the problem (more on this in chapter 9). Moreover, my history almost certainly influences my perspective on business luck, which will also show up in chapter 10.

However, this book is not about a personal struggle against adversity. It is about business owners harnessing personal motivation, and channelling energy into realising their vision by achieving the right outcomes at the right times. Hopefully, the lessons I've learnt will be helpful in illuminating the clear and actionable roadmap I outline in the following chapters, for breaking through the 'steel ceiling', and achieving sustainable success in infrastructure engineering and construction.

Introduction

What needs to change for your business to grow sustainably?

Over a 30-year career in infrastructure engineering and construction, I've witnessed a steadily increasing number of good small-to-medium businesses in the industry fail to break through the 'steel ceiling' to become great and sustainable enterprises.

Australia faces a great challenge in developing and articulating a coherent strategy for taking its place in the modern world of technology-driven change. Long-overdue disruption in infrastructure engineering and construction will continue to transform the industry, accelerated by the fallout from COVID-19. Small and medium businesses generate the energy and innovation that drives construction, which is the third-largest industry in Australia by number of employees, generating 9 per cent of total GDP in 2022.[1]

Australia in the mid-1980s was internationally respected in infrastructure engineering and construction and, in my opinion, has the potential to achieve greatness again. However, the period since the mid-1980s has seen a steady decline in public sector capability and expertise. More recent times have been characterised by ever more complex 'mega projects' controlled by an exclusive group of international contractors. The industry is now beset by delays, cost blow-outs and blame-shifting. The cost of mediocre industry outcomes translates to an enormous waste of scarce time and money, derailed careers and lost opportunities.

I've experienced first-hand the industry's continuing struggle to transition from adversarial 'bully boy' behaviour that all too frequently shows up reflecting win/lose contracting mentality, to a more inclusive, collaborative and attractive place for tomorrow's business talent. Mental health issues are endemic in the industry,[2] and the traditional support provided to site workers has broken down. In my considered view, the root cause of the win/lose mentality is the 'feast or famine' nature of the industry. This mentality is at the root of the 'steel ceiling' challenge, and businesses need to understand the risks of falling in line with the dysfunctional industry behaviour in this regard.

What's missing and what's at risk?

What makes infrastructure engineering and construction such a challenging environment in which to operate? Why are the major players in the industry reportedly losing money on 'mega' project after 'mega' project, when the demand for project services and volume of work to be undertaken is at a generational high?[3] And, equally importantly, why are good small- and medium-sized businesses in the industry struggling to mature into sustainable enterprises?

When formulating answers to these questions, I am reminded of a conversation with a colleague from an investment banking background, during which he stated categorically that he would never invest his own money in the infrastructure engineering and construction industry. Why? His reasoning was based on his assessment that the potential return on investment wasn't worth the industry-typical risk. (Interestingly, he later revealed his highly volatile Bitcoin play. The rationale behind his argument: he had only bet an insignificant portion of his investment portfolio on an 'asset' class with the chance of a huge return.)

Infrastructure engineering and construction is exposed to an array of risks that every involved business needs to understand. Infrastructure engineering and construction is, in many ways, a 'mug's game' (a profitless or futile activity) if businesses don't have a broad and deep understanding of the context in which the industry operates. The industry is highly exposed to 'boom and bust' economic phases, characterised by the potential for extreme volatility. Many businesses new to the industry take on enormous risks, exposing themselves to potential consequences (that should rightly be borne by the client or by more senior involved parties) for no other reason than 'everyone else seems to be accepting it'. And the pay-off in terms of profit for taking on these risks is more than likely heavily constrained by the competitive tendering processes through which the work is secured.

I've spent a considerable amount of time dwelling on what's really missing in the industry. A common theme showing up in this current era of abundant work is the lack of collaborative behaviour displayed by many industry participants. A scarcity-based mindset is not particularly helpful in the context of growing a sustainable business. However, this mindset is understandable in an environment where the 'pie' of work is shrinking, and everyone is seeking to secure their piece. Scarcity-based behaviour, though, makes absolutely no sense when the size of the 'pie' is increasing.[3]

The infrastructure engineering and construction industry in Australia is defined and shaped by the central role of government. Key, then, to predicting — or at least anticipating — the future, is gauging governments' evolving responses to the challenge of maintaining Westernised living conditions on the edges of a massive land mass with a vast semi-arid centre. Government planners are charged with the responsibility of responding to urban sprawl and transport-related congestion resulting from population growth, as well as enhancing connectivity between our capital cities and regional centres. Infrastructure solutions that have traditionally evolved from this work must also increasingly be informed by the imperative of a de-carbonised future.[4]

The industry has historically struggled to be informed by and learn from history. This leads to contextual deficiencies in dealing with problems as they arise. Time spent understanding the contemporary history of infrastructure engineering and construction in Australia reveals that many of the challenges that appear surprising and new could have been predicted. Many of the issues the industry grapples with have been faced before and either dealt with or consigned to the 'too hard' basket for future generations.

Understanding the infrastructure engineering and construction industry

Part I of this book explores the uniquely Australian context for our infrastructure engineering and construction industry. The Macquarie Dictionary defines context as 'the circumstances or facts that surround a particular situation, event etc.'[5] Context enables us to make sense of content, creating clarity out of confusion. The use of context as a communication tool is a fundamental technique that effective coaches learn to help clients make sense of the situations they find themselves in. The lesson of context is, in many ways, the most important of all lessons to learn. Understanding the corporate context in which good small- and medium-sized businesses in infrastructure engineering and construction find themselves in, goes a very long way towards untangling the conundrum of why good mid-tier businesses struggle to move up to first grade in the industry.

Thus, the first part of this book will consider the history of infrastructure projects in Australia: the evolution of our urban sprawl and how our transport and utilities sectors have been shaped accordingly. It will look at how boom and bust periods influence infrastructure engineering and construction; the internal and external factors driving consolidation; our shifting infrastructure needs; areas of investment; and the role of government in regulating, monitoring and driving the industry. Through an understanding of the many factors that influence our industry today, it becomes possible to better see how infrastructure engineering and construction businesses are impacted by external factors — and to account for those factors in enabling a business to grow sustainably.

Your roadmap for growing a sustainable business

The following parts of the book will be your roadmap to building a sustainable business in today's industry. Key to the framework I lay out is recognising where your business is in relation to the 'tipping point' through which every good business must transition if it is to become a great and sustainable enterprise (see figure A). This framework will enable you to identify which pieces of the puzzle your business might be missing.

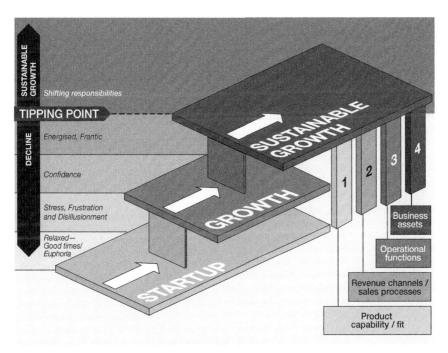

Figure A: Tipping point framework

Part II: The Why explores the key elements that owners must take personal responsibility for in setting the agenda and enabling change in their business.

Part III: The What details the process of creating a strategic roadmap for the journey through the 'tipping point' from good to sustainable business enterprise.

Part IV: The How describes the 4 Pillars of the business management system that must be in place to enable sustainable growth.

Part I

The Context

The science and art of building a sustainable business in infrastructure engineering and construction needs to be informed by the effects of changing economic circumstances. Why is this of particular importance? Because infrastructure engineering and construction is exposed to the effects of the economic cycle to an extent that only a handful of other industries can claim. Unfortunately, the seemingly simple exercise of forecasting when industry 'boom' turns to 'bust', and vice versa, is, in practice, quite difficult to achieve with any degree of precision.

At the time of writing, the industry was in the midst of a major boom phase, fuelled by government investment. However, whilst the projects pipeline across Australia was at a generational high, there were widespread concerns regarding project delays, cost blow-outs and consequent project losses. The medium- and longer-term effect on the industry, borne of COVID-19 related disruption, is also yet to be fully understood.

The local industry has internationalised and consolidated to an unprecedented extent over the last 15 years. The 'Top 4' contractors now dominating the industry in Australia comprise internationals CIMIC (ultimate owner Spain's ACS), John Holland Group (owned by China's CCCI), Acciona (from Spain) and WeBuild (from Italy). Between them, they access and control the cash flow associated with the major proportion of industry revenue.

The forecast volume of project work over the coming decade, mature legal system and pipeline of technically complex 'mega' projects will in all likelihood ensure the ongoing local presence of these dominant contractors.

On the other hand, competitive forces in the mature infrastructure engineering and construction industry continue to exert significant downward pressure on project margins. This is most unexpected, particularly when taking account of the large number of projects currently underway and the high level of demand for project services. All other things being equal, one would expect, at a minimum, for the dominant contractors to be able to maintain reasonable project margins. Reportedly, though, this is not the case.[1]

Of arguably greater concern for the local industry are the flow-on effects arising from margin pressure on project sub-contractors, suppliers and professional service providers. The squeeze on sub-contractor margins arises from cost, time and other potentially unmanageable risks being passed on by head contractors. Damaging, longer-term consequences for the health of the small-to-medium sector of the industry include:

- constrained opportunities for lower-tier infrastructure engineering and construction businesses to build internal capability and step into and progress through the 'big league' of direct client contracting

- reduced opportunities for investment on a cost/benefit basis in local capability, for instance in technology-based efficiencies or productivity transformation

- perpetuation of the cycle where procurement processes reward acceptance of mega project risk to an extent where only the largest contractors can participate.

Government as a market shaper can play its part in maintaining a balanced and sustainable industry with strong local capability. It is incumbent on governments, as industry shapers and procurers of infrastructure project services, to act as 'circuit-breakers' and lead an industry shift towards greater sustainability of engineering and construction as a critical local industry sector.

Matching shifting needs and demands

The industry's current growth phase has been fuelled by increasing demand for major project works since 2015.[2,3] Interest rates were at a historic low point in their cycle and were maintained at low levels for a significant period of time thanks to substantial increases in money supply by the Federal Reserve. Low interest rates on borrowings enabled state and federal governments to continue to fund substantial infrastructure investment programs.

The demand curve was further extended by delays in project approvals and commencements — commonplace in the industry — and disruptions due to the productivity-related effects of COVID-19. Labour, equipment and materials shortages also limited the industry's ability to fully meet demand across the country. Accordingly, an inevitable tail-off in project works appears to remain comfortably in the future.

Boom times don't last forever, though. Downswings in economic circumstances are typically set off by unanticipated events, as has been witnessed with the series of financial crises that occurred in the 2000s. A significant rise in local interest rates would be highly likely to trigger a broader economic downturn and consequent widespread government project cancellations. In the meantime, niche businesses in the industry need to be aware of the peaks and troughs in demand for their particular works and services, which can easily be obscured by the many projects currently in procurement and delivery.

Of interest, too, should be alterations to government project requirements, driven by changes in user demand. Whilst traditionally longer term in nature, changes in underlying demand may well prove to be disruptive to the industry in the wake of COVID-19. For instance, increased usage of remote communications technology has prompted what may or may not be a long-term migration from capital cities to regional locations. A close eye should also be kept on the inevitable technological disruption associated with productivity improvement– enabling technology.

As an industry directly exposed to both the short- and long-term impacts of government policy, one of the biggest (and most common) difficulties is predicting the time it will take for government investment promises to translate into projects on the ground. Nowhere is this more prevalent in Australia than the much-discussed regional development strategies and associated regional infrastructure investment funds.

Investing in the right infrastructure

Building the right infrastructure has flow-on benefits. It is generally accepted that infrastructure investment with a positive benefit cost ratio that takes appropriate consideration of environmental effects boosts an economy's multi-factor productivity.[4] And productivity is vital to Australia's ongoing prosperity, being the underlying driver of economic growth.

On a more practical level, this relationship between infrastructure growth and productivity improvement also seems logical. For instance, much of the visible investment in roads, rail and other enabling infrastructure across Australia in recent times has been targeted at reducing travel congestion and improving the workability and liveability of our major cities. Most would agree that the improved roads reducing trip times for, say, the truck drivers making deliveries from distribution centres to businesses across the cities and suburbs are a positive contribution.

'Mega projects', a term commonly used for projects with values greater than \$1 billion, have become a new normal for infrastructure engineering and construction in Australia.[5] This approach to nation-building has increasingly dominated government attention, with the consequences of a reduced focus on comparatively minor works becoming increasingly apparent.

Mega projects, however, take years rather than months to develop and deliver. Key to the development of a business case for a major project is a prediction of user demand for the service provided by the built infrastructure. What, then, if user demand fundamentally changes in the intervening period between project approval and delivery?

Key to better understanding the industry is observing how governments and their respective agencies go about responding to the challenge of providing infrastructure more closely aligned with user demand in an increasingly volatile environment.

CHAPTER 1

Infrastructure engineering and construction in Australia

A sustainable business in infrastructure engineering and construction must be well informed about the environment in which it operates.

Every day a myriad of urgent business issues arises. Delayed materials deliveries, last-minute alterations in client schedules, staff sickness, resignations and so on noisily announce themselves as problems that need to be resolved and are mostly sorted out 'just-in-time'.

Businesses, though, are typically less likely to immediately pick up on and respond in a timely manner to longer-term shifts in environmental circumstances. A slow-down in requests for tender may be the first sign of change to a key client's procurement strategy, preferred contracting model or broader change to relevant government policy. By the time the change is noticed, it may already be too late to avoid a detrimental effect on the business.

A delve into the recent history of the industry reveals that a great deal of what appears surprising and new could well have been predicted as a developing challenge, or at least flagged as a potential concern. History can be a source of valuable lessons in this respect.

Time spent developing an in-depth understanding of the history of infrastructure engineering and construction in Australia adds value to a business in the industry. The information that follows provides a contextual overview of the recent past. The intention here is to stimulate interest in further research into the rich history of infrastructure engineering and construction as an integral part of Australia's modern development.

The central role of government is the most obvious and defining characteristic of the infrastructure engineering and construction industry in Australia. The public sector remains primarily responsible for creating the market for constructing and maintaining the roads, railways, airports, water and electrical utilities, and other essential services that serve the needs of the population.

Australia's three tiers of government (federal, state and local) align with many countries worldwide in actively considering the extent of private sector involvement in asset ownership, financing, construction, operation and maintenance. Like the 50 states comprising the USA, Australia's state and territory governments preserve their autonomy in determining the private sector's role, informed by (some may say reacting to) political forces and wider public opinion. Accordingly, differences occur from state to state and between industry sectors (for example, water versus rail transport).

Federal, state and local governments are intimately involved in creating policies and adjusting policy settings, administering regulations and standards, procuring and managing service providers and — less frequently in this current era of government outsourcing — self-delivering works.

Key, then, to predicting future trends in infrastructure engineering and construction in Australia is gauging governments' evolving responses to the challenges arising from the context in which Australians exist. Australia is the driest inhabited continent in the world, with 70 per cent of the land mass either arid or semi-arid.[1] And the vast majority of the population live on or in close proximity to the coast.[2]

Today's outcome is our current lived experience: highly urbanised capital cities on Australia's seaboard in isolated locations where water enables fertile land, separated by considerable distances. Time and again, public sector planners are faced with three fundamental challenges:

- urban congestion arising from population growth

- urban sprawl as a response to congestion

- capital city/regional centres connectivity.

Considerable population growth from a base of 7.4 million in 1945 to 25.9 million as at September 2021[3] has underpinned increasing demand for power and water. Adverse weather events heralding the threat of climate change also signal the pressing need to moderate use of the planet's natural resources.

The baby boom driving the housing boom

More than 5.5 million Australians were born after World War II in the baby boomer era between 1946 and 1966,[4] with their accommodation requirements driving the major expansion of Australia's major urban centres. Building was accomplished with the assistance of an immigration program comprising over two million skilled, mostly European migrants who further boosted the population[5].

Motor vehicles and the Australian suburb

In the early 1950s, cars were too expensive for many families. In 1953, a typical Holden car, for example, would cost approximately $2000, or roughly 64 weeks' wages, leading most people to use public transport with urban development largely confined to rail and tram corridors[6]. However, as consumer wealth grew and credit availability expanded, more people were able to purchase their own means of transport and choose to live further than walking-distance from public rail and tram links. In this way suburbs expanded in a phenomenon known as 'urban sprawl'.

Public trams make way for cars

From the early twentieth century, suburban trains provided the bulk of the public transport heavy lifting in metropolitan Sydney and Melbourne, with the train systems in the other states more geared to enabling regional freight connectivity. Surface trip capacity was supplemented by tram networks.

Whilst the original Melbourne and Adelaide tram networks are largely intact today, the same cannot be said for the Sydney and Brisbane systems, which were casualties of increasing competition from private motor vehicles.[7]

By the late 1940s, Sydney's tram system carried 400 million passengers annually on a network of more than 250 km.[7] However, the explosion of car traffic in the post-war years persuaded the NSW Government of the day that urban freeways were the way of the future, with trams an impediment to that vision. Demolition of the tram network commenced in 1958, with removal of the Fort Macquarie depot at Circular Quay to make way for the Opera House, and the tearing up of lines along George Street.

The peak period for tram patronage in Brisbane was from 1944 to 1945, when almost 160 million passengers were carried. Decline in usage due to increasing competition from motor vehicles ultimately resulted in the last tram running from Balmoral to Ascot on 13 April, 1969. A 'Brisbane Transportation Study' recommending the replacement of all trams and trolley buses with diesel units was used as justification for Brisbane City to stop trams despite outrage from residents.[7]

The rise of motorways

Australia's major capital cities today are dominated by urban motorways. This is largely due to the strategic intent of the respective long-term urban transport plans commissioned in response to the challenges of urban congestion. In addition, private transport operators such as Toll Holdings (which began as a horse-and-cart, coal-hauling business in Newcastle in 1888), Brambles (established in Newcastle in 1875 by Walter Brambles), TNT (founded by Ken Thomas in 1946 with one truck) and Linfox (established in 1956 by Lindsay Fox with one truck in Melbourne) developed into powerful advocates for freeways expansion.

The 1969 Melbourne Transportation Plan (although badged a road and rail transport plan) was oriented towards an extensive freeway network, much of which has since been built.[8] More recent outer suburban freeway projects (under new branding) were procured by subsequent governments, including CityLink (by the Kennett government in the 1990s), EastLink (by the Bracks government in the 2000s) and Peninsula Link (by the Napthine government in the 2010s).

Sydney's current 110 km Orbital roads network (in progress as at 2022)[9] was formally conceptualised in 1962 as a key element of the County of Cumberland Planning Scheme.[10] Recent additions include the NorthConnex access to the Pacific Highway and the various WestConnex elements, including the in-progress Sydney Airport Gateway access and CBD connections from Rozelle via the Anzac Bridge.

Prior to the 1960s, Queensland Main Roads was focused on rural roads. In 1965, the state government and Brisbane City Council jointly commissioned Wilbur Smith Plan proposed a 'ring-radial' freeway system for Brisbane. A 1981 check of Smith's underlying population-growth predictions revealed that urbanisation had expanded well past the boundaries of Brisbane and out into the surrounding local authorities. Consequently, whilst the eastern outer circumferential (the Gateway Motorway) and the south-east radial freeway elements of the Wilbur Smith Plan were built, more recent freeways and tunnels (including Clem Jones Tunnel and Airport Link) only loosely resemble the original plan.[11]

In 1955, Gordon Stephenson, Professor of Civic Design at the University of Liverpool (UK), and J.A. Hepburn, the Town Planning Commissioner, released their plan for the Perth and Fremantle metropolitan region. The Stephenson Plan proposed a road network to cope with a projected 400 per cent traffic increase, and recommended the construction of eight new highways with a total length of approximately 130 km. The Narrows Bridge (opened in 1959) was a key element, crossing the Swan River to connect the Perth CBD to South Perth and areas beyond.[12]

The 1990s onwards: Urban sprawl

Continued population growth and accelerating 'urban sprawl' throughout the 1990s contributed to the overall growth in Australia's major cities. Over time, Australia has become highly urbanised, with approximately 90 per cent of the population today living near a capital city, compared with 60 per cent in 191[13].

With 'urban sprawl' however, comes the associated cost of connecting dwellings with the necessary transport, water, sewerage and electrical infrastructure needed to service the community. Governments around the world, including Australia, have sought to manage this ever-rising cost by restricting the rate of urban expansion through planning-related controls and making better use of existing urban areas through consolidation.

Australia's approach to urban sprawl and congestion management appears to remain largely as it has been for decades: anchored in capital investment in hard infrastructure to manage the effects of an ever-increasing number of motor vehicles on roads.

In fairness to those involved in transport planning, there seems to be a much more developed sense of roads and rail as complementary— rather than competing— modes of transport. Consider more recent examples of urban rail investments, including the Sydney Metro in NSW (curiously a separate rail system to the heavy rail network that has served greater Sydney for over a century), the 'back to the future' Sydney Light Rail CBD extension, the Melbourne Metro augmentation of the City Underground Loop, Cross River Rail in Brisbane and the continued works on Perth's Urban Rail network.

It's hard, though, to get away from the idea that much of what's actually constructed at the time of writing remains largely reactive to ever-increasing urban traffic demand. For instance, we do seem a bit short on 'new' ideas regarding how best to support regional development by alleviating capital city/regional centre connectivity challenges. Of specific relevance here is the concept of high-speed rail, which remains the subject of seemingly endless studies.[13] Of less apparent interest are the adjustments to government funding/cost recovery policy settings that will be required to enable high-speed rail to effectively compete with road and aviation alternatives.

At a more practical level, development of the enabling infrastructure for inland rail to facilitate the shifting of freight from road to rail continues — albeit at a slow pace. Developments, such as the largely automated port, rail and road freight transfer facility at Moorebank in Sydney's southwestern suburbs, will reduce truck pressure on the urban and regional roads network.[14]

There seems to be increasing interest in the debate regarding the implications of electric, driverless vehicles, and the consequent impacts on traffic demand and built infrastructure. There is an opportunity on offer for a switch to zero-emissions vehicles to make a significant contribution to lowering transport's share of greenhouse gas emissions.

A Grattan Institute report, `Towards net zero: Practical policies to reduce transport emissions', proposes zero-emissions electric light vehicles to be the most effective way to reduce transport-related carbon emissions. The major impediment to this shift, however, is the lack of national regulations enforcing reduced vehicle emissions[15]. Accordingly, global automotive manufacturers are choosing to devote time and effort to developing new models that meet new standards in larger markets such as United States, the European Union (EU), and Japan[16]. Vehicles built to existing standards will continue to be supplied to Australia, with limited incentive for manufacturers to develop new models that satisfy local challenges such as travelling long distances across remote terrain between urban areas.

The initial lockdown-related effects of COVID-19 have provided a glimpse into what real disruption to travel demand looks and feels like for Australia's urban roads and public transport systems (more on this in chapter 2).

Water supply and the millennium drought: 1997 to 2009

Australia's climate is characterised by intermittent periods of low rainfall. Between 1997 and 2009, much of southern Australia experienced a prolonged drought, with the most densely populated regions most heavily affected (see figure 1.1). In contrast and again as illustrated in Figure 1.1, large areas of northern and outback Australia experienced above-average rainfall.

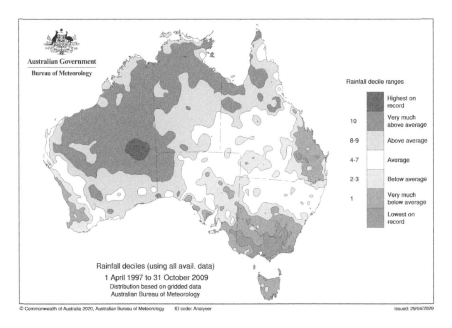

Figure 1.1: Rainfall deciles for the millennium drought (1997—2009)[17]

Source: © 2020 Commonwealth of Australia. Australian Bureau of Meterology

This prolonged and severe event triggered a wave of investment in freshwater generation infrastructure. In 2006, Perth became the first Australian city to operate a seawater desalination plant, the Perth Seawater Desalination Plant at Kwinana. Sydney's Kurnell Desalination Plant was completed in 2010, the Victorian Desalination Plant at Wonthaggi in 2012 and Adelaide's Desalination Plant at Port Stanvac in 2013. The Gold Coast Desalination Plant at Tugun was completed in 2010 in anticipation of significant population growth on Queensland's Gold Coast. The timings of these various investments were not without controversy. Plant commissioning coincided with above-average rainfall levels and floods in 2010, resulting in some plants being operated in expensive 'stand-by' mode.[18] However, it is becoming increasingly clear that further investment will be required in desalinated water generation, along with increased dam storage, to secure sufficient water supply for Australia's foreseeable needs.

Water recycling

On the demand side, and with Australia's supply of freshwater increasingly vulnerable to droughts, increased attention is being paid to water recycling.

Australian cities and developed regional areas are typically served by either trunk sewerage or septic systems. These arrangements have progressively replaced open sewer systems that had Melbourne (as Australia's largest city in the late 1800s) dubbed 'Smellbourne' thanks to the city's unsanitary waste disposal system.[19]

Melbourne's Water Corporation now operates a tertiary wastewater treatment plant at Werribee, producing recycled water for industrial and agricultural use. In South Australia, septic tank effluent drainage schemes bring together effluent for further treatment, and in some cases produce recycled water. Sydney Water's planned Upper South Creek Advanced Water Recycling Centre will support the development of the new Western Sydney International Airport and surrounds.[20]

Progress has been slower in relation to recycling for drinking water purposes. In 2006, Toowoomba residents rejected a Toowoomba Water Futures referendum regarding reuse of recycled water for drinking purposes.[21] The Western Corridor Recycled Water Scheme in south-east Queensland, developed to produce drinking-quality water suitable for release into the Wivenhoe Dam as Brisbane's principal water storage, was completed in late 2008. The treatment plants were put into 'care and maintenance mode' in 2013 and have yet to be implemented.[22]

To date, only Western Australia, with its recent declining rainfall, has managed to garner significant community support for use of recycled water for potable purposes via replenishment of Perth's groundwater supply. This followed WA Water Corporation's three-year demonstration project, concluding in 2012, investigating the feasibility of reclaiming water from the Beenyup wastewater treatment plant for injection into the Leederville aquifer. Stage 1 of the Beenyup Advanced Water Recycling Plant was commissioned in 2016 with approval to recharge granted in August 2017.[23]

Electricity transmission

Australia's trunk electricity transmission network traditionally connects large power generators, such as coal-fired power stations, to the lower-voltage distribution networks in cities and towns, as well as to industrial users.

What was once a network of poles and wires operating a one-way electricity supply, is evolving into a two-way system enabling commercial — and increasingly consumer — exporters to feed wind, solar and stored energy back into the grid.

Australia's east coast has one of the longest interconnected electricity system in the world.[24] Increasingly complex network load-balancing needs, borne of differences in regional weather, are driving investment in interstate interconnectors to enable sharing in firm capacity. Ageing coal-fired electricity generation is progressively being retired, to be replaced by wind and solar in different locations. Overall management responsibility for the integrated system plan lies with the Australian Energy Market Operator.

Concerningly, self-serving politics and vested interests have combined over the last two decades to disrupt multiple attempts to implement effective market signals regarding the cost of carbon pollution.[25] This combination of market uncertainty, increasing network complexity and rapid technological change has resulted in a highly volatile infrastructure investment landscape. Notwithstanding, the Australian Government in October 2021 formally committed to a net-zero emissions target by 2050[26], which was subsequently ratified by the incoming Federal Government following the election in May 2022. To achieve this, significant investment, by historic standards, will be necessary for the expansion of the electrical transmission and distribution network[27]. New sources of power, such as remote solar and wind farms, as well as battery and pumped hydroelectric storage units, will require connection to the transmission grid. This investment, however, will lead to a stronger and more resilient network that is better able to integrate the distributed energy elements.

Australia's gas network

Australia has more than 39 000 km of natural gas transmission pipelines that connect production to the outskirts of urban centres. Pipelines also act as storage vessels, assisting in managing peaks and troughs in demand. The 440 km Roma to Brisbane pipeline, commissioned in March 1969, is Australia's oldest natural gas pipeline.[28]

The East Coast pipeline transmission system covers Queensland, New South Wales, Victoria, South Australia, Tasmania and the ACT. In recent years, most transmission pipelines comprising the East Coast grid have been made bi-directional, enabling more flexible arrangements in support of gas supply and trading.

The Northern Territory's Amadeus pipeline accesses gas from fields in central Australia's Amadeus Basin. Darwin is also a liquefied natural gas (LNG) hub, with multiple offshore gas fields delivering gas to the two LNG facilities. The Northeast Gas Interconnector Link, completed in 2018, connects the Northern Territory's gas fields with the East Coast network.

The onshore gas transmission pipeline system in Western Australia is dominated by Australia's longest pipeline, the 1539 km Dampier to Bunbury pipeline servicing Perth and southern population centres[29]. The Mid-West and South-West Gas Distribution systems are also connected to the Dampier to Bunbury pipeline as well as the 1378 km Goldfields Gas Pipeline[30]. The APA Group-owned Pilbara Pipeline System (PPS) services mining requirements in the Pilbara[31].

The demands of meeting Australia's commitment to net zero greenhouse gas emissions by 2050 will in all likelihood necessitate a move from natural gas to renewable energy sources. Notwithstanding, plans have been developed to construct an additional 12 200 km of gas pipelines.[32]

Renewable gas: The hydrogen story

Hydrogen-production technology is promising to complement natural gas in the gas network, providing reserve energy as an analogous means to battery technology.

Hydrogen can be generated emissions-free from natural gas, creating what is commonly referred to as 'blue' hydrogen. However, this process has challenges around the high costs required for carbon capture technology to reach the scale required with no atmospheric damage, and the potential for methane, a byproduct of the extraction process, to leak.

Alternatively, producing 'green' hydrogen via electrolysis requires vast amounts of energy to achieve at scale. The approach may well provide an effective energy storage answer in the future, although it will require major additional investment in renewable energy production.

Successful development is likely to drive additional investment in gas pipelines, as referenced earlier, which could, in the future, carry a blend of natural gas and hydrogen[33].

Conclusion

Taking a step back, it is not difficult to foresee the end of this current era of major investment in mega road and rail projects. The imperative of addressing greenhouse gas emissions will drive significant developments in renewable technologies and enable electrical infrastructure. The timeframe over which net-zero greenhouse gas emissions must be achieved appears likely to result in an infrastructure program far exceeding the current quantum of works across the country.[27]

Key takeaways for sustainable businesses

1 Australia's public sector retains primary responsibility for constructing and maintaining roads, railways, airports, water and electrical utilities, and other essential services. Accordingly, public sector policies and strategies in relation to combating urban sprawl will continue to shape the nature of the land transport network.

2 Security of water supply remains a key potential limitation to Australia's ongoing development. Increased storage, reclamation via desalination and recycling remain the major means of improving Australia's situation in this regard.

3 Australia's public sector response to the challenge of minimising greenhouse gas emissions will fundamentally shape the form of the nation's future electricity transmission grid. Similar policies — be they proactive or reactive — will also influence the extent of ongoing investment of the national gas network, as well as the evolution of hydrogen and/or additional alternative energy technologies.

CHAPTER 2

The economics of boom and bust

The science and art of building a sustainable business in infrastructure engineering and construction needs to be well informed by the effects of changing economic circumstances. Why is this of particular importance? Because infrastructure engineering and construction is exposed to the effects of economic cycles to the extent that very few other industries are.[1]

Business owners in the small-to-medium space rarely find the time — or create the opportunity — to take a step back and observe the prevailing economic circumstances. Sometimes you might find that focusing on the daily news cycle can be quite misleading.

One of the more common questions people with experience in the industry raise is along the lines of: 'Why is the infrastructure engineering and construction industry always either in boom or bust?'

There are fundamental reasons why the industry is regularly subject to feast followed by famine periods that make it a particularly tough place in which to survive and thrive. Economic cycles are the expansions and contractions that market economies (as opposed to planned economies) experience on a regular basis.

A country's economic performance is commonly measured using gross domestic product (GDP), being the total monetary value of the finished goods and services domestically produced over a given time period (typically measured per quarter). As a broad measure of overall domestic production, relative change in GDP from quarter to quarter functions as a scorecard of a given country's economic health.

Demand for goods and services rises with increasing GDP and decreases as GDP falls away. What this means in practice for infrastructure engineering and construction is that as an economy enters an expansionary period, demand for infrastructure engineering and construction services increases. This drives demand for materials, and the equipment and workers who perform the work on the ground. As an economy contracts, the process reverses.

In a perfect world, and as demand for construction services rises, infrastructure engineering and construction businesses would procure people, plant and equipment, and materials to deliver the services clients require. Increased costs incurred in supplying resources to clients are passed on via increased rates and prices. As demand falls away, businesses shed costs by reducing headcount, equipment and inventory.

In the real world, however, rising costs are difficult to fully pass on in competitive tender situations, whilst surplus labour and equipment costs money to offload when demand falls away. In circumstances where a spike in demand is followed by an equally precipitous drop, over-capacity can rapidly morph into a cash crisis.

Let's consider in more depth then, the reasons why changing economic circumstances are experienced in a cyclic pattern.

Construction industry boom and bust cycles are influenced by global and national economic circumstances. These cycles, as for most industries, typically trail the broader economic cycle — as measured by relative changes in GDP — anecdotally by around six to nine months. Note, too, that construction industry cycles are further influenced by exogenous (external) effects, such as changes in interest rates, government policy intervention, technological change and — as recently encountered — global pandemics.

Understanding the economic cycle

Ray Dalio is the founder of Bridgewater Associates Investment Management, a company he launched out of his two-bedroom apartment in New York in 1975. In 2011, Bridgewater was listed as one of the largest hedge funds globally, with assets under management in excess of US$100 billion. In 2020, Bloomberg ranked Dalio the world's 79th-wealthiest person (noting that Bridgewater reported significant losses at the time due to COVID-19–related market volatility, with the flagship pure Alpha II fund losing in excess of US$12 billion in 2020).[2] Dalio is regarded as a major innovator in the finance world. He is also a prolific, clear and engaging writer in the space of economics and investment strategy, sharing lessons learnt in growing his business.

Dalio uses Monopoly — the game of acquiring properties and extracting rent from other players to fund the acquisition of more properties until all the properties are owned by the winner — to explain how economic cycles come about. He describes how Monopoly would work if (more akin to the real economy) the bank was allowed to make loans for property purchases and take deposits rather than the game restricting the players to holding idle cash. Dalio further explains thus:

> *The amount of debt-financed spending on hotels would quickly grow to multiples of the amount of money in existence. Down the road, the debtors who hold those hotels will become short on the cash they need to pay their rents and service their debt.*

Absent external intervention (the role of central banks in the real economy), as depositors withdraw more cash to pay more debts, banks and debtors eventually become insolvent and the economy accordingly starts to contract.

So, each phase of credit-based economic growth is inevitably followed by a period of economic 'shrinkage'. As noted earlier, construction industry revenues grow relatively quickly in boom periods and fall hard during the bust cycle. Smaller construction firms are less able to downsize to meet contracting demands, but can expand as fast, if not faster, than larger firms in response to a boom cycle.

Boom times in infrastructure engineering and construction are characterised by intense project activity and heightened competition for skilled staff and workers. Bust periods are the opposite.

Dalio notes a particular challenge experienced by economies whose growth is significantly supported by debt-financed building of fixed investments, real estate and infrastructure. This is particularly true of Australia, as a net importer of capital needing to fund investment in infrastructure to overcome the vast distances between major cities. Countries such as ours are particularly susceptible to large cyclical swings, because the fast rates of building long-lived assets are not sustainable. This type of cycle — where a strong growth upswing driven by debt-financed real estate, fixed investment and infrastructure spending is followed by a downswing driven by a debt-challenged slow-down in demand — is also typical of emerging economies, because these economies typically have a great deal of pent-up demand for building works.

Boom and bust: Predicting the cycle

An awareness of the effect economic cycles have on the infrastructure engineering and construction industry highlights the importance of understanding the stage at which a cycle is at. Of even more importance is the ability to forecast the next major inflection point: when boom is turning to bust and vice versa. Unfortunately, this seemingly simple exercise is, in practice, quite difficult to undertake with precision. Let's explore in more depth why this is so.

For example, businesses may rely on GDP as the broad indicator of economic health for an indication of where the economic cycle is at. The GDP quarterly reports allow us to look back at what happened over the last three months, but do not provide sufficiently timely data to enable effective tracking of economic performance on a weekly or monthly basis.

Let's consider, then, stock markets as a timelier indicator of economic health. Value investing pioneer Benjamin Graham is credited with describing the stock market as a short-term voting machine, but a long-term weighing machine.[3] In this way, the two different drivers of stock market value are captured: investor confidence and business value.

Companies publicly listed on a stock market are valued based on the most recent price at which their shares have been traded. Taking account of the virtually instantaneous nature of modern computer-based trading systems, the valuation of a given company is a 'real time' reflection of the market's opinion of that business. Of course, the market's opinion is also influenced by company results and other statutory announcements such as mergers and acquisitions and capital restructures, which must be publicly disclosed. Over time, the pattern of the company's historic performance becomes apparent and is reflected in market opinion.

Groups of share prices are consolidated into market indexes, which may be adjusted (weighted) by, for instance, the relative size of individual share prices within the index. The calculation of the index value is derived from the prices of the underlying holdings.[4]

We can use, then, a broad index such as Australia's Stock Exchange (ASX-500) Index as a dynamic indicator of Australia's economic health. The key challenge here, of course, is volatility, with the index constantly varying as a reflection of stock price trading activity. In practice, economic performance is divined using a range of indicators, with GDP and the stock market on top of a list, as well as:

- unemployment as well as underemployment: a measure of how well the labour force is being utilised in terms of skills, experience, and availability to work

- Consumer price index (CPI): the average change in prices over time that consumers pay for a basket of goods and services

- Producer price index (PPI): a family of indexes gauging the average fluctuation in selling prices received by domestic producers

- balance of trade: the difference in value between a country's imports and exports

- housing starts: new residential construction projects

- interest rates: typically movements in the Reserve Bank of Australia's official cash rate.

Diagnosing the situation

One particularly interesting contributor to the measurement of economic performance is the concept of confidence. The Consumer Sentiment Index measures how a sample of households are currently feeling about the economy. The index is a compilation of five sub-indexes measuring how a surveyed sample of households are currently feeling about the economy, reflecting their views regarding anticipated economic conditions and their preparedness to purchase major discretionary items. A reading of 100 in each sub-index means that the number of positive and negative responses is equal.

Recent COVID-19 lockdown-related disruptions provided a stark illustration of how the index works. Figure 2.1 illustrates the Consumer Sentiment Index for Sydney, NSW, slumping by 13.6 per cent as the June 2021 lockdown commenced, plunging the population into another round of intense anxiety and uncertainty.

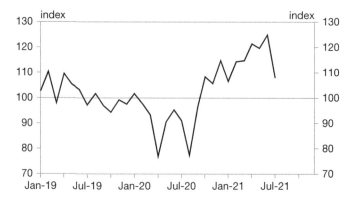

Figure 2.1: The confidence of Sydney's consumers plummeted during the winter lockdown.[5]
Source: Westpac Economics, Melbourne Institute

You can get your own sense of how this measure works.

In late 2012 I attended AusRail, Australia's premier rail industry conference, in Sydney. It was very illuminating to spend time 'taking the temperature' of the attendees. This period followed Australia's version of the 2009 global financial crisis (GFC), with the stock market initially falling, stabilising and then falling again in what is commonly associated with a 'W' type recession. The index had not yet shown strong signs of recovery (see figure 2.2). Broad opinion was divided regarding whether recovery would continue or a further slump would signal the onset of economic depression.

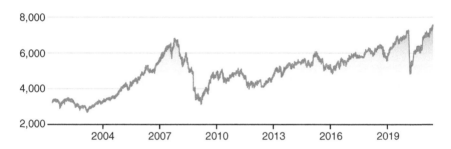

Figure 2.2: Worldwide GFC 2009, then by 2012 hesitant and uneven recovery[6]

There were two distinct groups in the conference hall: those for whom business remained tough and who were struggling to see the light at the end of the tunnel; and those who were dealing with so much activity that they were desperate for a break at the end of the year.

Another technique in getting a sense of what the wider business community is feeling by way of confidence, is to open a copy of the *Australian Financial Review* and count the number of 'good news' and 'bad news' stories and compare the two.

This uncertain sentiment is typical of the times following a downturn. Periods of hesitant, uneven recovery are characterised by good and bad sentiment in almost equal measure. This tends to create confusion and uncertainty in the minds of business owners and makes achieving internal consensus around (for instance) investment decisions very difficult. In this way, confidence (or lack thereof) feeds into measured economic performance in a reinforcing cycle.

The overriding issue in 2012 was that it was the first time many business owners had experienced a protracted flat spot in 30 years of uninterrupted economic growth in Australia. Five years of sideways movement in the market had occurred since the GFC in 2008. Most were confident that a recovery would eventually arrive, however, most were equally unsure as to when it would materialise.

Consider the following as a way of gaining perspective on the situation at that time. The US Dow Jones Industrial Average (as a measure of US stock values) had regained its pre-GFC levels. There were signs of recovery in the UK after five years of the deep recession that Australia had been fortunate enough to avoid. Historic records indicate that Australia is typically a follower rather than a leader when it comes to economic cycles.

Records reveal that after the prolonged period of sideways movement following the GFC, the ASX in 2012 commenced a multi-year growth cycle that abruptly ended with the onset of the COVID-19 pandemic (refer figure 2.2). The ASX trend was reflected by a precipitous reduction in growth of the broader Australian economy (with a six- to nine-month time lag as mentioned earlier) as illustrated by relative changes in GDP (see figure 2.3).

You might note in figure 2.3 that average growth in GDP had been trending downwards from approximately 3.0 per cent in 2000 to below 2.5 per cent in the decade since 2012. This indicates a more fundamental growth challenge that will be dealt with later in the book.

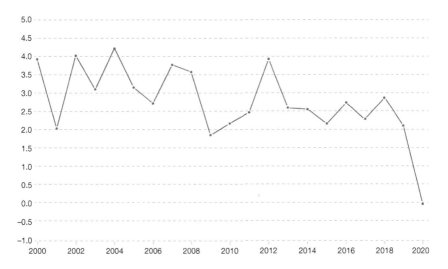

Figure 2.3: GDP Australia[7]
Source: The World Bank

The Investment Clock

The difficulties encountered in accurately forecasting economic growth cycles gave rise to a 'rule of thumb' technique termed the Investment Clock.

The concept of the Investment Clock was purportedly first published in London's *Evening Standard* in 1937.[8] While not flawless, the clock can be quite accurate at predicting the sequence of events that lie ahead in each economic cycle. The major source of judgement involves determining exactly where the hand on the clock should be placed at any given time, as an indication of the phase in which the economy currently lies.

The clock amalgamates the individual cycles of rising and falling share markets, interest rates, commodity prices and so on that comprise an overall economic cycle. Each of the component cycles interrelates with the others, thus resulting in a predictable chain of events that may be illustrated using the clock in figure 2.4. Consider a journey from 12 o'clock at the top of a boom cycle marking the end of an economic expansionary period, through 3 o'clock during a slow-down period to 6 o'clock at the depth of recession:

- 12 o'clock: Rising real estate values feed into inflation, which typically triggers a response from those charged with managing monetary policy (in Australia, the Reserve Bank of Australia (RBA)) by raising interest rates to avoid the damaging effects of uncontrolled inflation.

- 1 o'clock: Rising interest rates puts pressure on business returns (as an investment class), which, in turn, puts downwards pressure on share prices (2 o'clock) as investors reduce their exposure.

- 3 o'clock: Falling business values results in reduced capital to fund business investment, which triggers a reduction in demand for materials (comprising input commodities, such as steel for building structures, copper for electrical cabling and the like).

- 4 o'clock: Falling business demand requires the RBA to draw upon its store of foreign currency (countries such as Australia with a floating exchange rate system use Forex reserves to manage the relative value of the local currency in comparison with foreign currencies).

- 5 o'clock: Similarly, reduced money supply by the RBA results in less money circulating within the economy, which ultimately feeds into reduced credit availability and, ultimately, declining real estate values (6 o'clock).

- 7 o'clock: External market stimulus in the form of reduced interest rates is required to 'kick start' the economy, encouraging business investment and the commencement of the next economic expansion period back to 12 o'clock.

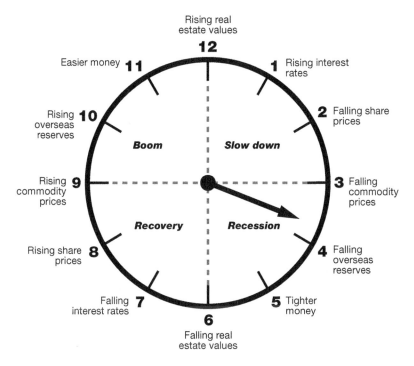

Figure 2.4: The Investment Clock[8]

The sequence of events depicted by the clock have proven to be quite accurate over the period since the mid-1930s. However, the elapsed time between the 'hours' on the clock face can vary substantially between economic cycles. As a recent (overview-level only) illustration of how the clock works, the Federal Reserve Bank's response to COVID-19 comprised increasing the supply of money in the economy to avoid the damaging impacts of economic slow-down and recession. This action drove interest rates downwards and improved credit-based affordability of assets. Cheaper money has enabled governments at all levels to implement expanded infrastructure investment programmes, which have flowed through to historic high levels of industry. Accordingly, rising asset prices (particularly shares and real estate) have signalled boom economic times, from which the direction of the next cycle can only be downwards.

Conclusion

Recent external interventions in market-based economies around the world (including Australia) have temporarily distorted economic circumstances from country to country. However, market fundamentals of supply and demand still drive the underlying cycles of growth and recession.

Key takeaways for sustainable businesses

1 Market economies are subject to economic cycles, which are regular expansions and contractions in growth. This is fundamentally why infrastructure engineering and construction is regularly subject to feast followed by famine periods that make it a particularly tough place in which to survive and thrive. Understanding the current phase of the broader economy informs the upcoming conditions likely to be faced by business.

2 An awareness of the effect economic cycles have on the infrastructure engineering and construction industry informs the importance of understanding the stage at which a given cycle is at. Forecasting the next major inflection point (when boom is turning to bust and vice versa) is, in practice, extremely difficult to undertake with precision.

3 The Investment Clock is of value in predicting the sequence of events that lie ahead in each economic cycle. Whilst each economic cycle has a similar sequence of events, the elapsed time between events can vary substantially. It is this 'shifting' that causes the change in character of one cycle to the next as well as the length of a given cycle.

CHAPTER 3

External forces and industry consolidation

As explored in chapter 1, Australia's story in infrastructure engineering and construction is synonymous with overcoming vast distances across largely uninhabitable terrain to enable connectivity between our urban centres. Commercial and residential builders such as Lendlease, Queensland's Hutchison Builders, Richard Crookes and, more recently, Watpac and Built, have made major contributions to the modern urban centres in which we live.

Central to our story though are the organisations, such as Baulderstone, John Holland, Thiess, Hornibrook, Leightons and Abigroup, that provided the infrastructure foundations for the industry that exists today. Typically, these entities were founded by visionary locals or immigrants and grown from humble beginnings to become significant local entities (see chapter 8 for more on this subject).

Similar companies operating today are in varying phases of growth. Successful entities, such as WA's Georgiou Group (formed from Direct Drainage and Geocrete via an acquisition of Roadpave) and Queensland-based BMD, are vying for local 'Tier 1' status.[1] These businesses also take advantage of boom periods in mining and/or the commercial sector to expand and diversify.

Increasingly though, international players now dominate the local market. The reasons for the underlying nature of the local industry become apparent when:

- taking a snapshot of recent history and the key circumstances that have given rise to the current situation

- introducing a strategic framework known as the Five Forces Model to make better sense of what's going on

- exploring the implications for businesses, considering risks, returns and potential government actions.

International involvement in Australia's infrastructure engineering and construction industries

Australia has a long history of international company involvement in infrastructure engineering and construction. For decades, international participants have provided local companies with financial backing, resources and connections to enable local growth and diversification as well as successful regional expansion. Indeed, and as a net importer of capital, Australia's ongoing prosperity depends upon international participation in the industry.

The following analysis concentrates on the infrastructure sector of the engineering and construction industry, being the major element of the industry comprising civil infrastructure, commercial and residential building and mining services.[2] Infrastructure engineering and construction is a predominant driver of growth and a significant attractor of international investment in the local industry.

Whilst over the years many foreign organisations have established an entity in Australia, only a handful have developed a significant local business. A long list of organisations, including the ones listed here, have established a local presence with varying degrees of minor success and/or failure:

- Great Britain's Costain Group (de-listed in Australia in 1988[3]) and Balfour Beatty plc (exited Australia following the 2014 sale of the Parsons Brinckerhoff services division and exiting a bid in 2015 for the Sydney CBD and South East Light Rail project[4])

- New Zealand's Fulton Hogan (active across Australasia)

- France's Citra (incorporated in Australia in 1969[5]), Dumez (subsequently merged with Vinci SA who maintains a local presence via Seymour Whyte[6]) and Bouygues (active in Australia since 2008 via Colas' acquisition of Australia's SAMI Bitumen Technologies and consolidated via acquisition of AW Edwards in 2018[7])

- Japan's Obayashi and Kumagai Corporations (both established a presence in the 1990s via Transfield Kumagai for the Sydney Harbour Tunnel project and Transfield Obayashi for Melbourne City Link ring roads, with Obayashi remaining more active locally, teaming with Australia's Built in 2016 for building projects[8])

- Korea's Samsung (active locally including the award of the WestConnex M4 East Tunnels contract in 2015[9])

- Germany's Walter Bau (local entity Walter Construction went into liquidation in 2005 along with the parent group[10]) and Bilfinger Berger (acquired by Lendlease in 2010)

- Austria's Strabag SE (undertook water industry projects in the early 2000s and maintains a minor local presence[11])

- USA's Dillingham (exited Australia following participation in the Snowy Mountains hydroelectric scheme in the late 1960s[12])

- Italy's Rizzani (involved locally since 2010 including WestConnex M4 Widening in NSW[13])

- Malaysia's Gamuda BHD (a recent entrant successfully securing a Sydney Metro West Western Tunnelling contract in Joint Venture with Britain's Laing O'Rourke who retains an active Australian presence[14]).

International domination

Spanish entity OHL established an Australian presence in 2011[15] and exited in 2018. Spain's Ferrovial sold their local investment Broadspectrum to CIMIC Group (ultimate owner ACS) in 2020,[16] apparently signalling a wavering commitment to an Australian presence.

Conversely, Spanish entities ACS and Acciona have established a solid platform in Australia. Why then have these Spanish contractors, in particular, been successful in making their presence felt in Australia?

One key reason lies with the economic circumstances experienced in Spain, following the recession triggered by the 2007–2008 global financial crisis (GFC).[17] In the decade prior to the GFC, Spain flourished, with economic growth much faster than the rest of Europe, and a high level of employment.

Spain's associated construction boom abruptly reversed via a credit crunch, borne of a collapse in real estate prices. Local banks absorbed huge losses as property owners struggled to repay mortgages. The crisis was devastating for the Spanish economy, with a protracted downturn resulting in a severe increase in unemployment.

Spain's economic troubles culminated in 2012, necessitating an application for a rescue package from the European Stability Mechanism (ESM)[18] — the Eurozone's provider of financial assistance programmes for member states in financial difficulty.

Accordingly, major Spanish engineering and construction contractors (particularly those with international operations) finding themselves with significant local idle capacity, turned their attention overseas for opportunities. Their expansion efforts were greatly assisted by access to the aforementioned European Union funding arrangements, which was largely provided in the form of guaranteed up-front tariffs for power generated via local renewable energy projects.

In the case of Spanish company ACS, market entry into Australia was via buy-in and then progressive takeover of German constructor Hochtief, with majority ownership achieved in 2011. Hochtief possessed a controlling interest in local Leightons Holdings (which in turn comprised Leightons Contractors, Thiess and John Holland). Leightons Contractors and Thiess merged to form CPB Contractors under the umbrella of CIMIC Group. CIMIC remains the dominant player in the local market.[19]

Acciona established an initial presence in Australia in 2002 in the renewable energy market (constructing wind farms and waste-to-energy facilities).[20] The company delivered Legacy Way in Brisbane, the Adelaide Desalination Project and acquired the Geotech Group in 2017[21] whilst delivering projects, including Sydney Light Rail CBD and Southeast Extension, Toowoomba Range Second Crossing and Harwood Bridge as part of the Pacific Complete upgrade of the Pacific Highway from Woolgoolga to Ballina. In 2020, Acciona acquired Lendlease Engineering from Lendlease Group to consolidate a position as a Tier 1 contractor in Australia.[22]

John Holland, formerly part of the Leightons Group, was acquired by China Communications Construction International Holding Limited (CCCI) in 2015.[23] Despite CCCI shelving its Singapore-based South-East Asian expansion plans to re-focus on its reportedly loss-making Australian operations, John Holland has retained its position as a major local player.[24]

Italy's Webuild SpA (formerly Salini Impregilo SpA) was founded in 2014 via merger of Salini into Impregilo.[25] Acquisition of Alstaldi SpA, aligned with an Italian Government–supported consolidation of the construction sector known as Progetto Italia (Project Italy),[26] is intended to improve Webuild's competitiveness in international markets. This, along with Webuild's 2021 successful Northeast Link tender in Victoria and involvement in the Snowy 2.0 pumped Hydroelectric project[27] appears to signal the establishment of a fourth major local player.

The structure of the local industry

Consider figure 3.1 illustrating the share of transport infrastructure project work awarded to major engineering and construction contractors since 2005, grouped by ultimate corporate ownership. The underlying data, drawn from reported major transport project values and first collated in May 2020, is broadly representative of the proportion of infrastructure work awarded to major contractors over the previous decade and a half. The chart plainly illustrates the results of the local industry consolidation that has occurred over the last 15 years.

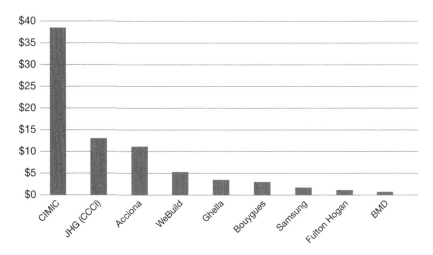

Figure 3.1: Major transport infrastructure projects work won by $bn since 2005 (updated June 2021).[28]

The chart closely resembles the typical structure of a mature industry, shaped by market forces. The local infrastructure engineering and construction industry is currently dominated by four major participants, who access around 80 per cent of the available project revenue.

The attractiveness of the local industry

A related question concerns the extent to which the current situation will remain the status quo, with international contractors remaining invested in Australia and dominating the local market for the foreseeable future.

To a large extent, this depends on the relative size and attractiveness of the future pipeline of infrastructure projects on offer in Australia in comparison with other jurisdictions, taking into consideration relative sovereign-, political-, regulatory- and currency-related risks.

Most importantly, though, contractors evaluate market attractiveness from the perspective of return on investment as well as volume of work (projects) on offer. All other considerations being equal, international contractors will logically deploy their resources in the jurisdictions that maximise their risk-weighted return on deployed capital and resources.

Referring to figure 3.2 (overleaf), as at 2022 the volume of work across Australia announced (approximately $181 billion) and under procurement (approximately $71 billion) remains significant by international standards.

The NSW 2020 10 Year Civil Infrastructure Report is one of several sources flagging consistently elevated infrastructure expenditure, forecasting an estimated NSW Civil work spend of $246 billion in 2020 (up 23 per cent from the previous year) with minor adjustments of -5 per cent and +1 per cent in subsequent 2021 and 2022 Reports.[28]

Infrastructure developments such as Sydney Metro in NSW (Sydney Metro West and Badgerys Creek), Sydney's Western Harbour Tunnel and Northern Beaches Link, Victoria's Melbourne Airport Rail Link and ARTC's Inland Rail programme, are attractive 'mega' projects for international contractors.

In broad terms, Australia remains a desirable destination for construction companies, with a mature legal system and projects with a level of technical complexity that attracts international capabilities.

However, whilst the projects pipeline across Australia has remained robust since the mid-2010s, specific concerns are being raised locally regarding project delays, cost blowouts and consequent poor project returns, citing a wide range of recently completed and in-progress projects. Broader effects borne of COVID-19–related disruption are also yet to be fully understood. These issues will be explored in depth in chapter 4.

For the time being, though, let's briefly consider what alternative work is on offer for international contractors elsewhere across the globe.

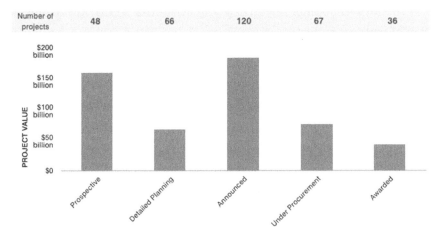

Figure 3.2: Infrastructure pipeline by project status[29]
Source: Infrastructure Partnerships Australia

The economics and politics of infrastructure demand

Public infrastructure, whilst taking time to develop and bring to market, is extensively publicised during government elections.

Accordingly, project initiations are heavily influenced by electoral cycles, in addition to being exposed to general economic circumstances. Major project announcements are a typical part of election campaigns, and a significant proportion of countries around the globe have major public infrastructure programmes in train.

Public sector investment (commonly referred to as fiscal stimulus) is currently a popular method utilised by governments to counteract economic slow-down conditions. Accordingly, and to counteract the considerable recent damage to local economies borne of COVID-19, many countries are widely expected to implement infrastructure expenditure programmes over the next decade to stimulate growth.

Let's illustrate the international trends with a brief snapshot around the globe.

USA

A major, USA-wide infrastructure investment and rehabilitation program was a feature of the 2016 presidential elections. However, it took until late 2021 and a change in government for the programme to be approved.[30] This is expected to boost major projects, such as the California High Speed Railway, which continues to inch forward with escalating overall costs.[31]

Spain

The Coalition government elected in 2020 is expected to moderately increase public construction and civil engineering investment, albeit off a small base compared with the period since 2012.[32] Uncertainties remain regarding political stability and the ongoing effect of the major deficit reduction measures negotiated in 2012 as a key component of the ESM rescue package discussed earlier.

United Kingdom

A December 2019 snap election and subsequent confirmation of Britain's exit from the European Union (Brexit) delayed confirmation of the timeframe for major public infrastructure projects, in particular the Northern Powerhouse Rail upgrade program, which interfaces with the in-progress London–Birmingham HS-2 High Speed Rail project. A scaled-back version of Northern Powerhouse Rail was announced in November 2021.[33]

Asia

The Rapid Transit System Singapore–Malaysia Link project remains on hold as at early 2022 following a Malaysian Government review of the local construction sector.[34] Notwithstanding, Singapore's investment in infrastructure and civil engineering works remains relatively high, with several mega projects currently underway or in the pipeline, including the Thomson–East Coast MRT Line, the new Tuas Mega Port and Changi Airport Terminal 5.

The Middle East

A major focus is on the Qatari economy, which has strengthened with increased infrastructure and construction activities associated with the 2022 FIFA World Cup.[35]

The local competitive environment

Over the course of 2020, I carried out a survey of regular blog readers to get a sense of what was happening in the local infrastructure engineering and construction market. This was prompted by the following anecdotal evidence at that time:

- Lendlease was reportedly seeking to exit infrastructure engineering and construction based on poor returns and significant unforeseen write-downs on in-progress projects (as noted earlier LendLease's engineering arm was subsequently sold to Acciona)

- Fulton Hogan reportedly had its local business up for sale (as of 2022, no transaction has occurred)

- international entrants were withdrawing from the local scene (most notably Spain's OHL).

The issues identified by readers included:

- reported cost overruns and declining profitability for Tier 1 contractors

- over-use of inexperienced resources on in-progress projects, potentially compromising performance across the industry

- time- and cost-intensive procurement processes limiting participation in larger tenders to major contractors

- significant transfer of risk (and in some cases unmanageable risk) to contractors, creating a concentration of commercial, financing and insurance/reinsurance risk.

These issues still characterise the local industry today. How then do we go about better understanding what's driving the current circumstances?

Identifying the competition: The Five Forces Model

Theoretical models can be very helpful in analysing a problem or considering an issue from a strategic perspective. One relevant model in this instance (my favourite because of its simplicity) is known as the Five Forces Model. The underlying framework draws upon industrial organisation economics to identify five 'forces' that determine the competitive intensity of an industry, and therefore its overall attractiveness for business seeking to generate sustainable returns on investment.

The analysis was developed by Michael Porter of Harvard University, who described the model in his 1979 *Harvard Business Review* article 'How competitive forces shape strategy'.[36] Porter developed his Five Forces analysis in reaction to the widely used strengths/weaknesses/opportunities/threats (SWOT) analysis, which he believed lacked appropriate rigour.

Porter identified five factors that act together to determine the nature of competition within an industry. These are typically presented as per figure 3.3, and comprise the:

- bargaining power of customers (buyers)

- threat of new entrants to an industry

- bargaining power of suppliers

- threat of substitute products

- intensity of competitive rivalry within an industry.

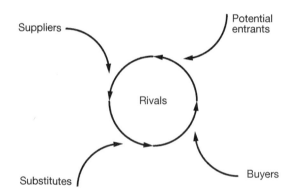

Figure 3.3: Five Forces Model[36]

Porter referred to the Five Forces as the micro-environment, consisting of those factors impacting a company's ability to serve its customers and make a profit. A significant change in any of the forces normally requires a business to reassess its industry position. Porter proposed that overall industry attractiveness does not imply that every organisation in a given industry will return the same profitability. Businesses can apply their core competencies, business model, network and/or innovative capability, and achieve a profit ideally above the industry average.

Consider infrastructure engineering and construction as an industry. This industry is fundamentally created and shaped in Australia by Commonwealth, state and local governments and their agencies. These *Buyers* procure infrastructure, such as roads, railways, water storage and delivery, electricity assets, on behalf of citizens as the users and beneficiaries of the works. The *Suppliers* are the consultants, contractors and equipment and materials suppliers, large and small, who compete (largely by tender) to design, construct and/ or maintain these assets directly for the *Buyers* or as sub-contractors to larger *Suppliers*.

Infrastructure engineering and construction is a mature industry and, therefore, characterised by intense competition between existing *Rivals*. As explored in chapter 2, the industry is also subject to regular episodes of feast and famine in line with rising and falling economic conditions.

The industry is progressively embracing technology such as integrated design and construction data systems, mechanised construction methods, improved materials and recycling methodologies (more on this in chapter 4). Viable *Substitutes* (such as alternative transport) have yet to fundamentally alter the demand for physically constructed transport infrastructure assets. Climate change–associated water scarcity and the demand for carbon-neutral forms of energy generation are in the process of disrupting demand for enabling utilities such as electrical, water and gas services.

Barriers to entry to an industry are important in determining the threat of *Potential Entrants*. As outlined in table 3.1 (overleaf), Porter defined six major sources of barriers to entry.

Table 3.1: Porter's Five Forces—barriers to entry[36]

Barrier	Description
Economies of scale	Lower unit costs make it difficult for smaller newcomers to break into a market and compete effectively
Product differentiation (including branding)	Existing products and services with strong unique service propositions and/or brands increase customer loyalty and make it difficult for newcomers to gain market share
Capital requirements	High investment cost will deter new entrants to an industry and can restrict entry to larger organisations
Cost disadvantages independent of size	Other elements may create barriers, such as learning curve effects, proprietary technology, access to raw materials, government subsidies or favourable locations
Access to distribution channels	A lack of access to distribution channels will make it difficult for newcomers to enter an industry
Regulatory and legal restrictions	Government-enacted rules, as well as legal protections, such as patents, can provide the beneficiary with protection

Infrastructure engineering and construction in Australia is historically characterised by a relatively benign regulatory framework, allowing foreign establishment of local operations with only minor restrictions. A significant increase in public sector investment in infrastructure projects over the last decade has resulted in an influx of foreign companies establishing a local presence and competing for work.

Shifts in capital requirements and a reduction in regulatory and legal restrictions have provided international organisations with opportunities to establish and consolidate their local position.

Capital requirements

The relative strength of the Australian economy in comparison with global conditions and the sizeable pipeline of work on offer by international standards appear to justify the initial investment required by new entrants. Most new entrants minimise initial costs by establishing a small local presence staffed by a combination of ex-patriates and locally procured resources.

The packaging methodologies increasingly employed by governments in procuring mega projects provides multiple opportunities for businesses to secure work that fits within balance sheet constraints.

The key initial hurdle to be overcome is the tendering process, where specific standards, client expectations and procurement approach (including probity requirements) create unexpected surprises for those companies inexperienced with local processes. The cost and time commitments associated with tendering for major projects in Australia is significant by international standards. High tender costs are driven by bespoke contracting models and elevated client expectations regarding demonstration and documentation of capability, previous experience and proposed methodology. This barrier has been acknowledged to some extent via (limited) government funding of unsuccessful bidder costs.

Regulatory and legal restrictions

International organisations have been encouraged to enter the local market via government relaxation of regulatory and legal restrictions, particularly in relation to stipulated minimum local content requirements.

Local industrial relations requirements create specific challenges for new entrants seeking to import a skilled workforce. This typically results in successful new entrants initially utilising local sub-contractors. Whilst local sub-contractors have grown largely organically to meet industry demand, resources do not always keep pace with demand. This creates further challenges for new entrants in competing with the established players with similarly established networks.

History indicates that consolidation via local business investment/ acquisition is a key step most entrants must make to successfully achieve a sustainable industry position.

Competitive pressure

Let's evaluate the status of the industry from the perspective of existing suppliers (contractors) in the market. The key is in evaluating in relative terms how 'powerful' the existing suppliers are.

Referring again to Porter's work,[36] suppliers find themselves in a powerful industry position when:

- there are only a few large suppliers (and referring to figure 3.1 earlier, four major contractors dominate the market, with one of the big 4 dominating the other three when measured by work secured over a significant timeframe)

- the product or service being supplied is unique or at least differentiated (in this case the services provided are not strongly differentiated, given the major contractors are largely sourcing equipment and materials and delivering services using sub-contractors drawn from the same local pool)

- the cost of switching to an alternative supplier is high (in this circumstance switching from contractor to contractor potentially occurs each time a new project is awarded; the domination of the big 4 in the market indicates government buyers perceive high economic and psychological costs associated with appointing contractors outside of the 'usual suspects')

- the supplier can threaten to integrate vertically (in this circumstance, major contractors overwhelmingly avoid vertical integration to take advantage of price tension within the sub-contractor pool)

- the customer is small and unimportant (certainly not the case here as government buyers retain the means to reshape the market by altering procurement strategies and tactics; more on this later in this chapter)

- there are no or few substitute resources available (of particular relevance when considering current restrictions on accessing off-shore labour).

Supplier power appears to be increasingly concentrated with the big 4, with the emergence of CIMIC as the dominant contractor a particularly noteworthy development. This creates pressure on the remaining minor players to retain their share of the available work. In circumstances where it is difficult to clearly differentiate services and where government buyer relationships are constrained by probity considerations, price-based competition for the available work is likely to result.

Margin squeeze: The consequences

The available evidence points to a perhaps unsurprising conclusion. Competitive forces in infrastructure engineering and construction are exerting significant downward pressure on project margins.[37] This is unsurprising as one would expect margin pressure in mature industries.

The unusual circumstances arise when taking into consideration the historically high levels of demand for project services. All other things being equal, one would expect, at a minimum, for the dominant contractors to be able to maintain reasonable project margins.

A key contributor to this situation lies with the trend towards major contractors' adoption of joint ventures of 'convenience'. This approach enables a contractor to access shared resources and reduce balance sheet stress when responding to a larger volume of project requests for tender than might otherwise be accessible. This approach increases tendering competition and enables contractors outside the big 4 to compete via joint venture with a major contractor for larger projects. This approach appears to be strongly supported by clients across the country as a means by which competitive pressure is maintained in an environment with high project demand.

Interestingly, a rise in big 4 contractors aligning with each other for mega project tenders suggests a shift towards consolidating industry control. Exits by unsuccessful minor international players would further shift the balance of power in favour of the major contractors. These developments may result in some reduction in margin pressure. Exit or failure of a major contractor (particularly the dominant contractor) would result in major industry disruption and a re-think by the buyers of infrastructure services. However, in the absence of major events, active government market intervention and/or a change in procurement policy, downwards margin pressure is likely to remain an industry reality for the forseeable future.

Setting aside closer analysis of the nature of industry demand for the time being (more on this in chapter 4), let's return to my 2020 survey of blog readers, and consider in more detail the experiences of smaller contractors in the industry. Readers reported flow-on consequences arising from margin pressure on major project sub-contractors including:

- a squeeze on sub-contractor margins due to cost, time and other potentially unmanageable risks being passed on by head contractors

- constrained opportunities for lower-tier infrastructure engineering and construction businesses to build internal capability and step up into the big league of direct client contracting

- reduced opportunities for investment on a cost/benefit basis in local capability, for instance in technology-based efficiencies or productivity transformation

- perpetuation of the cycle, where procurement processes embed mega project risk transfer to an extent where only the largest contractors can participate.

What to do: Business response to competitive pressure

Returning to Porter's work, the Five Forces theory proposes that, having assessed the forces affecting competition and their underlying causes, a strategist can identify a given company's strengths and weaknesses to devise a plan of action. This builds on the concept that the attractiveness, or otherwise, of an overall industry does not imply that every organisation in a given industry will return similar profitability. Businesses can apply their core competencies, business model, network and/or innovative capability to achieve superior profits in comparison with the industry average. Accordingly, strategic responses to industry pressures that might be considered include:

- repositioning so that the company's capabilities provide a better defence against the competitive force

- influencing the balance of the forces through strategic moves, thereby improving the company's position

- anticipating shifts in the factors underlying the forces and responding to them, with the hope of exploiting change by choosing a strategy appropriate for the new competitive balance before opponents recognise it.

What does this mean for smaller enterprises in mature markets, such as infrastructure engineering and construction? In answering this question, we will refer to another Porter theory regarding competitive advantage whereby contractors can exploit their relative agility in seeking competitive niches where lower overheads offer the opportunity to compete effectively with larger businesses. We will return to this subject in detail in chapter 9.

Government procurement intervention

When evaluating potential strategic responses to a given situation, it is important to consider the potential for the forces currently affecting the industry to fluctuate in strength.

As flagged earlier, governments, as the buyers of infrastructure engineering and construction project services, are in a prime position to influence the industry. Evidence over recent decades indicates that public sector agencies have adopted a relatively non-interventionalist stance in relation to the industry, allowing market forces to play out. This reflects an approach aligned with the Australian National Competition Policy established in the 1990s, reflecting the principle that competitive markets generally best serve the interests of consumers and the wider community.

The evidence discussed here indicates that the infrastructure engineering and construction industry is currently dominated by four international organisations (see figure 3.1). Domination by a big 4 is not unexpected for a mature industry; however, major industry issues have become evident including:

- the relative domination of one major contractor

- a lack of involvement in mega projects by capable local contractors.

In relation to the first concern, the signs are that unmanaged competition is resulting in a concentration of increased project risk across multiple projects with one dominant contractor. This in turn ramps up pressure on the other industry competitors to take on additional project risk to retain their respective industry position and market share, increasing the potential for contractor failure and/or broader market disruption. Anecdotal evidence indicating significant unresolved contractor claims across multiple projects leads to broader concerns regarding major contractor balance sheets.

In relation to the second concern regarding reduced industry involvement by local entities, a similar trend may be observed in relation to the providers of technical engineering services. Major international technical professional services companies, such as Jacobs, AECOM and Bechtel (US), WSP (Canada), Arcadis (Netherlands) and Arup (UK), have subsumed Australian-founded consultants and now dominate the local scene, with GHD Pty Ltd and BG&E the remaining locally owned organisations providing design services for major projects.

The risk of changing the status quo

Given the importance of infrastructure engineering and construction to Australia's economic prosperity, as one would expect there are a wide range of opinions regarding what's going well and what — if anything — needs to change.

The argument for industry non-intervention advanced by many over the years since the mid-1990s, was most recently put forward by Grattan Institute's report, 'Megabang for megabucks: Driving a harder bargain on megaprojects'.[38] The report supports robust competition as a means for maintaining downwards pressure on construction costs and encouraging innovation, calling the approach fundamental to procuring public infrastructure at the lowest cost to taxpayers.

An alternate view regards local contractors as a core element of a healthy industry, supported and enhanced by international businesses, as has been the case in Australia for much of our modern history. However, it appears to be increasingly challenging to maintain a sustainable local industry for all bona fide participants.

In relation to foreign ownership of local contractors, by its very nature, infrastructure construction work will, for the foreseeable future, continue to be delivered by locally sourced labour, regardless of which entity holds the contract for project delivery. However, as long-anticipated productivity improvements in labour utilisation begin to reshape the industry (more on this in chapter 4), the resulting benefits will increasingly accrue to the overseas-domiciled holders of project contracts.

There are indications of increasing government awareness of these issues. By way of example, in 2021, the NSW Government released 'Premier's Memorandum M2021-10: Procurement for large, complex infrastructure projects'.[39] The memorandum sets out expectations for the procurement of large, complex infrastructure projects, to enable sustainable delivery of the infrastructure pipeline as set out in the Infrastructure NSW document, 'Framework for establishing effective project procurement'.[41]

The NSW Government's stated intention is to evaluate procurement form, size contract package(s) and allocate risk to facilitate competitive bids from a wide range of participants (for instance Tier 2 contractors on a stand-alone basis or in joint venture with a Tier 1 player). There is also an acknowledgement that:

> ... a stable and sustainable infrastructure sector is in the public interest as, when projects experience stress, it can undermine public confidence in infrastructure investment and also reduce enthusiasm amongst contractors, subcontractors, and professionals to pursue further work with the NSW Government.[40]

Anecdotal evidence suggests an improved way forward.

The Southwest Connex Alliance (Acciona, NRW Contracting and MACA Civil, as well as AECOM and Aurecon), as proponent for the design and construction of Western Australia's AU$852 million Bunbury Outer Ring Road, is required by Main Roads WA to allocate approximately $300 million of sub-contract works to local businesses.[41]

The $5.3 billion duplication of 155 km of the Pacific Highway between Woolgoolga and Ballina engaged Laing O'Rourke and Parsons Brinkerhoff as delivery partners on behalf of NSW Roads and Maritime Services (now Transport for NSW).[42] The works packaging strategy enabled smaller contractors, including Quickway Constructions, SEE Civil and Bielby Hull Albem, to contract directly with RMS alongside major contractors, such as CPB and Acciona.

The approximately $10 billion Sydney Metro West underground railway connecting Parramatta and the Sydney CBD is a 24 km section of the wider Sydney Metro network. Gamuda Australia and Laing O'Rourke Australia (GALC JV) in March 2022 were awarded the $2.2 billion Western Tunnelling Package,[43] one of three tunnelling packages. This was the first significant local contract for Malaysia's Gamuda.

A similar package-based approach has been adopted for Melbourne's Suburban Rail Loop project, a 90-km rail loop of the Melbourne metropolitan area that will transform Melbourne's rail network from its current radial status to an orbital network.[44]

Industry-disruptive tendering tactics are occasionally employed by the major contractors, such as bidding for projects with a view to replenishing working capital (as opposed to targeting a reasonable risk-weighted project margin). Project and wider industry risks are only realistically manageable via capable government procurement processes, including informed and accurate pre-assessments of bidder financial strength and responsible risk-adjusted bid evaluation processes.

Informed project packaging strategies and judicious application of local content requirements by government procurers are available tools to create opportunities for 'up and comers' to build internal capability and move through the grades.

In this way, the government can play its part in maintaining a balanced and sustainable industry with strong local and international capability. There is a widespread industry sense that it is incumbent on governments, as buyers of major infrastructure project services as well as market managers, to act as 'circuit-breakers' and lead an industry shift towards greater sustainability of infrastructure engineering and construction as a critical local industry sector.

An alternative perspective regarding market consolidation: Passenger railcar industry case study

A transport infrastructure–related case study concerning the Australian passenger railcar manufacture industry provides a different industry perspective. This topic is of personal interest, as my first industry experience was in the mid-1980s as an undergraduate cadet engineer, an employee of what was then known as the NSW State Rail Authority. At that time, passenger railcars were still locally designed, manufactured and assembled by a duopoly of A Goninan & Co and Clyde Engineering.

Like automobiles, passenger trains are made up of complex sub-assemblies and component parts, such as traction (propulsion) and braking systems, air-conditioning units, wheel and axle units, seats and so forth. These items are mostly procured from specialist rail equipment suppliers from around the globe. Builders such as A Goninan & Co and Clyde Engineering typically designed and manufactured the body shell, ensured optimisation of the drivers' cab layout, procured sub-assemblies and vehicle fit-out items, and completed testing and commissioning of the assembled unit.

A brief history of railcar manufacturing

As historical context, much of the foundation design development work for Australian-manufactured rail carriages produced from the mid-1980s onwards was undertaken by an enterprise known as Comeng.[45] This enterprise was founded as Sydney-based company Waddington Body Works. During World War II, the Commonwealth took control of Waddington to enable completion of government orders during a time in which the business was in financial distress. The enterprise was renamed Commonwealth Engineering (later shortened to Comeng) in 1946 and opened manufacturing facilities in Rocklea, Queensland (1949), Bassendean, WA (1952), and Dandenong, Victoria (1954), prior to the Commonwealth divesting its interest in 1957. In 1982, Comeng was taken over by Australian National Industries, with the Granville factory closing in 1989 and subsequently being demolished. The Dandenong plant was sold in 1990 to ABB Transportation and is now operated by Bombardier Transportation, whilst the Bassendean facility was sold to A Goninan & Co.

A Goninan & Co Limited was founded in 1899 by Cornish brothers Alfred and Ralph Goninan as an engineering and manufacturing company for the coal industry[46]; it was then incorporated in 1905. It entered the rail business in 1917 via Commonwealth Steel, a Newcastle-located wheel and axle manufacturer, because those items could no longer be imported from Belgium due to World War I. A Goninan & Co built a business in general engineering at Broadmeadow, NSW, which expanded into a national railcar manufacturing business. Works included manufacture of K-, S- and C-set passenger carriages, as well as Tangara and OSCAR passenger trains for NSW Railways, Sprinter diesel railcars for Victoria's regional public transport operator V-Line, and railcars for WA's regional equivalent Transwa. A Goninan & Co was sold in 1999 to United Group, and in 2016, the renamed United Group Rail (UGR) was taken over by CIMIC.

Clyde Engineering was founded in Granville in 1898[47]. Early contracts included supply of railway and tram rolling stock, as well as a 1907 contract for steam locomotives for NSW Railways. Post-recovery from the Depression and following a diversification into munitions during World War II, Clyde Engineering secured an exclusive Australian Electro-Motive Diesel supply licence and built diesel locomotives for the Commonwealth Railways under a contract awarded in 1950. Following completion of a wide range of locomotive and rolling stock contracts for freight and passenger fleet customers across Australia,

Clyde Engineering was subsumed into Evans Deakin Industries in 1996. In 2001 Downer Group acquired Evans Deakin Industries to form ASX-listed Downer EDI.

Recent developments

Moving forward to 2006, and by the time the AU$3.6 billion Waratah Trains Public Private Partnership contract with NSW Railcorp (now Transport for NSW) was executed,[48] Downer had commenced a journey from train builder to local importer and maintainer of offshore manufactured and assembled passenger rail vehicles. UGR's most recent local build, comprising the Outer Suburban (OSCAR) fleet for Railcorp NSW, was completed in 2012. Waratah Series 2 passenger trains (manufactured by China's CRRC)[49] and replacement Outer Suburban cars (manufactured by Hyundai-Rotem)[50] were sourced offshore, with Downer and UGR, respectively, providing local maintenance.

A trend towards offshore manufacture has been (at least temporarily) curtailed by local content and local job creation requirements, implemented by the state governments of Victoria and, more recently, Western Australia. In both cases, this has resulted in manufacture being undertaken by local enterprises (such as Hoffman Engineering in Bendigo and head contractor Downer at Newport Workshops for Metro Trains Melbourne's High-Capacity Metro Trains fleet)[51] or in local facilities set up by offshore firms (such as Knorr-Bremse for air-conditioning and brake components as part of the WA Railcar Program for the Metronet rail system).[52]

Without active intervention by governments in the procurement process, it seems clear that there would be very little (if any) local rail passenger car manufacturing activities. Setting aside arguments regarding the appropriateness (or otherwise) of Australia's ongoing participation in this industry sector, the case study makes abundantly clear government's ability to influence a market sector in which it participates as buyer.

Conclusion

To revisit the central theme of Part I of the book, good businesses seeking to become sustainable organisations in infrastructure engineering and construction must understand the:

- forces that impact on the competitive dynamic of the industry

- relative impact these forces have on the industry

- extent to which the forces are subject to change in strength or impact.

Australia's relatively open approach to international business means that mature local industries are subject to the effects of international competition as well as local consolidation. History provides both context and useful indications for what may transpire in the future. Good local businesses in infrastructure engineering and construction need to take both recent history and industry analysis into strategic consideration when seeking to map out a journey towards becoming a sustainable enterprise (more on this in Part III).

Key takeaways for sustainable businesses

1   Australia has a long history of international company involvement in infrastructure engineering and construction; however, international companies now dominate the local industry to an unprecedented extent.

2   The extent to which international contractors remain invested in Australia depends on the relative size and attractiveness of the future pipeline of infrastructure projects on offer in Australia in comparison with other countries. Whilst the projects pipeline across Australia is at a generational high and has remained robust since the mid-2010s, concerns are being raised locally regarding project delays, cost blowouts and consequent poor project returns.

3 Public infrastructure investments are heavily influenced by electoral cycles, in addition to being exposed to general economic circumstances. To counteract the considerable recent damage to economies after COVID-19, many countries, including Australia, are expected to maintain infrastructure expenditure programmes over the forseeable future to stimulate growth. Australia will be competing with other countries to retain the interest and services of the international players in engineering and construction.

4 The dominance of the big 4 in Australia creates pressure on the remaining minor players to retain their share of the available work. Competitive conditions are exerting significant downward pressure on project margins, even in an environment with a high volume of available work.

5 Flow-on effects to major project sub-contractors include 'margin squeeze', which constrains opportunities for lower-tier engineering and construction businesses to build internal capability and step up into the big league of direct client contracting. The longer-term risk lies in perpetuation of the cycle, where procurement processes reward mega project risk transfer to an extent where only the largest contractors can participate.

CHAPTER 4

Analysing shifting demand, needs, and investment imperatives

Before diving into this topic, let's consider this extract from an article by Robert Puentes on the importance of infrastructure:

> *Tremendous growth … will place new demands on already over-taxed infrastructure. Rooftop solar panels have rattled electric utilities, which are scrambling to keep the grid operating. High-profile natural disasters draw attention to problems with infrastructure.*[1]

This quote highlights just a few of the disruptive forces authorities are faced with when looking to plan and manage infrastructure investment programs. The new normal arising from the extended COVID-19–related disruptions will create even greater challenges for decision-makers seeking to accelerate economic recovery. So which country do you think the extracts above refer to? Here's a hint:

> *America's ability to realize its competitive potential depends on making smart infrastructure choices.*[1]

It is apparent that Australia is not the only country struggling with these challenges.

Mid-2010s industry growth cycle

Let's look more closely at the profile of forward demand for infrastructure engineering and construction project services across Australia. Much can be learnt from this current industry growth cycle:

- commencing in the mid-2010s with the cessation of the mining boom

- expanding via major infrastructure investment in roads and rail transport

- disrupted by COVID-19.

Interest rates have been at a low point over the cycle and have been maintained at low levels by substantial increases in local money supply by the Federal Reserve. Low interest rates on borrowings have enabled state and federal governments to fund substantial infrastructure investment programs.

A combination of delays in project approvals and commencements (not an unusual occurrence) and recent disruptions due to the productivity-related effects of COVID-19 have further extended the demand curve. Looming labour, equipment and materials shortages are also likely to limit the industry's ability to fully meet demand across the country. Accordingly, an inevitable tail-off in project works still appears to be comfortably in the future.

Of course, our understanding of the cycles that drive the infrastructure engineering and construction industry suggests that boom times do not last forever. Downswings in economic circumstances are typically set off by unanticipated events, as was witnessed with the series of financial crises that occurred in the 2000s. A significant rise in local interest rates would be highly likely to result in widespread government project cancellations.

In the meantime, niche businesses in the industry need to remain informed of the peaks and troughs in demand for the sub-contracted works and specific project services disguised by the headline demand profile.

Overlaid on this demand profile are government-triggered alterations to project requirements, driven by changes in underlying user demand. This element, whilst traditionally longer term in nature, may well prove to be industry disruptive in the wake of COVID-19.

Transition from mining to transport infrastructure

Reflecting on the commencement of this industry growth phase in 2015 provides a useful perspective regarding the challenges likely to be faced in the foreseeable future.

The period around 2015 marked the tail end of the most recent mining boom. Major expansion works were undertaken, predominantly in WA by BHP Biliton and Rio Tinto, alongside the Fortescue Metals Group becoming the fourth-largest iron ore producer worldwide. Major investments were enabled by high commodity prices. As illustrated in figure 4.1 (overleaf), the period from 2013–2016, saw the effects of a drop-off in global resources demand became rapidly apparent, flowing through to delayed and cancelled mining projects.[2]

Accordingly, WA-focused infrastructure contractors turned their attention to the eastern seaboard in anticipation of the commencement of new transport infrastructure projects. As illustrated in figure 4.1, major project work in progress had built steadily since the early 2000s, before levelling off at around $5 billion per annum through to 2015. All available evidence pointed to a major upswing in project demand; however, the evidence was viewed with scepticism at that time by an industry used to experiencing long lead times and frequent delays with major infrastructure projects in Australia coming to market. The reality as shown in figure 4.1 shows a rapid increase to just below $14 Billion in 2021.

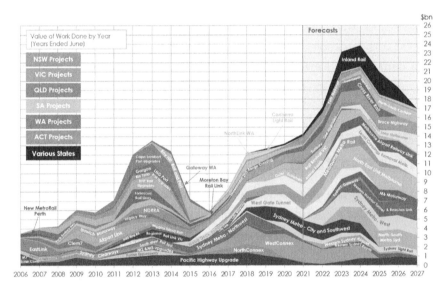

Figure 4.1: Major transport infrastructure projects – Australia[3]

Note: This chart includes projects with a value of work done greater than $300 million in any single year.
Source: Macromonitor

Looking to figure 4.2, it is apparent that the forecast upswing in major projects indeed materialised, with 2022 quarter 3 work in progress at approximately $14 billion.

The industry has, since 2015, completed significant transport infrastructure projects, including the remaining Pacific Highway works from Ballina to Woolgoolga (NSW), WestConnex Stages I and II (NSW) and Sydney Metro Northwest (NSW). Progress has also been made with Cross River Rail in Brisbane, Metronet Stage 1 in Western Australia, Westgate Tunnel in Victoria and Inland Rail in multiple states. In 2015, this appeared to be an almost unachievable outcome.

What is the current supply and demand outlook for the industry?

In evaluating the forecast pipeline of work, additional expansion in industry capacity would be required to meet and sustain 2024 peak demand of $19 billion shown in figure 4.2.

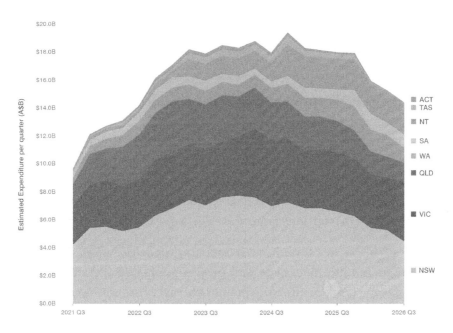

Figure 4.2: Pipeline forecast by expenditure[4]
Source: © Infrastructure Partnerships Australia

When considering the broad industry including government procurement, it is highly unlikely that a peak demand of $24 billion as shown in figure 4.1 will eventuate. Given the delays manifested in major projects thanks to COVID-19 work restrictions, it appears likely that peak work output will flatten in line with delivery schedule slippages being experienced by most major projects. Using recent industry history as a guide, the current project work profile is likely to be further flattened and extended by yet-to-materialise issues, including scope creep and schedule delays.

Evidence points to the major contractors across Australia approaching maximum capacity. Extensive use of sub-contracting services from the same local pool to deliver major projects indicates that local sub-contractors could be a source of delivery-capacity limitations.[5] The local small and medium contractors typically expand organically to meet peaks in demand (and are forced to contract when work dries up). Contractors also seek to access overseas-sourced skilled labour to supplement local capacity. Larger contractors on occasion partner with smaller businesses, leveraging balance sheet strength to secure exclusive access to scarce additional resources from the limited pool.

However, in the current circumstances of restricted overseas labour supply (borne of COVID-19–related international border closures), the local contractors have limited scope for additional expansion. COVID-19 supply-chain-related disruptions have created similar restrictions in procuring new equipment. Adequate supply of raw materials (sand, gravel etc.) is also challenging, again, exacerbated by supply-chain disruptions from the effects of COVID-19.

The predominant limitation on industry capacity, however, is a lack of skilled and locally experienced project managers and supervisors. This chronic issue is affecting major contractors as well as small and medium businesses.

Governments are also limited in their ability to source additional skilled personnel to plan, procure and manage projects and pro-grammes. This is felt to a greater extent in the minor projects and programs space, reflecting the current industry focus on mega projects. It is fair to observe that the challenge here is not access to funding, with programmes such as WA Recovery: Infrastructure,[6] the Queensland Reconstruction Authority (QRA)[7] and Restart NSW[8] in place to deal with infrastructure requirements, including disaster recovery and improved resilience. Challenges appear, though, when it comes to detailed planning and procurement, with many of the smaller projects slow in coming to market.

On the supply side, and referring to McKinsey & Company's publication 'Australia's infrastructure innovation imperative',[9] construction industry research and development investment is historically less than 1 per cent of its revenue, in comparison with, say, the aerospace industry investment at 4.5 per cent of revenue. Considering that, for advanced economies, 80 per cent of long-term productivity growth is due to advances in 'technological innovation', it appears inevitable that industry adoption of productivity-improvement-enabling technology will accelerate.

McKinsey proposes 'industry disruptive', technology-based solutions that the engineering and construction industry could embrace, including:

- higher-definition surveying and geo-location

- 5D building information management (BIM): linking 3-D information models to scheduled time (4-D) and cost (5-D)

- digital collaboration and mobility supported by the widespread use of handheld devices

- the Internet of Things and advanced analytics, enabled through adoption of 'smart' design principles at the front end of developments

- future proof–based design and construction.

If we consider the persistent cost pressures experienced on major projects, I'm inclined to believe that we will also see a much greater focus on input costs and, more specifically, labour inputs going forward.

Local wages and, to a lesser extent, salaries are not directly exposed to the effects of international competition. In this sense, Australia operates as a relatively 'closed' economy without the competition that occurs between more mobile workforces across, say, the European Union. Accordingly, the key drivers of productivity improvement are most likely to be greater augmentation and/or replacement of labour with mechanised solutions and technology-enabled improvements in the way site labour is organised and integrated with equipment and materials.

With the current evidence pointing to the industry operating at or near to a capacity ceiling, governments will likely be cautious to not over-stretch the industry, recognising that an over-supply of work typically leads to an increase in poor project outcomes.

Signs, therefore, point to an inevitable, and potentially sudden, drop-off in demand and the industry cycle moving from a 'build' to a 'maintain' phase. This is characteristic of the industry, leading to more aggressive feast or famine behaviour that typically shows up when the pipeline of work starts to decrease.

This inevitable drop-off can be offset with additions to federal and state government project pipelines. However, well-developed major infrastructure projects in Australia inevitably take years for governments to properly plan, scope and assess, so that necessary consultation can be undertaken, and for funding and approvals to be secured.

Additional challenges arise when poorly scoped projects that have been rushed through the preliminary planning and procurement stages are prematurely released to market. Fast-tracked projects could be deemed necessary or desirable by governments as a means of offsetting the effects of a general slow-down in the wider economy. Unfortunately, these projects are typically at a heightened risk of delay, re-scoping and associated claims for variations. Problems multiply when these projects are not procured under the appropriate contract model for the circumstances (more on this in chapter 5).

How important is it to build the right infrastructure?

Let's tackle the broader question of whether building the right infrastructure matters.

On face value, this might appear to be a disingenuous question. When considering funding allocation for infrastructure projects involving many billions of dollars of expenditure, the significant interplay between process and politics must inevitably be taken into consideration.

There's a long-running industry debate regarding the extent to which decisions relating to infrastructure investment should be managed on an independent basis via Infrastructure Australia and the various state-based infrastructure agencies. Indeed, Infrastructure Australia was established in 2008 for the express purpose of providing independent advice to government and industry regarding investment in Australian infrastructure. This was enshrined in the *Infrastructure Australia Act 2008* (subsequently amended in 2014).

The alternate view regarding the government's overriding role in determining what should be built and where, is that decisions should be determined based on representations from government members representing the needs of their constituents. This view was expressed quite bluntly by the ex–NSW Premier Gladys Berejiklian when addressing questions posed by counsel assisting an Independent Commission Against Corruption (ICAC) inquiry termed Operation Keppel. Crikey reported Ms Berejiklian saying that she found nothing unusual about a government spending money to keep a seat during a by-election. Further and as recorded in Operation Keppel transcripts:

> *Asked by counsel assisting the ICAC, Scott Robertson, whether Ms Berejiklian was interested in funding projects for political reasons without necessarily being concerned about their merits, she said: 'I don't think they're mutually exclusive.'*[10]

Setting aside the political aspect of this issue (occasionally labelled 'pork-barrelling'), the debate is fundamentally about the criteria by which investment decisions are made. Consider then, the importance of investing in the right infrastructure.

Referring to analysis contained within a 2014 Australian Commonwealth Bureau of Infrastructure, Transport and Regional Economics Information Sheet, 'Infrastructure, Transport and Productivity',[11] a positive link can be established between investment in the right transport infrastructure and improved productivity.

What is productivity?

Let's look more closely at some key definitions.

Productivity is the efficiency of transforming inputs (capital and labour) into outputs (goods and services). The two main measures of overall productivity employed by statisticians are:

- labour productivity: a partial measure calculated as real GDP or gross value added per hour of labour worked

- multi-factor productivity: a broader measure determined as real GDP or gross value added per unit of combined labour and capital inputs.

When interpreting productivity trends, it is important to distinguish these productivity concepts from the measured productivity indices (for instance reported changes in GDP). Whilst productivity statistics aim to measure technical progress or changes in the efficiency of production, in practice they measure the volume of outputs versus inputs. This gives rise to measurement limitations, including being affected (at least in the short term) by fluctuations in external factors, such as weather, changes in capacity utilisation and population growth due to immigration.

Why is productivity important?

As explored in some depth in chapter 2, countries with open economies experience cycles of economic growth and recession. However, improved productivity is a long-term driver of sustained economic improvement.

In broad terms, and as illustrated in figure 4.3, productivity trends are relatively stable and do not fluctuate much over time. In comparison, the effect of credit on economies is much more volatile, typically playing out as recurring growth (borrowing) periods followed by corresponding recessionary (pay-back) periods.

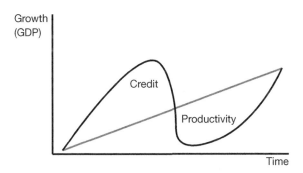

Figure 4.3: GDP versus productivity and credit cycles[12]

Productivity improvement matters, not for its own sake, but because the consequential growth it generates flows through to the sustainably higher incomes and government revenues needed to raise living standards. Or stated another way, increased productivity in the way people, capital and technology are applied improves community welfare, rectifies disadvantage and enables economies to maintain their relative global competitiveness over the longer term.

NSW Treasury in 2020 issued a green paper for discussion titled 'Productivity drives prosperity'.[13] To quote:

> *Productivity is the most powerful tool we have for improving our economic wellbeing.*
>
> *Our future prosperity depends upon how well we do at growing more productive – how smart we are in organising ourselves, investing in people and technology, getting more out of both our physical and human potential.*

Consider too, economic growth is also affected by additional elements, such as fluctuations in terms of trade and worker participation rates. As illustrated in figure 4.4, a declining trend in Australia's terms of trade since 2009–10 (which is, in turn, linked with the cessation of Australia's 'mining boom' and associated reductions in commodities prices), as well as the general ageing of the population, have worked against growth in incomes over the period since 2009–10. Expectations are that improving productivity will need to provide the heavy lifting over the foreseeable future in maintaining and enhancing real wages and future living standards for Australians.

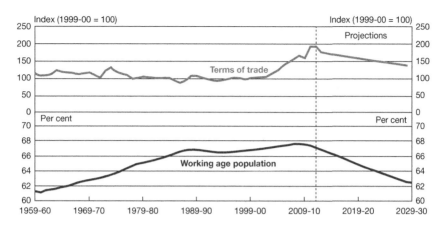

Figure 4.4: Contributions to growth in average incomes[14]

What is Australia's recent productivity trend?

As illustrated in figure 4.5 (overleaf), Australia's multi-factor productivity index rapidly increased from the beginning of the 1990s until 2003–04, whereupon it levelled out and began to decline from 2007–08 onwards. Strong growth in incomes in the 2000s was fundamentally driven by rising terms of trade. From March 2004, the mining boom boosted Australia's terms of trade by almost 50 per cent up to and beyond the GFC in 2007–08. Decline in terms of trade post the GFC (most recently weighed upon by COVID-19's disruptive effects on global supply chains as well as trade disputes with China) was expected at that time to exert additional negative pressure on average income growth.

The more recent figure 4.6 (overleaf) aligns with this expectation, with both labour and multi-factor productivity growth rates (whilst fluctuating year-to-year) trending downwards since 2012.

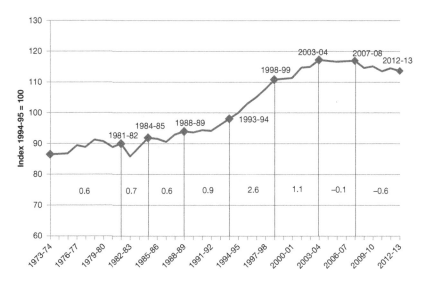

Figure 4.5: Market sector multi-factor productivity, 1973–74 to 2012–13[15]

Source: Australian Bureau of Statistics

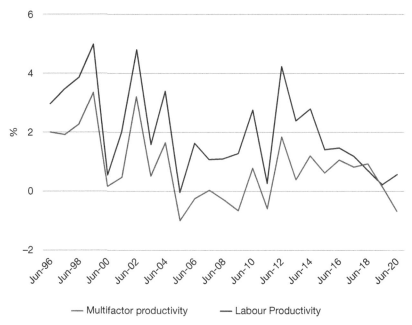

— Multifactor productivity   — Labour Productivity

Figure 4.6: Market sector, productivity growth—hours worked basis[16]

Source: Australian Bureau of Statistics

How does transport infrastructure investment contribute to overall productivity?

As illustrated by figures 4.7 and 4.8 (overleaf), declining overall productivity has coincided with a significant increase in private and public sector capital investment in the transport sector.

Investment post 2012–13 dipped in the period (roughly) from 2015 to 2017, coinciding with the cessation of the mining boom. Figure 4.9 (overleaf) illustrates a strong rebound from 2017 in government investment in major transport infrastructure and private sector investment in transport, postal and warehousing. This aligns with the 'hump' in major transport infrastructure projects explored in some depth earlier in this chapter.

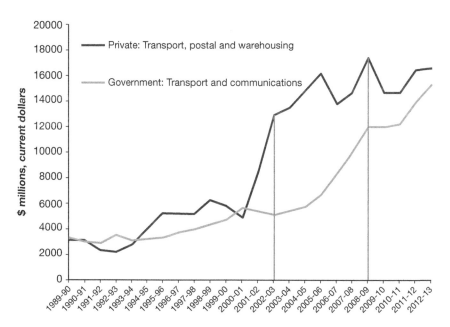

Figure 4.7: Gross fixed capital formation, transport related 1989–90 to 2012–13[17]

Source: Australian Bureau of Statistics

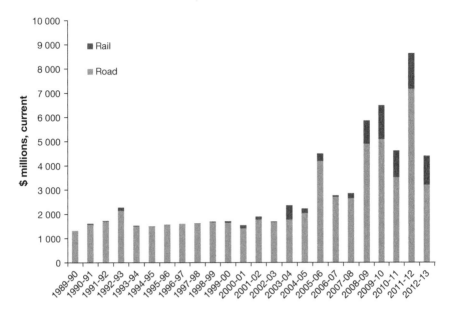

Figure 4.8: Australian Government investments in rail and road, 1988–89 to 2012–13[18]

Source: © Commonwealth of Australia

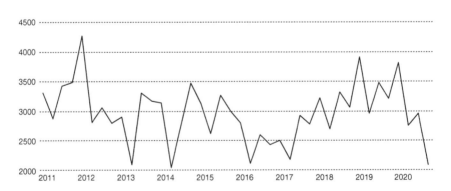

Figure 4.9: Private new capital expenditure: Actual transport, postal and warehousing[19]

Source: Australian Bureau of Statistics

What are the challenges in delivering the right infrastructure projects?

Let's extend the analysis to the more problematic link between increased productivity and enhanced community benefits. Evaluating this concept requires taking account of the alignment between enhanced infrastructure and the reality of changing community needs and expectations. This becomes a particularly topical consideration during times of disruptive change, such as occurred during the volatile times borne of COVID-19.

One of the ongoing effects of COVID-19 became apparent with major alterations in travel demand. Closed international borders resulted in stalled net overseas migration from a multi-decade high of 190 000 people per annum,[20] effectively halting worker-age population increases in the major cities across Australia. This created a significant hole in travel demand as well as wider economic growth forecasts. At the same time, plummeting use of public transport systems shifted demand to urban roads. Work-from-home has reduced the number of daily commutes and many of these work trips have morphed into school drop-offs and pick-ups (albeit at different times of the typical workday). Decades of public transport travel data indicates that the shifting of travel behaviour from the convenience of cars to buses and trains is a slow process. Recovery to pre-COVID levels of public transport usage is therefore likely to be some years away. In the shorter term major spikes occurred in roads usage as the states progressively reopened.

There is widespread community uncertainty regarding how long the COVID-19 effects will last and what a 'new normal' might be. We may be seeing a generational shift in the way we go about business and life.

As the 'new norm' of our working lives becomes evident, community concerns will inevitably be raised regarding the appropriateness of the transport infrastructure projects in the pipeline (and even those currently under construction). Concerns will be fuelled by the daily inconveniences associated with the plethora of projects, large and small, still under simultaneous construction, evoking a recent time when the major cities' public transport systems struggled to keep up with skyrocketing travel demand.

Major transport projects, such as the Level Crossing Removal Project in Victoria, WestConnex Motorways in NSW and Cross River Rail in Queensland, were intended to alleviate chronic congestion across the road and rail transport networks in the major cities. Time will determine the extent to which these projects were the right investments for the respective governments of these major cities to have made.

A particularly topical case study regarding the link between technology and productivity concerns the recently completed National Broadband Network (NBN) rollout. As chance would have it, finalisation of this long-awaited project coincided with an abrupt COVID-19 shift in travel demand. It remains to be seen whether temporary work-from-home arrangements and, in some cases, relocation to regional locations morphs into a permanent reset of working arrangements. It is clear, though, that this shift could not have occurred in the absence of the increased network capacity of the NBN without a major effect on business productivity.

What is the 'right infrastructure' for the future?

Mega projects have become a new normal for infrastructure engineering and construction in Australia.[21] This approach to nation-building has increasingly dominated government attention, with the consequences of a reduced focus on comparatively minor works becoming more apparent.

How might governments and their respective agencies respond to the challenge of providing infrastructure more closely aligned with the needs of the community in an environment with rapidly changing community requirements?

Smaller projects can be developed and implemented relatively quickly to resolve issues at specific locations. Flow-on effects on the surrounding network can then be assessed and responded to accordingly. This incremental approach to resolving localised transport congestion issues vastly decreases the risk (as well as the consequences) of making mistakes. An essentially reactive approach to network improvement has, for decades, been a core strategy for transport authorities across Australia. This approach should be considered as an essential means of enhancing — rather than a source of funding for — the current mega project program.

TfNSW's Easing Sydney's Congestion program is a case study for responding to congestion management challenges across Greater Sydney's roads network.[22] Typical initiatives include:

- pinch point projects addressing upgraded capacity requirements, incorporating increased CCTV monitoring for sections of road that are prone to congestion

- smart motorways elements, such as traffic flow management on entry ramps, variable speed limit signage and hard shoulder lane usage

- extended clearways to reduce congestion during busy periods.

The Level Crossing Removal Project (LXRP) was established in 2015 by the Victorian Government to oversee one of the largest rail infrastructure projects in the state's history.[23] Elimination of 85 level crossings across metropolitan Melbourne by 2025 is intended to mitigate the risk of collisions by separating trains from vehicles as well as reducing road and rail network congestion and delays.

Brisbane City Council's version of a congestion alleviation and safety improvement program is the Better Roads for Brisbane Fund, incorporated within a Commonwealth Urban Congestion Fund. This involves upgrading major road corridors in multiple locations. Safety improvements at several open-level crossings are also planned.[24]

It is also worth noting that not all investment of an incremental nature needs to be in 'visible' infrastructure. Ross Gittins, in his 2014 *Sydney Morning Herald* article 'How the econocrats can lift their game',[25] highlighted technological investment as an effective enabler of improvement, particularly if productivity is considered from the perspective of 'technological progress' as a means of generating improvements in the welfare of the population.

Pursuit of the economies of agglomeration across Australia has resulted in vast numbers of the population clinging to urban areas on the coastal edges of the country, with resultant urban congestion, compromised open spaces and loss of amenity. Technological improvements can mitigate the effects of these policies and overcome the natural disadvantages of the vast distances across Australia between urban centres. In this way, government can adopt the role of micro-economic reformer, targeting the way that our cities are organised and operate.

A plethora of existing and emerging technologies can be utilised in this space. A particularly noteworthy transport management–related example is SCATS (Sydney Co-ordinated Adaptive Traffic System), a system originally developed in Australia over 40 years ago to control traffic light phasing and optimise traffic flow.[26] A range of additional technologies aim to mitigate the negative effects of traffic congestion, including real-time public transport information flow, variable time tolling of major urban roads, and automated parking monitoring and infringement issuing systems.

What are our future needs?

Infrastructure engineering and construction businesses face a complex challenge in anticipating what the industry will look like in the wake of COVID-19.

As an industry directly exposed to the both short- and long-term impacts of government policy, one of the biggest (and common) difficulties is forecasting the pace at which investment promises translate into projects on the ground. Nowhere is this more prevalent than with the much-discussed regional development strategies and associated regional infrastructure investment funds.

I was lucky enough to spend a weekend at Mudgee in central west NSW just prior to the advent of COVID-19 travel restrictions in March 2020. Mudgee, a regional town in the middle of wine country, is very much geared towards tourism. It did seem apparent, though, that an increasing number of younger people are making the local area their home.

This shift towards regional growth is occurring counter to what has been a broad trend towards urbanisation and the growth of major cities in Australia and around the world.

The NSW example of what's being done to support this shift is outlined in various state government documents such as 'A 20-year economic vision for regional NSW'[27] and 'Making it happen in the regions: regional development framework'.[28] These documents provide contextual frameworks to enable sustainable regional development. Special Activation Precincts (SAPs) are a foundation element of the State Government's regional plans. The first SAP was Parkes in central west NSW, recognising its unique location at the intersection between key road (Newell Highway) and rail (ARTC Inland Rail and East-West Interstate rail) trunk routes. Coordinated Government support for land use and infrastructure planning will assist in creating appropriate centres such as Parkes to support sustainable business growth.

The Wagga Wagga SAP (incorporating Bomen Business Park and the Riverina Intermodal Freight and Logistics hub) is also intended to capitalise on Inland Rail and will focus on advanced manufacturing, agribusiness, and freight and logistics.

The Moree SAP (with road, rail and air transport links, including connection to Port of Newcastle) is intended to take advantage of its location in the middle of the most productive grain region in Australia.

There are of course additional underlying issues to consider.

The following was offered by demographer Bernard Salt at a Committee 4 Wagga seminar (as reported by *The Daily Advertiser* in 2019[29]) organised in response to the state government's 20-year economic vision for regional NSW, which endorsed the city's planned growth by 33 000 residents in 19 years.

> *There has been significant job growth … but … job loss in manufacturing, agribusiness and agriculture. Wagga is more than just the local municipality, it is its own territory, it's the whole Riverina. And when the Riverina does well then Wagga does well … it can't do that on its own.*

There are 14 cities across Australia with a population greater than 100 000 but under one million. Very few are located inland; some examples are Wagga, Albury-Wodonga and Toowoomba in Queensland. The commonality between these cities, as identified by Salt, are that they command their own territories and are generally very well-watered. Accordingly, the greatest obstacle in the way of sustainable growth for cities such as Wagga is likely to be episodes of drought.

Acceleration of the work-from-home trend during COVID-19 and completion of the NBN project have created opportunities for those with mobile jobs to relocate. Of these, millennials making the move to a small town is the most likely group to make the move a permanent one for themselves and their families. Millennials typically crave affordable living, and enjoy new experiences and being part of a community.[30] On the other side of the coin, many of these same people hold legitimate fears about themselves and their families finding work; for example, the unemployment rate for those under the age of 25 living in regional Australia can be as high as 25 per cent according to charity The Brotherhood of St Laurence.[31]

Regional infrastructure construction projects are typically smaller in scale and value and less complex in comparison with works in confined metropolitan sites. Well-selected projects generate jobs for skilled and unskilled workers, creating flow-on benefits for local communities. Investment in the right roads and rail-improvement projects mitigate traffic congestion, the effects of which those who move around Australia's metropolitan areas are familiar with.

Water access and security remains a major restriction to regional development. This does, however, create opportunities in the infrastructure space. For example, the National Water Grid Authority (NWGA) works with the states and territories to identify, plan and deliver a programme of national water infrastructure investments focused on improving the reliability and security of water for Australia's regions and agriculture and primary industry sectors. Under this arrangement, state and territory governments are responsible for developing project proposals for business case development or construction funding. National water grid priorities are guided by the National Water Grid Investment Framework and informed by the NWGA Science Program.[32]

Finally, the challenges of achieving net zero greenhouse gas emissions by 2050 will drive an increasing volume of regional projects associated with the reconfiguration of Australia's energy generation and distribution network. Figure 4.10 (overleaf) illustrates the forecasted increase in expenditure on energy projects across Australia to 2026.

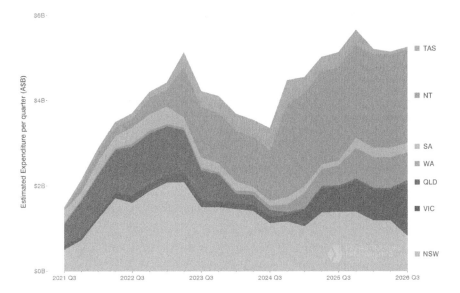

Figure 4.10: Pipeline forecast by expenditure: Energy sector projects[33]

Source: © Infrastructure Partnerships Australia

Conclusion

Many in the industry expect a continuation of increased demand for infrastructure for the next decade and beyond. History shows, however, that demand for infrastructure falls just as quickly as it rises in line with fluctuations in broader economic circumstances. Whilst governments have sound economic rationale for continuing to invest in infrastructure when broader economic circumstances deteriorate, the need to maintain fiscal discipline tends to constrain governments' ability to maintain high levels of investment regardless of the health of the broader economy.

Key takeaways for sustainable businesses

1   An in-depth understanding of the industry growth phase that commenced in 2015 with the tail end of the mining boom provides a useful perspective regarding the future demand for infrastructure engineering and construction services in the foreseeable future. An understanding of the cycles that drive the industry informs the reality that boom times do not last forever.

2   The forecast peak in project demand is well in excess of current industry output. However, the current market is seeing project delays due to COVID-19 work restrictions, additional delivery schedule slippages due to ongoing supply-chain disruption, an industry approaching a peak of capacity and labour and materials cost increases.

3   Governments are likely to hesitate before releasing a large volume of additional projects into an overheated market. Consequently, small- and medium-sized businesses, in particular, need to be vigilant regarding upcoming gaps in demand for their specific works and services.

4   Governments recognise the benefits of investing in the right infrastructure and the wider economic benefits of boosting multi-factor productivity. Choosing the right projects in the

right locations with the right benefits for the community is problematic in the current environment with rapidly changing community needs and expectations.

5 Nowhere is the challenge of building the right infrastructure in the right locations more prevalent than with the revitalisation of Australia's regional centres. This challenge may drive a move away from 'mega projects' towards greater investment in smaller works programmes and technological innovations, which can be implemented relatively quickly and flexibly.

CHAPTER 5

The evolving role of government in infrastructure

Let's look in more depth at the government's role as buyers of infrastructure engineering and construction services. Looking back, it becomes apparent that this evolution, which began in the late 1990s, of government from in-house deliverer of works to informed procurer is a relatively recent phenomenon. This shift aligns with the rise in popularity of competitive tendering for public sector–managed services. The trend also corresponds with a reduction in governments' technical capability and experience in procuring engineering-intensive products and services. As outlined by Engineers Australia in a 2012 report, 'Government as an informed buyer',[1] key technical staff have progressively migrated from the public sector to private contractors and service providers. Consequent knowledge imbalances between public and private sector are at the root of the breakdown in trust between the parties, so characteristic of this cycle.[1] To a certain extent, the inexorable growth of bureaucratic processes reflects modern societal expectations of institutions, such as the engineering profession, where trust in professional competence has been replaced by an expectation of proof regarding compliance with defined standards.

The ongoing push for collaborative (as opposed to adversarial) approaches to contracting and risk transfer reflects widespread dissatisfaction with the current state of the industry. Unfortunately, those with long industry memories recall instances where parties have taken advantage of collaborative arrangements, with a view to short-term gain. Governments' concern regarding this behaviour surfacing again is one of the key issues holding the industry back from achieving lasting improvement.

Focusing on sustainable business and choosing when to engage (and when not to engage) in opportunities is how good businesses can break their dependency on the endemic and destructive feast or famine industry cycle.

Competitive tendering of services

Since the 1980s, competitively tendered public services have become increasingly common throughout the Western world.

What has caused the shift to competition in service delivery? And, more importantly, is it a positive development? To answer these questions, it is necessary to go back some 200 years.

The contracting of public services is not a new phenomenon. The First Fleet, which sailed into Sydney Harbour in January 1788, was, in fact, a contract prison managed by private operators under contract, with the ship's captain, Arthur Phillip, acting as the prison warden.[2] There was nothing extraordinary about this arrangement, as the contracting of public services was commonplace around this period.

By the nineteenth century, contracting had gone into decline concurrent with a realignment in economic activity, as industrialisation enabled local services to be consolidated and managed at a national level. Accordingly, a range of services, such as roads, railways, electricity, telecommunications and prisons, were nationalised. Put simply, local contracting was no longer able to meet the needs of the national community. Moreover, due to poor accountability levels, contracting had, in many instances, been plagued by corruption and political pork-barrelling.

The end of the twentieth century saw another upward shift in focus of economics and politics, in this case to the global level. Just as the rise of the nation-state saw a reorganisation of public services in the eighteenth century, globalisation prompted a rejigging of public services in the late twentieth century. While bureaucracy was suited to the industrial age, it appears less well equipped to handle the information age, which demands public services that are flexible, adaptable and responsive to people.

Economic theory rests with one key principle: competition is better than monopoly. It follows then that a properly designed competitive tendering regime will produce better results than a bureaucratic monopoly. This proposition can be explored using the example of public transport systems.

With the trend towards contracting out services, governments respond by shifting focus to tendering some of their more substantial budgetary challenges, such as public transport services. Urban railways require significant capital investment to develop, operate and maintain. Transport costs inevitably rise over time and in most, if not all, jurisdictions, costs rise well in excess of farebox revenue.

This gap between costs and revenue occurs for two main reasons. Firstly, public transport is intended to provide low-cost services to the 'transit-dependent market', those people on low incomes and people with physical and age-related disabilities who are dependent on transit services. Second, public transport offers an alternative to people who would normally travel by car. Any increase in the discretionary market contributes positively to the broader community by decreasing car usage. That is, the urban environment is enhanced by improved air quality, decreasing energy use and reduced traffic congestion.

Of course, the public interest is best served by providing cost-effective and quality transit services. If a transit service is not provided at a cost-effective rate, the transit authority cannot provide as much of that service as they may have desired, especially to the transit-dependent market. A public transit system that does not provide a high quality of service (measured in terms of on-time services, cleanliness, safety, frequency and breadth of service) is unlikely to attract the discretionary market, thereby impacting adversely on the urban environment.

Accordingly, governments of various political persuasions around the world have turned to competitive tendering in the interests of closing the gap between revenue and costs, and ideally expanding services into new areas.

Privatisation: Make or buy

Given the principle that competition is better than monopoly, it is interesting to consider that contracting out state-owned services is not widely popular. At the same time, though, and as pointed out by Gary Sturgess in his *Australian Financial Review* article 'History has turned the page on state ownership', research in Britain and Australia has consistently shown that most people are opposed to privatisation of government-owned services before they occur.[3] Six months later, as long as the privatisation has been well managed, they typically don't care.

So is private-sector contracting good or bad? An easier question to answer might be whether privatisation achieves results in terms of higher industry productivity and better service to consumers? Ross Gittins explored this question in his *Sydney Morning Herald* article 'Searching for our salvation in privatisation'.[4] He asserted that deregulating an industry to foster competition within it (for instance, exposing a government-owned monopoly to private-sector competition) is far more important in driving reform than privatising a public sector business. This is certainly true of the major industry transformations since the late 1990s in the airline, railway, electricity and water sectors. Once greater competitive pressure has been achieved, selling the business on behalf of taxpayers for a reasonable return can then be considered as an option.

To return to the question of whether public ownership versus privatisation is essentially 'good' versus 'bad': If we consider Gittins again in the *Sydney Morning Herald* article 'Take rational measures on electricity privatisation issue',[5] he reminds us that mindless prejudice is no substitute for rational analysis of the pros and cons.

On the question of 'asset recycling' being considered by governments with businesses left to sell, Gittins suggests that careful analysis is essential. One must cover all the relevant major considerations for and against privatising a public sector asset, taking account of opportunity costs as well as actual costs and avoiding any double counting.

But is it possible to simplify an evaluation of whether privatisation will result in a beneficial outcome in a given circumstance? I believe history demonstrates that a successful privatisation requires three pre-conditions:

- well-developed government procurement capability

- well-developed private-sector capability in providing the required services

- a fair and effective way of incentivising performance via both monetary and non-monetary means.

Privatisation has been used in the past as a blunt instrument to address poor service provision by public sector monopolies with entrenched work practices built up over decades. It's probably not surprising then that initial outsourcing efforts have had a chequered history, as both the public and private sector lacked capability in managing transformational change as well as administering and providing services in these industries.

Public sector capability

Infrastructure engineering and construction has experienced an evolution since the late 1990s, with the public sector shifting from procuring public assets to ensuring public access to essential assets. Let's look more closely at the extent to which the public sector, as buyers of infrastructure engineering and construction services, has effectively managed this shift in role and responsibilities.

The following excerpt is taken from an article by J.W. Holliman, Department of Public Works, Sydney, published in *New South Wales: the mother colony of the Australias* (1896).[6]

> *Although much good work was done by the early road-engineers, the real engineering history of the colony dates from the formation of the Public Works Department in 1859.... Since that time, the Government have been actively engaged in improving roads already in existence and opening new means of communication to meet the demands of the increasing population.*

Since the 1980s, and following decades of developing in-house expertise and experience, public sector engineering departments across Australia have undergone a dramatic shift in capability.

As previously mentioned, I commenced my working life in the mid-1980s as a cadet engineer with the NSW State Rail Authority. At this time, the NSW State Government offered a range of technical cadetships in the transport, water, electricity and other sectors. If I recall correctly, in 1985, over 50 cadetships were offered by State Rail alone. The year after, 14 cadetships were offered, and the year after that only three cadetships were available. This reflected a wider collapse in the number of cadetships offered by the various public sector authorities at that time.

Referring to the issues identified in the Engineers Australia report, 'Government as an informed buyer'[1]:

> *Since the 1980s, Government engineering departments have undergone a dramatic shift in capacity ... The core of the issue is a dramatic 'hollowing out' of government engineering as successive Governments have driven a strategy of outsourcing ...*

The identified consequences are wide-ranging and go to the heart of government's ability to evaluate the engineering implications of projects and to properly document procurement requirements. Ineffective procurement is highly likely to reduce the cost-effectiveness of a project in the long run. A particular manifestation of this issue is scope creep, with significant cost implications via variations, disputes between client and contractor and poor project outcomes.

An even more fundamental challenge arises with the loss of governments' ability to evaluate standards for conformance with the local regulatory environment and suitability in meeting local performance challenges. An inability to assess new materials and construction methods for their applicability to the local environment, and adjust standards accordingly, stifles industry innovation, which is at the core of productivity improvement.

Commercial models

Effective procurement begins with selecting the right commercial model for the project circumstances.

Alliance agreements are applied in circumstances where the final project outcome is broadly defined but not fully specified, and where collaboration and trust-based behaviour is required to achieve an equitable commercial outcome. The project is typically subject to significant unknowns, the effect of which are difficult and costly to quantify prior to commencement and may result in significant change to the project requirements. Alliances enable the parties to share risks and work to incentivises them to reach a common goal. Alliances also enable projects to commence prior to being fully developed, thus enabling the parties to work together during the scoping phase[7]. Contractor procurement assessment and selection is primarily based on capability rather than price.

Alliances are underpinned by risk-sharing mechanisms with varying degrees of complexity. These mechanisms are typically characterised by the reimbursement of pre-disclosed contractor costs with its margin 'at risk' based on assessed performance. These risk-sharing arrangements reflect the extent of collaboration sought between the parties, which may vary from simple partnering to fully integrated 'pure' alliancing models.

Early Contractor Involvement (ECI) contracting models can be considered a 'part-way' solution when a full alliance is determined to be unsuitable or undesirable. The preliminary phase of the arrangement is collaborative in nature, with the principal seeking timely and honest input from the contractor during the design development phase of the project to finalise scope, cost and timeframe. The contractor is procured based on capability and may be engaged on a cost reimbursable or fee basis.

Upon completion of the preliminary phase, the contractor is typically provided with an opportunity, such as on a first-right-of-refusal basis, to procure and deliver the project. In this way, the client moves from a collaborate role in the preliminary phase, to an arms-length relationship in the delivery phase. This ideally reflects the reduction in unknowns as the project advances towards completion.

At the other end of the contracting spectrum is the public-private partnership (PPP). This contemporary model was developed as a working framework for private and public sector contracts that involve private financing. Solidifying this, in 1992, the United Kingdom introduced the private finance initiative (PFI), the first systematic program aimed at enabling public-private partnerships[8]. PPPs have since been applied in a range of circumstances, from the provision of new assets in 'greenfields' environments to transfer of responsibility of rehabilitation of existing assets in 'brownfields' environments, as well as a mix of the two.

PPPs involve multiple project phases, typically design, build/ rehabilitate, finance, operate and/or maintain elements. To allow this to work harmoniously, a special purpose vehicle (SPV) is typically created to enable the private sector entities to segregate assets and liabilities in relation to the specific works and services. A key element of the PPP model is the allocation of risks and establishment of performance-based outcomes to incentivise both parties. Performance is typically assessed in accordance with a complex payment mechanism involving fixed and variable incentives and penalties, including the potential for contract termination.

Choosing the right commercial model for the project circumstances is not without its challenges.

Alliancing as a commercial mechanism can mitigate a lack of client-side expertise and experience by drawing on the engineering expertise of a private-sector participant early in the project development phase. Accordingly, the inability of government to finalise technical solutions during the procurement phase was a significant factor in the rise of public sector alliancing in the early to mid-2010s, sometimes in circumstances where alliancing proved to be an inappropriate commercial choice.

So too, the application of the PPP model in Australia, particularly the approach of adopting layers of legal protection, based on my own previous contract experience, in favour of the public sector has progressively resulted in an environment characterised by significant, and sometimes unreasonable, risk transfer to the private-sector provider[9]. This position is entrenched by the inflexible nature of the PPP model once financing has been finalised, where modifications to the works typically require approval from multiple parties to the transaction.

Complex infrastructure procurement: Commercial implications

The prevailing reality of mega projects in Australia is that they are typically conceptualised on a design development and construct basis, within a risk regime oriented towards protecting the client's interests.

Accordingly, the ongoing challenge for clients is in selecting the right contract model on a best-for-project basis, where the temptation is to fall back on the model providing maximum client protection.

As a long-time supporter of public transport as an enabler of urban regeneration, I'm really pleased to see the Sydney CBD and Southeast Light Rail up and running following completion of the line extension construction works in late 2019.

As a complex greenfield/brownfield project procured under a PPP model, the overall success of the project won't be fully apparent until substantial completion of the 15-year Operations and Maintenance phase in 2034. One prevailing question will be: how flexible is the service agreement and will it cater for potential longer-term impacts on patronage demand due to COVID-19?

It is hard to assert, though, that the build phase — which culminated in a public dispute between constructor and the NSW State Government — was a rousing success. It's reasonable (in my view at least) to say that the complexity and inflexibility of the private finance-based contract model was a key contributor, if not at the heart of the dispute.

It appears that similar issues were in play, for example, with the delayed opening of Sydney's NorthConnex project[10] as well as the agreed responsibility for costs associated with contaminated material disposal for the Westgate Tunnel in Melbourne.[11]

So why does it seem so difficult for project proponents to decide on the right contract model and key terms for the right circumstances?

My own experience, from the late 1990s to the early 2010s with Serco (a British services company), then GHD and latterly with Transfield Services (now Ventia), included extensive exposure to Australia's move from procurement of engineering and construction services using traditional design and construct or construct-only models, to construction and private-sector financing, and then to the integration of asset provision with service delivery.

Hard lessons were learnt by clients and contractors regarding packaging and delivery on complex projects, such as Melbourne Trains and Trams Franchising, Brisbane Light Rail Project, Epping–Chatswood Rail Link, Waratah Trains PPP, and the NSW Country Regional Network.

As a mature industry, it is reasonable to expect that we should, by now, be much better able to align the contract model with the project risk profile.

The Australian Constructors Association (ACA) released a response to Infrastructure Australia's 2019 Infrastructure Audit investigating the major challenges for infrastructure in Australia over the next 15 years.[12] In the report under 'Better Risk Allocation' are the following statements:

> ...industry noted that the single biggest threat to sustainable infrastructure delivery was inefficient risk allocation on projects... Increasingly, clients are transferring greater risk to industry based on its bargaining position rather than the principle of who is best able to manage (or pay for) that risk.

What, specifically, is going wrong?

The available evidence suggests that the issue is not one of stated intention by the project owners. For instance, the NSW Government, way back in November 2001, published 'Working with Government' guidelines for privately financed projects, following industry consultation via a green (consultation) paper. Specifically, Section 5: Risk Management[13] leads with the following:

> Government's aim is to optimise risk allocation so that value for money is maximised in each project on a whole-of-life basis; the aim is not to maximise risk transfer from government to the private sector.

More recently, Point 2 of the NSW Government's June 2018 10-point 'Commitment to the Construction Sector' states: 'Adopt partnership-based approaches to risk allocation.'[14]

Nor does the issue appear to stem from a fundamental misuse of private finance-based contract models. Since the late 1990s, when

PPP projects were commonly 'off government balance sheet' items, there is now widespread recognition that private financing does not represent a 'magic pudding' by which to procure additional public works. However, when we step back and consider what success fundamentally looks like for all parties working on a complex infrastructure project, the key issue associated with ineffective risk management does become apparent. Indeed, as the ACA argues:

> *The increased complexity and risk embedded in modern infra-structure projects, combined with potential constraints on the capability and expertise of the client to evaluate and manage these risks, requires clients to adopt a more agnostic approach to their choice of procurement model.*[13]

An appropriate contract model and key terms is at the heart of effective risk management for complex projects. Well-designed and-documented contracts properly address the following key elements.

Value-for-money drivers

At the top of the list of value-for-money drivers is appropriate risk allocation, ahead of elements such as output-based specifications, appropriate length of contract, performance measurement, and incentives and opportunities for innovation.

Alignment of incentives

A quality outcome should be a matter of contract specification and incentivisation, rather than a stick-based approach to identifying and rectifying issues. Well-designed bundling of operations and asset management services with construction should provide effective incentive against cost-shifting, and create an environment for optimising up-front investment. Service providers prepared to invest in better-quality assets up-front should be able to benefit from reduced costs downstream.

Trust between the parties

Referring again to the ACA, it notes the need for trust to be established at the start of the tender process, continuing:

> *Just as bidders must be able to rely on the information received as complete and sufficient to develop an accurate costing, clients should also be able to rely on the tenders received in that the method and costing are accurate and not over-engineered.*[13]

The increasing tendency for government buyers to issue tenders with key documentation subject to very limited or no reliance does not encourage the submission of fully transparent pricing.

The way forward

Game theory offers the 'prisoners' dilemma': a paradox in which two rational parties acting in their own self-interests do not produce the optimal outcome. The typical prisoners' dilemma arises when both parties are constrained by a lack of trust that the other party will act in a cooperative manner that ultimately benefits both. The results leave both in a worse position. Unfortunately, this is exactly the situation in which the industry finds itself each time a new mega project is launched.

This situation is not confined to Australia. In the US, recent experience is characterised by contractors losing money on major projects.[15] There is a move in the US jurisdiction towards preliminary development agreement (PDA)–based arrangements as a means of more equitably sharing risk during the initial stage of a PPP project, at the time where scope and cost are yet to be accurately defined.

A PDA allows a selected bidder to assess the feasibility of a given project. This enables the design to progress and for applicable development, completion and life cycle risks to be better understood prior to fixing the price. Bidders submit development plans to the owner, who retains the right to terminate the project whilst selecting a preferred scheme. The preferred proponent is incentivised to successfully develop the project by the offer of a first right of refusal for completing the project. Bid and preparation costs incurred are typically reimbursed.

Returning to the Engineers Australia report (2012),[1] two key recommendations hint at a potential way forward towards improved procurement capability.

Recommendation 3 recognises the challenges government agencies face in accessing the right engineering expertise to support procurement. Government-imposed limitations on recruitment, in-house staff reductions and a heavy reliance on contracted staff create hidden costs, particularly when manifested as delays in key procurement activities.

Recommendation 8 recognises the need for agencies to implement longer-term strategies to address shortages of engineers in areas in which they are a significant market player, through recruitment and training of graduate engineers. However, the reality of an ageing workforce creates an opportunity for the public sector to tap into the wealth of knowledge and experience retained by this group by providing latter-stage career options within the key agencies. Just as a number of the major contractors have tapped into the knowledge and experience of senior professionals to advise and mentor up-and-coming executives, so too the infrastructure agencies can strategically and tactically rebuild internal capability.

There is evidence of shorter-term actions being undertaken in addressing deficiencies in public sector engineering capability.[16] For instance, the NSW Transport sector is increasingly utilising early contractor engagement processes, for instance a 'market sounding' phase for significant projects, enabling private sector input to inform the project development team prior to commencement of the formal tendering process. The challenge here is in the public sector engaging with private contractors in a way that respects the proprietary knowledge held within these businesses, as opposed to collating best practice from individual contractors and then disseminating the information to the market via tender.

Conclusion

Procurement expertise has a major impact on project success, be it a mega or less-substantial project. Unresolved issues identified during the procurement phase may (due to time constraints or inability of the parties to reach consensus) find their way into sub-contracts. This transfer of responsibility, whilst apparently effective in mitigating the risk of the head contractor, still poses risks to the ultimate success of the project. Small and medium businesses need to be aware of the nature of risks being taken on in these circumstances.

Key takeaways for sustainable businesses

1   Infrastructure engineering and construction is exposed to an array of risks making it a 'mug's game' without a broad and deep understanding of the context in which the industry operates. The industry is highly exposed to boom and bust economic phases characterised by extreme volatility.

2   Of great concern for the local industry are the flow-on effects arising from margin pressure on project sub-contractors, suppliers and professional service providers. The squeeze on sub-contractor margins arises from cost, time and other potentially unmanageable risks being passed on by head contractors.

3   A common theme showing up in this current era of abundant work is the lack of collaborative behaviour, encouraged by a scarcity-based mindset and in some cases driven by the adoption of an inappropriate commercial model in procuring the project. A scarcity-based mindset is not helpful for growing a sustainable business.

4   Building the right infrastructure has flow-on benefits, with the right infrastructure boosting an economy's multi-factor productivity. Productivity is vital to Australia's ongoing prosperity, being the underlying driver of economic growth and prosperity.

5 Changes in underlying demand for government projects may be industry disruptive in the wake of COVID-19. For instance, increased take-up of remote communications technologies has prompted people to migrate from capital cities to regional locations.

6 Mega projects with values greater than AU$1 billion have been driving industry demand. With changing user requirements in the wake of COVID-19, sustainable businesses need to remain vigilant for signs of an industry shift to smaller projects and programs as governments respond to changing user needs.

Part II

The Why

Before launching into Part II of this book, let's return to the roadmap for building a business in the infrastructure engineering and construction industry.

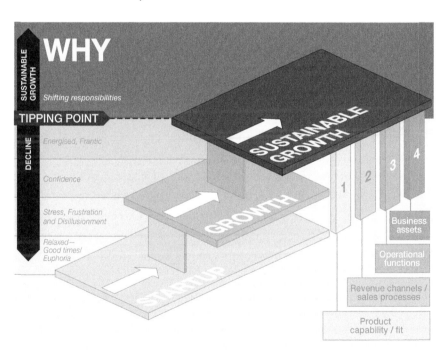

The journey a good business must undertake to become a sustainable enterprise can be thought of as a transition phase through a 'tipping point' from one state to another. In evaluating the capability of a business to transition to this new and improved state, we first must consider the environment in which the transition will occur. Accordingly, Part I of the book explored the challenges and opportunities presented by the environment in which infrastructure engineering and construction businesses in Australia exist. Part II of the book now considers the internal state of the business as defined by the 'why', providing you with an opportunity to assess how ready you and your business are for the journey ahead.

Part II explores the key elements business owners must take personal responsibility for in setting the agenda and enabling sustainable growth in their business.

This section of the book explores the process by which a vision is embedded in a business. A common vision aligns staff behaviour and provides context for the business strategy and supporting management system in circumstances where the size and complexity of an organisation renders persuasive one-on-one conversations unrealistic.

Creating a great and sustainable business seems challenging. Competitive pressures in the mature industry that is infrastructure engineering and construction are such that the business needs to be a good one just to survive the initial flush of success. As a business develops and its success becomes apparent to others, competitors become interested onlookers of the business' journey from a good to sustainable endeavour. Easily replicable initiatives can be readily identified and copied by competitors, occasionally with active encouragement from those larger organisations who exert significant control over the industry as it is currently configured. A good business needs more than clever ideas to become a sustainable enterprise, as chapter 11 will explain.

Business building requires the owner's full commitment as well as a great deal of resilience. If building a business were easy, then the intense satisfaction borne of creating a sustainable business would be much less likely to show up! When faced with day-to-day challenges and in the depths of problem-solving mode, it is quite easy for an owner to lose sight of the 'why' for their business.

Where does vision as the foundation of a business come from?

The source of the business vision comes from the founder as business owner. Accordingly, the fundamental role of the owner is to unify those tasked with implementing the vision. For a small business, the owner has direct face-to-face access to employees and more organic opportunities to reinforce the business vision, which can make it easier to maintain alignment across a small team. The larger the business, though, the more complex the challenge of creating and maintaining alignment becomes. With more complex layers of leadership and management that separate the business owner from the people who need to execute the vision, comes a greater challenge to keep everyone focused on the same goals.

Most of us are familiar with an internal dialogue: a constant commentary in our head as we weigh up the pros and cons before finally converting our intentions into actions. In circumstances where our actions appear to be triggering more negative results than positive, why-related questions naturally show up in our consciousness. A business owner with a strong internal sense of 'due north' possesses an effective contextual compass for the relentless stream of decisions that business owners need to make. In this way, a powerful vision can generate clarity, confidence and focus for the business, and inspire employees to align their behaviour with the vision.

Harnessing behaviour in aligning values

Behaviour, unlike values, is readily observable. Accordingly, an effective way of aligning people with an organisation's values starts with conversations about behaviour. Indeed, the task of establishing and maintaining behaviour in alignment with the organisation's values is best achieved through extensive formal and informal consultation with employees. Agreed behavioural norms, once established, are powerful drivers that enable individuals to champion those behaviours and demonstrate their commitment to the company's values.

Trust: The key to building relationships

Trust is the glue that cements relationships together and enables sustainable enterprises. By way of example, the extent to which your management team has historically taken care of your needs and concerns determines the level of trust you, as owner, currently have in your team and in the broader business. If trust is the key to effective interpersonal engagement, then it stands to reason that leaders need to be focused on building high levels of organisational trust.

Leadership and sustainable enterprises

By exploring effective leadership behaviour from a range of different perspectives, much can be learnt about the key role leadership plays in building a sustainable business. High-performance leadership is not attained by developing one skill or leadership style. It requires multiple components of an individual's abilities, strengths and self-belief. An effective leader needs to understand the strengths and weaknesses of their people, the interdependencies between the people that arise from their strengths and weaknesses, and the overall effect on the capability of the enterprise.

CHAPTER 6
Personal lessons in business

My business journey aligns with the private sector outsourcing process undertaken by many government-owned entities since the late 1990s (outlined in chapter 5). Australia's railways transformation is typical of other privatised industries in the transport and utilities infrastructure industry sector, including roads, water, electricity and telecommunications. In describing my first-hand experience (including the ups and downs typical of many careers), I trust the common thread that led to where my business and my career are today will become apparent over the course of this chapter.

From government to private sector

My business story starts in 1994 with my resignation from the NSW State Rail Authority (State Rail) and subsequent employment at a privatised railway maintenance facility in Auburn, NSW. Maintrain was set up by State Rail as an early phase partnering-style services contract. This approach represented a concerted attempt to fundamentally shift the way railway services were conducted. At that time, State Rail, along with equivalent railways around the country, remained entrenched in a long-standing adversarial relationship with the various transport unions who controlled railway work practices.

Goninan, the Newcastle-based builder of State Rail's Tangara passenger rail fleet, was awarded a 10+5-year contract in 1993 to provide railcar maintenance services, minor vehicle refurbishments and component rebuilds for the passenger car fleet, as well as freight wagon components for FreightCorp (the NSW Government–owned freight rail operator). The services utilised an existing facility, which was refurbished with the addition of a multi-car lifting system to enable multiple bogie replacement, and a weighing system (which incidentally provided no end of trouble in the set-up phase).

Immersion in the initial stages of this contract was a real eye-opener, in terms of the on-the-ground challenges that show up when the private and public sector are tasked with working together. Maintrain, as a private contractor, faced two major hurdles in getting up and running. The first involved stepping into a highly unionised environment and achieving sustained change in work practices. The second required re-establishing transparent work standards in an environment where much of the configuration and maintenance documentation for State Rail's (old and in some cases technologically obsolete) fleet assets had been lost due to lack of care in maintaining paper-based documentation over the course of various internal re-organisations.

My role connected me with the operational part of the business (passenger car servicing and repairs) as well as the technical support for procurement and subcontracts. Consequently, I became intimately acquainted with the effects of Maintrain's challenges as they played out across the business.

Maintrain was set up as a 'one union' shop with a multi-skilling agenda in direct conflict with the prevailing public sector approach of strict job demarcation between, for example, the mechanical versus electrical activities performed by fitters versus electrical mechanics who belonged to the Rail Trams and Buses Union or the Electrical Trades Union, respectively. The employees were sourced, in most cases, from outside the industry, and the resultant workforce required extensive training in railcar servicing. Indeed, I was employed as a depot maintenance engineer largely because of my knowledge of the Intercity Passenger fleet based at Flemington Maintenance Centre.

Servicing of railway passenger car equipment is an activity involving extensive logistical coordination. RailCorp's intention in setting up the partnership contract was to move away from a workshop-based approach to servicing. The dark days of NSW Railways involved railcars with undiagnosable problems being parked in the Electric Car Workshops (Elcar) in Chullora, where they were often cannibalised to provide spare parts for operational vehicles. The more modern approach involved exchanging the sub-assemblies that required servicing with refurbished units. The removed sub-assemblies were then sent out to a network of companies for servicing.

One of Maintrain's key initiatives was to expand the pool of contractors authorised to service the various sub-assemblies. What this looked like in the early days was another huge task in assembling technical standards and developing output specifications. Sourcing of parts, particularly those out of production by the original manufacturer and without fully detailed manufacturing drawings, created additional challenges. Many problems surfaced during this exercise, each of which required investigation and rectification. It became apparent over time that many of the resultant problems that surfaced with faulty refurbished equipment (such as leaky air compressors, traction motor rewiring issues etc.) had clearly been encountered previously. The root of all of this was a lack of access to a full body of knowledge by either party.

The partnership agreement that defined and governed Maintrain's activities included key performance indicators (KPIs) that were intended to incentivise appropriate commercial behaviour. Unfortunately, and as with many KPI regimes, the opposite behaviour was incentivised. This played out most tellingly in the initial phase of the contract in the achievement of cost reductions in comparison with benchmark prices for procured parts and refurbished sub-assemblies.

Price reductions (in the form of volume procurement when the quantities were not justified by demand or sourcing of re-manufactured parts that, in some cases, were not fit for purpose) were rewarded under the contract arrangements. Modifications to the partnership-based agreement were subsequently made to address these issues.

I would hasten to add here that there were many people on the public sector as well as the private sector side of the fence who recognised the challenges in shifting decades of old-school thinking. Many of these people also remained committed to the partnering principles of the agreement and continued to work together despite challenges and mistakes on both sides. It would be remiss of me not to acknowledge the public sector representatives who contributed to the eventual success of the arrangements, even though this was to the detriment of their own employment. The fact that the arrangement continues today, whilst in a substantially modified form, is a testament to the efforts of these people and those who have replaced them over the years.

Key lessons learnt

Two key lessons stand out from my time at Maintrain. The first concerns transformational change, being extremely difficult to achieve in an environment with entrenched dysfunctional behaviour. Committed leadership performs an essential role in these circumstances in holding the vision and maintaining the course (see chapter 8). The second lesson relates to KPIs associated with financial incentives, which are powerful motivators of behaviour. Great care must be taken in designing and then monitoring KPI frameworks, keeping an active eye out for signs of unwanted behaviour (see chapter 13).

The transformation of Australia's national railways

Once most of the angst associated with the initial stage of the contract had passed, I realised that, after three-plus years, I needed to move on. The thing that really signalled my need to change the situation was waking up most mornings at 4 am with a feeling of impending doom, and the memory of a recurring dream about the upcoming walk across the bridge from the staff carpark to the office. I'm certainly more aware these days of the mildly depressive state these symptoms indicate, and am very fortunate not to have experienced this persistently.

Having made the decision to find a new job, I set out to leverage my operational experience at Maintrain to secure a position in production management. Many applications and the occasional interview later, I felt close to success. It took a close colleague (a direct report in fact) to point out that I was chasing an area of local industry in the process of rapid contraction. Manufacturers across Australia at that time were rationalising overheads by removing production management positions and consolidating functions into fewer operations management roles. This process has evolved into the significantly reduced local manufacturing capability seen today (see chapter 3).

One day in late 1997, and completely out of the blue, parent company Goninan's manager of the newly established South Australia business arrived at Maintrain looking for due diligence and, ultimately, transition services assistance for a maintenance contract for the about-to-be-privatised Australian National Railways. This turned out to be my second major experience of outsourcing and privatisation, which were transforming the rail industry across Australia.

Australian National Railways, re-branded Australian National (AN), was established as a Commonwealth Government-owned entity in 1975. The entity initially comprised the loss-making state railway services of Tasmania and South Australia (bar the Adelaide metropolitan network) which were transferred to AN under a Commonwealth-States agreement. The interstate freight services were subsequently transferred to National Rail Corporation (formed in 1992).

In November 1997, *The Ghan, Indian Pacific* and *Overland* passenger services were sold to Great Southern Rail (GSR), a consortium comprising GB Railways, Legal & General, Macquarie Bank, Rail America, G13 and Serco. The South Australian intrastate services were sold to Genesee & Wyoming Australia and AN Tasrail was acquired by Australian Transport Network (a joint venture comprising NZ Tranz Rail and Canada's Wisconsin Central Ltd).

My involvement in this industry transformational outsourcing process concerned Goninan's provision of maintenance services to the newly privatised Great Southern Railway for *The Ghan* and *Indian Pacific* carriages at Keswick Terminal located just outside Adelaide's CBD.

The due diligence phase consisted of trawling through a vast data room full of documents in a rented office in Sydney, and extracting information of relevance to maintaining the existing passenger fleet. This documentation was eventually consolidated into fleet servicing plans, which were provided to the maintenance personnel at Keswick. The work itself might sound quite boring, but the access to this bigger railways game turned out to be a fascinating experience. Moreover, the experience brought me into contact with the Australian-based people at Serco, a British facilities management and systems engineering company.

Serco and transport outsourcing

Serco began its journey in 1929 as RCA Services Limited, the UK division of the Radio Corporation of America. Acquired in 1985 by General Electric, a management buyout saw a name change to Serco in 1987. From its UK Stock Exchange listing in 1988, Serco rapidly expanded in the provision of a diverse array of outsourced public services in the UK and internationally, including in Australia. At one time, Serco simultaneously provided parks and gardens maintenance in Melbourne[1] and a nuclear weapons contract in Britain, the latter as part of a consortium including Lockheed Martin and Jacobs Engineering[2].

From 1997 via acquisition and until 2015, Serco in Australia owned Great Southern Rail. In March 2015, the business was sold to Allegro Funds.[3]

In the late 1990s, Serco was on an upwards growth trajectory globally with various contracts in Australia, with a strategic intent to consolidate the Australian business in transportation. Accordingly, the main target for business expansion was the multi-year Melbourne Trains and Trams operations franchises.

Melbourne trains and trams franchises

In 1999, in what was publicly stated as 'the pursuit of greater efficiency and service quality', and privately rumoured to be ongoing enmity between the Transport Unions and the Victorian Liberal Government, Melbourne's state-owned train and tram system was split into five franchises. Following a competitive tender process, the franchises were awarded to three private sector entities for periods of between 12 and 15 years.[4]

Serco participated in the process, bidding for the two trams franchises on offer as well as one of the trains opportunities. My contribution to Serco's ultimately unsuccessful involvement in the franchising process was with the Hillside Trains bid in joint venture with Singapore Mass Rapid Transit, with financing via Macquarie Bank. The bid involved an initial submission followed by a subsequent best and final offer phase, ultimately consuming six months of my life in Melbourne.

As a footnote, it soon became clear post-award that the franchisees' agreed revenue and cost targets were unrealistic, resulting in unsustainable franchise operations. The franchisees experienced various degrees of financial difficulty, culminating in December 2002 with National Express Group Australia handing back three franchises to the state. This triggered a process of government restructure of the metropolitan train and tram system into one train and one tram franchise, followed by bilateral negotiation with Connex Melbourne and MetroLink Victoria for management of the combined trains and trams franchises, respectively.[4]

International opportunities

Serco's unsuccessful experience in Melbourne was followed by bids for the Brisbane Light Rail Project (cancelled by Brisbane City Council in 2000 after tender lodgement and eventually morphed into Brisbane Metro in 2020[5]), a surface Light Rail scheme in Koto Ward, Tokyo,[6] championed by the Tokyo Privately Financed Initiative Association (not progressed) and a proposed privatisation of the Estonian Railways in 2001 (ultimately awarded to Ed Burkhardt's Rail World and subsequently repurchased by the Estonian government in 2007).[7]

The most interesting for me concerned an operations and maintenance opportunity for a viaduct-based metro rail system in the Philippines. President Ferdinand Marcos created the Light Rail Transit Authority (LRTA) in July 1980,[8] giving birth to what was then dubbed the Metrorail. Metrorail Line 1 consists of two parts, the first from Baclaran to Central Terminal and the second from Central Terminal to Monumento. Line 1 was fully opened by 1985 with the LRTA retaining overall responsibility for operations, planning and governance. Daily operations were undertaken by Meralco Transit Organization (METRO Inc.).

Overcrowding, structural issues and poor maintenance took its toll on the metro rail system[9], so much so that by 1990 trains approaching Central Terminal station were heavily speed restricted to minimise additional stress on the cracking support structures.

In the late 1990s, Canadian firm SNC-Lavalin developed a proposal for extension of the existing Line 1 to Cavite in the southwest of Manila. In 2000, Serco was invited to participate in a combined construction and operations and maintenance submission to LRTA. In mid-2000, employees of METRO Inc. had gone on strike,[10] paralysing Line 1 operations from 25 July to 2 August 2000. Consequently, the LRTA had not renewed its operating contract with METRO Inc. and had assumed all operational responsibility for the metro rail. The Arroyo administration rejected the combined SNC-Lavalin/Serco submission in 2005,[11] with the scheme eventually proceeding in 2015 with Light Rail Manila Corporation as the joint venture project proponent, comprised of Metro Pacific's Metro Pacific Light Rail Corporation,[11] Ayala Corporation's AC Infrastructure Holdings Corporation, and the Philippine Investment Alliance for Infrastructure's Macquarie Infrastructure Holdings (Philippines) PTE Ltd (MIHPL).

My participation in Serco's in-country due diligence work included one memorable stay in the Westin Philippine Plaza in Makati City (now a Sofitel-branded establishment) that coincided with tropical storm Bebinga (Seniang) hitting Metro Manila on 1–2 November 2000, resulting in 26 deaths.[12] The storm took out hotel power and resulted in extensive building flooding. I recall the band in the hotel lobby continuing to play after the lights went out in a scene eerily reminiscent of the legend of the *Titanic*. Nevertheless, deal negotiations progressed to the extent that I contemplated moving the family to Manila for the transition stage of the project.

Negotiations eventually stalled and the deal did not proceed, which, in hindsight, was a blessing as, subsequent to our in-country involvement and in late December 2000, the metro was subject to a terrorist attack. As part of the Rizal Day bombings, 11 people were killed when a bomb went off in a train entering Blumentritt station.[13]

Following an extended and refreshing non-transportation assignment implementing an asset management system at the Australian Defence Force medical and dental facility at Randwick Barracks in eastern Sydney, I was identified as surplus to Serco's requirements and moved on.

Key lessons learnt

My Serco experience taught me a great deal about the drivers behind private and public sector deals, the long lead times and many twists and turns often associated with infrastructure development projects, and the challenges in finalising workable arrangements between governments and the private sector in complex industries such as transportation. Serco as an organisation was a private sector product of the UK Government's outsourcing and privatisation agenda in the late 1990s. Serco's early success and rapid expansion globally from the late 1990s reflected the rapid adoption of government outsourcing world-wide. A precipitous decline in late 2014 and 2015 reflected the increasing maturity of UK Government clients in transferring risk to the private sector, a trend seen in other jurisdictions including Australia[14] (see chapter 5).

GHD infrastructure consulting

My next job at Australian-owned engineering firm GHD involved exposure to the world of consulting and the concept of deadlines.

My transformative experience in this sphere was as an independent engineer, engaged over an almost two-year period from 2005 to 2006 by a consortium bidding for a major train supply contract to RailCorp NSW. The client-defined public-private partnerships (PPP) contract comprised railcar supply, maintenance facility works, railcar through life support (maintenance) and financing.

Reliance Rail Waratah Trains PPP

Modern passenger trains are comprised of components sourced from various places around the globe. Components are selected to comply with specified performance requirements, supplier manufacturing capability and delivered costs. In this case, the traction equipment was sourced from Hitachi, Japan; the body shell manufactured by China North Rail (CNR) in its Changchun facility; the brakes from Knorr-Bremse in Germany; body shell steel from South Korea; manufactured wheelsets from Spain, and so on. The core of the train builder's job is sub-assembly integration as well as vehicle assembly, testing and commissioning. As one might gather, the project is, in essence, an international logistics management challenge.

The finalised commercial and legal relationships between RailCorp and the state of NSW; railcar builder Downer EDI; key suppliers, CNR and Hitachi; maintenance facility constructor John Holland; maintainer Downer (again); as well as our good selves at GHD, who were appointed as independent certifier for the rolling stock manufacture and through life support contract arrangements were a wonder to behold when fully sketched out.[15]

My task over the course of the bid was to prepare a technical due diligence report for reliance purposes in favour of the:

- bond underwriter ABN AMRO Bank and Bond Holders

- providers of bank debt financing facilities, including Westpac, NAB, Sumitomo Mitsui and Mizuho

- initial providers of equity capital comprising ABN AMRO, Babcock & Brown, Downer EDI and AMP Capital

- bond insurers Financial Guaranty Insurance Company and XL Capital US

- rating agencies Standard & Poor's and Moody's Investors.

Finalisation of the 260-page due diligence report needed to be squeezed between the preparation of the bid submission and submission sign-off by the various financial entities. I recall many heated conversations (mostly late at night) between the lead transaction arranger's representative and my report compiler as, what felt like, every word was exhaustively reviewed.

The tendering timeframes for these submissions are typically as short as they can reasonably be made. Both client and tender applicant support the approach in principle, as it is the most effective way to limit the obscene amounts of money spent on the bid and transaction finalisation stage.

In this case, the competitive process quickly became a two-horse race between Reliance Rail Consortium and Star Transit, a similar sized consortium arranged by Macquarie Capital. Unfortunately, and as appeared to be the norm at the time, the two parties were subjected to a best and final offer stage, which required further amendments to the report. Much of this work was done during a flight to the US for a meeting with XL Capital, who was recruited relatively late in the process to provide a second layer of insurance for the CPI bonds (bonds in which payment of interest is related to the consumer price index), thereby supporting the credit rating of the bonds at issue. I vaguely recall lifting my head from what felt like constant typing on the laptop to my first view of Manhattan. I'm sure I hadn't processed that I was actually staying in the Palace Hotel on Madison Avenue in Manhattan, New York, and spent much of the subsequent three-day trip on a bit of a high from the city's legendary energy.

Key lessons learnt

Those who know how to best utilise consultants effectively outsource their hard work to them. With experience comes an awareness that from a client perspective the expertise underpinning the consulting work undertaken is merely a given. I learnt the valuable lesson that meeting deadlines is how a competent consultant is judged, and the means by which mutually beneficial client relationships are established and maintained (see chapter 12).

Transfield Services: Back to outsourcing

The next engagement at Transfield Services was my first real exposure to the pressures of an ASX-listed entity.

Transfield was founded in 1956 by Italians Franco Belgiorno-Nettis and Carlo Salteri, who emigrated to Australia and secured an initial contract for Australian Iron and Steel (AIS) at Port Kembla, NSW. Initial works included construction of a powerline from Magill to Port Augusta in South Australia and the Merritts chairlift in 1967/68 at the ski fields at Thredbo NSW (only recently modernised to a gondola). Transfield expanded via a diverse range of major engineering projects across a wide industry spectrum, encompassing water, power, mining, transport and commercial building and community infrastructure. By the early 1980s Transfield had completed flagship projects including Sydney Harbour Tunnel and Brisbane's Gateway Bridge and was recognised as the largest engineering firm in South-East Asia.

In 1995 and following a dispute between the Belgiorno and Salteri families (more on this later) the Salteris split from the business to form Tenix, which concentrated on defence and maritime projects[16]. In 2001, and in response to the fallout from several loss-making projects, Transfield was separated into a construction division (sold to John Holland Group) and an operations and maintenance division (listed on the ASX as Transfield Services).

It became apparent upon joining Transfield Services in 2008 that the business remained consumed by the administrative challenges of shifting from a privately held company to a listed entity. The services model upon which the business had been founded had been a successful one, and Transfield's growth in this space was at the expense of early international adopters such as Serco Australia. However, the unsuccessful submission for a 10-year Northern Sydney Roads Performance Specified Maintenance Contract renewal (awarded to Downer Group) was a significant blow to the transport business division, raising questions regarding the lack of in-house supply chain capability in comparison with Downer who had accessed significant asphalt-laying capability via the acquisition of Emoleum in February 2006. The remaining portion of the transport division consisted of a South Australian–based rail alliance contract with ARTC and minor contracts in NSW and Queensland. Transfield's transport business required a significant additional contract — preferably NSW-based — and two major opportunities appeared over this period that aligned with these requirements.

NSW country regional rail network tender

The first of these was a rail network management contract for the state-owned and -managed Residual Grain network in western NSW. Grain logistics chains are a combination of storage, rail and road transport, and intermodal and port transfer facilities. The logistics chain is a complex network in which growers and service providers make choices about least-cost pathways and transport modes. Modal choice is fundamentally driven by the least transport cost to port, although external factors, such as road user safety and sources of funding for road and rail, play a part in the broader economic consideration.

The rail network across this region—and particularly on the Western edge—was originally constructed to minimal `pioneer' loading and speed standards, compared with more contemporary freight rail lines. Deteriorating rail condition—which necessitated further loading and speed restrictions—and comparative improvements in truck standards and capacities, had led to grain haulage progressively favouring road transport. Despite rail investment to attract an increased grain haulage share, these rail lines were at risk of falling into disuse and eventual closure.

In response to concerns raised by industry stakeholders and the community, as well as an ongoing NSW Government review of the cost of a Community Service Obligation (CSO) for maintenance of the regional network, the NSW Government established the Grain Infrastructure Advisory Committee (GIAC) to investigate the ongoing viability of the lower standard or `restricted' lines. The GIAC, chaired by senior public sector executive Vince Graham, comprised stakeholders including representatives from NSW Farmers' Association, NSW Grain Growers Association, AWB Limited, GrainCorp Limited, Pacific National Pty Ltd (PN), the Local Government Association of NSW and the Shires Association of NSW, the NSW Labor Council, Roads and Traffic Authority of NSW (RTA), Rail Infrastructure Corporation and the Office of Coordinator General of Rail.

GIAC's terms of reference encompassed:

- The structure of the NSW Grain industry and associated demand for grain haulage services.

- The effects of privatisation and deregulation on the freight storage and handling task and potential impacts on the future utilisation of the restricted rail lines.

- The likely road and rail network maintenance costs, considering potential upgrade(s) of the restricted lines.

In 2003, I undertook an assignment with GHD to develop a methodology for evaluating road and rail infrastructure which was compiled as a discussion paper for input to the final GIAC report[17].

In the subsequent 2008–09 NSW mini budget, the NSW Government determined to 'subject management services to competitive processes' in relation to the restricted network.[18] Accordingly, the Country Regional Infrastructure Authority (CRIA), as the responsible government entity, called for tenders in relation to a performance-based contract for the provision of CRN management, maintenance and operational services.

In 2010 I led the Transfield Services' submission for the 10+5-year, $1.5 billion CRN stewardship contract. Competitive submissions of this magnitude and complexity require a major commitment in terms of cost and time. Transfield Services invested in what was believed to be a strong bid team, with the capability and experience to form the basis of an effective contract management and delivery team. The bid process involved a series of interactive sessions with the client's representatives as well as a post-submission presentation to the CRIA team in Newcastle. Bid coaching and independent bid review services were provided by Wayne Seaward and Barry Harrison from Advanced People Systems, a Melbourne-based coaching and leadership services business. This was my first direct experience of services of this nature, with the learnings influencing my approach in this space to this day.

Unfortunately, our team lost out to John Holland, who at that time was widely regarded as the industry benchmark for competitive bidding and had planned and implemented its strategy well in advance of the formal EOI/RFP process. This enabled John Holland Group to establish strong connections with key influencers involved in the process prior to the establishment of formal bid probity requirements restricting access to the client's representatives. John Holland Group went on to deliver the services over a ten-year period before being replaced via re-bid by UGL from 2022.

Maintrain re-tender

The second major submission in late 2011 concerned a 7+5-year, $1-billion-plus re-bid for the UGL Maintrain services (referred to as the Rolling Stock Level 3 Maintenance and Logistics contract) discussed earlier. Whilst I obviously possessed expertise and previous experience with the works, Transfield Services lacked sufficient organisational experience in the space. Accordingly, the submission was formulated in joint venture with Bombardier Transportation, a Canadian-German multi-national with the requisite expertise as well as a strong local presence (albeit in states other than NSW).

Experienced bidders regard re-bids for multi-year services contracts involving incumbent service providers with considerable scepticism. In these circumstances, the client has typically discovered any major flaws in the services arrangements and has rectified said deficiencies in the updated contract arrangements. The client has built a working arrangement with the service provider through shared experiences (both good and not-so-good) over a significant length of time. Additionally, the incumbent service provider has both access and opportunity to strengthen relationships with senior representatives in the client's organisation. Unless the relationship at contract level is particularly toxic, the client is more than likely to stay with the incumbent provider and is therefore likely to use the re-bid as an opportunity to extract a lower price for the same services.

The Maintrain submission required a similar level of commitment to what was required for the CRN bid. Much of the organisational learning developed over the course of the CRN process was incorporated into the Maintrain solution, and Bombardier's bidding expertise and experience added significant value to the team.

The pricing requirements created an additional challenge that commonly arises with re-bids of this nature: timely access to information. In this case, the expectation of fixed pricing for refurbishment of more than 250 rotables (exchangeable assemblies) was unachievable within the tender and best and final offer (BAFO) period. The incumbent service provider, with full access to this information, had an obvious advantage in this circumstance.

As an interesting aside, an alternative view is that access to information is a disadvantage to an incumbent, creating a barrier to competitive pricing in circumstances where price is a key driver of the decision-making process. My view is that in a competitive tender, starting from a position of greater knowledge is always preferable. One can then choose to adopt a different price point and associated risk profile should circumstances warrant.

The interactive client process extended to a BAFO stage, which included the unusual step of pre-negotiating a full services agreement prior to being advised of the preferred contractor status. Right up until the end of the process, we continued to receive positive signals regarding our position. Again, we were unsuccessful and post-bid inquiries did little to allay concerns regarding the client's application of the tender criteria in the evaluation process.

In hindsight, there were obvious signals pointing to our team's eventual lack of success. Again, the incumbent's connections with the client's representatives at various levels were ultimately telling. Whilst not inferring untoward behaviour by anyone involved in the Maintrain re-bid process, release in 2014 of an ICAC report into what was termed 'Operation Spector' made for interesting reading.[19]

Key lessons learnt

Major multi-year services tenders like NSW CRN and Maintrain are hotly contested by a small number of organisations, possessing the capability of delivering the requirements and the financial resources to prepare a competitive submission. Enormous amounts of planning, effort and money are expended by the bidding parties in chasing an opportunity to secure a transformational contract for the successful organisation. Whilst competitive pricing is fundamental to preparing a winning submission, a host of other activities including client relationship building, team assembly and management, job planning and risk review, submission preparation, commercial and legal review and organisational governance make important contributions to success. Time pressure and hard deadlines play their part in creating a space for tremendous learning experiences (captured in chapter 12).

Business advisory and coaching

My experiences at GHD left me with a love of consulting, albeit with an interest in participating in the industry in a more distinctive way.

Towards the end of my time at Transfield Services, the concept of founding my own business began to take shape in my consciousness. Whilst with GHD, I had made contact with representatives from Shirlaws, a company named after the founder Darren Shirlaw and immersed in the early phase of the emerging business coaching industry. I was quite captivated by Shirlaws' methodology, and I spent time researching the industry and eventually resolved to become a business coach.

SamWilko Advisory was duly registered as a limited partnership on 22 June 2012. I recall this as a most exciting first day in the life of my new venture. I can visualise even more clearly the frantic energy that showed up when I realised that I needed to recoup the $6800 in set-up costs that I'd invested in the venture! Looking back, the investment seems trivial, but the amount was certainly a big deal at the time. A redundancy from Transfield Services in August 2012 was the additional impetus I needed to fully commit to my next phase as a business owner.

Given my interest in learning about the business coaching game, I formally associated with Shirlaws as a sub-licensee.

Lesson 1: Defining your business proposition

This gave rise to the first of many business learnings: the positioning lesson. In my efforts to get up and running in either the corporate consulting and/or business coaching space, I represented myself to prospects as both a Shirlaws business coach and a director of SamWilko Advisory, thereby creating instant confusion as to what I actually did. Following some sage advice from a colleague or two, I switched to adopting an appropriate position in alignment with what I perceived to be of most interest to the prospect and generated much better results.

Lesson 2: Following your instincts

My second major learning requires a deeper dive into the Shirlaws organisation. Darren Shirlaw, who had a background in funds management, founded Shirlaws as an entity providing business coaching services to small- and medium-sized enterprises. The approach to working with clients was based on a methodology developed by Darren, with the overall objective of increasing the value of each client's business and, ideally, providing the owner with an opportunity to exit the business via a sale transaction.

The business commenced in Australia in 1999 as Shirlaws Pty Ltd, with Darren and six associates jointly funding the enterprise. The business grew quickly, and by 2003, fee revenue was reportedly $6 million and the business was well-positioned in the rapidly expanding business coaching industry. The expansion of Shirlaws in Australia was via a franchise-based approach, comprising the sale of non-exclusive, territory-based licences to various subsidiary entities. The licence granted access to the coaching methodology and associated training as well as the Shirlaws brand, with associated obligations for remittance of a percentage of revenue to Shirlaws.

I met many talented coaches during my association with Shirlaws, and had the opportunity to learn the methodology which was the real 'secret sauce' of the enterprise. The approach influences the way I coach businesses today and I remain grateful for the benefits of their knowledge and experience.

I was also lucky enough to get to know colleagues from a variety of backgrounds who had become associated with the business at the same time. I was in a similar career inflection point to others and the Shirlaws approach and promise was an attractive proposition, as was Darren's methodology.

At the time, I was unsure about making an equity commitment and becoming a partner in the business. On the other hand, I learnt quite a bit about the power of an offer to be a part of what was represented as an exclusive club. I'm still grateful to Darren Shirlaw himself for calling me out during an internal workshop prior to a conference at SeaWorld on the Gold Coast in October 2015. His labelling of me as the longest-standing 'probationary' member in the business was the wake-up call that I needed in realising that it was time to sever my connection with Shirlaws and focus on SamWilko Advisory.

On the corporate project services side, in early 2015 I experienced a watershed moment in securing a contract with Capella Capital as Altrac Light Rail SPV's technical director and first representative for the Sydney Light Rail CBD and Southeast extension project. This was a time where major project work on Australia's east coast was particularly thin on the ground (see chapter 4). The sustained effort I put into securing the contract despite limited positive feedback from the market gave me the confidence to continue investing in the business, particularly in content marketing via industry articles.

From a business coaching perspective, in 2016 I made a significant business investment in hiring One Rabbit to advise and assist in implementing a digital marketing system. The separate website and SME-focused content marketing plan greatly enhanced the business, enabling me to access a broader audience. The opportunity to join Quickway Constructions in 2018 in a part-time board capacity solidified what was an ideal long-term relationship with one of my first SME clients.

Lesson 3: Hold your vision

The need to realign my split energy and focus on SamWilko Advisory was exactly what was required at the time to move my business forward. This echoes a vital small-business lesson concerning the value of holding a vision as a means of maintaining focus. The trick is in making the right strategic choices between developing proficiency in one service area and trusting in sufficient demand versus broadening the services offering to increase the size of the target market (more on this in chapter 11).

In the case of SamWilko Advisory, my work with corporate and SME organisations in engineering and construction, although related, serves two quite different market segments. I have tracked the revenue generated in these two segments from business inception. At various times, my work has veered more towards corporate; at other times business has been more SME focused. Interestingly, the times when the most significant progress has occurred coincided with when I've temporarily prioritised one service line over the other (for more on this, see chapter 14).

Conclusion

I've found exploring the common thread leading to where I am today to be extremely beneficial in understanding the 'why' for my business journey. Unlike the auto mechanic with the worst-maintained car in the street, I've diligently applied the business coaching and advisory concepts that will be set out in the balance of this book, in building my own business as a case study of what can be achieved.

Key takeaways for sustainable businesses

1. Transformational changes require committed leadership to maintain the vision and prevent entrenched dysfunctional behaviour from dominating.

2. Public and private sector deals in complex industries are commonly associated with long lead times, twists and turns and challenges in finalising workable arrangements between the parties.

3. Specialist consultants play a key role in the tendering process, and businesses who effectively utilise consultants have a key advantage — not the least in knowing that meeting deadlines communicates the competency and trustworthiness of a business.

4. While competitive pricing is critical to a successful tender submission, numerous other elements (such as building relationships with the client, job planning, governance and implementing the right team) are key contributors to success.

5. Committing to your endeavour as a business owner requires three key elements: 1. define your position, 2. follow your instincts, 3. stay true to your vision.

CHAPTER 7
Business vision and values

This chapter explores the process by which a business vision is promulgated throughout a sustainable organisation. Vision as a process aligns behaviour and provides context for the business strategy and supporting management system in circumstances where the size and complexity of an organisation renders persuasive conversations insufficient.

The most fundamental role of leadership in business is to establish and hold a context for the business. Effective leaders also take on feedback, recognising and testing useful input, and adjusting their own view of the world accordingly.

The importance of context

The Macquarie Dictionary defines context as: 'the circumstances or facts that surround a particular situation, event etc.'[1] Coaching is all about effective conversations, and establishing context is a vital element to having an effective conversation. To illustrate: how many times have you had an exchange with someone where you've spent pretty much the whole time rehearsing in your head your response to the first thing that was said? How well do you remember the rest of the conversation? And how well did your response land when you finally had the chance to launch it? More than likely, you walked away from the conversation with that slightly disconnected feeling borne of unfinished business. It's also quite likely the other party to the conversation experienced a similar feeling.

One of the most important techniques in coaching involves delaying a response long enough to establish the context for the conversation. The first few words of a dialogue rarely establish the circumstances surrounding the conversation, but how often do we find ourselves, anxious in our efforts to come up with an instant answer to the problem at hand, jumping to a conclusion? Listening is an under-rated skill in a fast-paced modern business, and can be a challenging but effective way of accessing context.

Applying context in business

Business owners, focused as they remain on getting things done, are typically reticent to engage their employees in conversations about the 'why' for their enterprise. This might sound like heresy: of course we all strive to be consultative and inclusive — surely this is what modern-day business demands?

What underlies this fear? Often, it's the potential for the conversation to mutate into a complaints session. What would that signify? In part, employee complaints are a manifestation of the typical stress associated with working with others and getting things done. And the opportunity, from time to time, for complaints to be heard can go a long way towards lowering the overall temperature of the business.

But there's something else at play here, a phenomenon with which we became intimately familiar via our extended experiences in a state of heightened anxiety thanks to the COVID-19 pandemic.

Have you ever experienced the feeling associated with walking into a room with a purpose and then stopping, realising you have completely forgotten why you're there? In 2011, researchers at the University of Notre Dame determined that a simple change of location, such as walking through a doorway into a new room, can cause a bout of instant amnesia. The researchers proposed that our working memory appears to have an effective capacity limit, and that the act of changing rooms forces us to reorient ourselves to our new surrounds. This process can displace the thought we were previously holding in our working memory and trigger distress at having forgotten something.[2]

Research has established a link between anxiety, changing circumstances and an impaired ability to focus.[3] Chronic, stressful situations and a deeply uncertain future are particularly hard on working memory, making even the simplest tasks feel more difficult than they normally are. The specific mechanism by which anxiety interrupts cognitive function is not fully understood. However, the cognitive load borne of the COVID-19 experience appears to be closely linked with widespread feelings of overwhelm.

When we are in overwhelm, our natural tendencies draw us towards specific issues that we can latch onto, channelling our anger and frustration with the broader issues and the uncertainty of the future, over which we have little, if any, control. A business vision describes what the future state of the organisation is intended to be. A well-articulated vision speaks directly to the overwhelm that can occasionally threaten to engulf even the most efficient business. It serves as a guiding beacon, depicting the kind of future to which the organisation aspires. Vision provides direction to everyone in the organisation, enabling the focused activity required to achieve the desired outcomes. Vision provides the ability to shape and influence the culture of the business into 'the way things are done around here'. The vision question is the most important of all to answer in relation to your business.

Consider the circumstances in which your business currently exists. It's more than the engineering and construction industry, with its boom and bust cycles driven by government and business investment and population demand. The context of your business relates to the fundamentals upon which it was established:

- whether your business produces products or services or distributes products and services that others produce

- the primary position your business has adopted in the industry, based on (best) product, (cheapest) price, (specific) market or (great) service (more on this in chapter 9).

Of relevance, too, is your personal (as owner) position within the business:

- are you oriented towards investing in or generating a return from your firm

- is the relationship you have with your business motivated by income, equity or control (more on this in chapter 14)

- has your 'why' changed over time, reflecting factors such as personal growth, changing external circumstances or influences etc.?

There are reasons why we do what we do. Investing time and effort in truly aligning with your 'why' raises consciousness of what we do, our source of personal energy and our purpose for being in business. It's about finding the passion and spark, and clarifying why you get out of bed every day! Accessing this for yourself, capturing the essence and articulating it in a way that others can grasp enables the people around you to participate in the journey.

The Golden Circle theory

Simon Sinek is perhaps best known for one of the most popular TED talks of all time: 'How Great Leaders Inspire Action'.[4] He has authored several books on the topic of leadership, including *Start With Why:*

How great leaders inspire everyone to take action, which first popularised his Golden Circle concept.[5]

The Golden Circle theory, heavily influenced by Sinek's marketing background, proposes a means by which business leaders can inspire cooperation, trust and change. His work is based on research into how successful organisations think, act and communicate when messaging is oriented around the why.

Sinek's methodology encourages you to start with the 'why' of your message. This allows for an immediate emotional connection by engaging the audience's limbic brain–the part of our brain commonly thought to process feelings such as trust and loyalty and to make decisions. For an organisation, the 'why' is its purpose or reason for existence and it can serve to encourage action in others. Sinek further argues that 'what' messaging only engages the rational part of the brain, the neocortex, while the 'why' engages the part that is passionate.

Sinek's concept serves as an effective communication anchor; starting with the 'why' for your business before describing 'how' and 'what' is a great way of creating an engaging and powerful dialogue.

Critical questions to help diagnose vision issues

Perseverance and grit are key to achieving success in any field[6], and infrastructure engineering and construction is no exception. Anyone who survives and thrives in this industry will face times of doubt and need to find the inner resolve to keep going. If you want to build a successful enterprise, 'sticking with it' is a critical trait to possess. However, successful people also possess the ability to recognise when something isn't working. They revise, adjust, pivot as needed. You may have heard of the saying, 'Insanity is doing the same thing over and over and expecting different results'.

Sustainable business requires being open to both possibilities. The key question is: how does an owner determine when to give up and when to stick with it?

An effective way of making this call is to consider your business from three contexts: the 'why', the 'what' and the 'how'.[6]

- The 'why': your vision, providing the context for your business strategy

- The 'what': the strategy comprising your business model and roadmap for where your business is headed; this provides the context for your business tactics

- The 'how': the tactics including management systems, processes and people who get things done.

Diagnosing a 'why' problem requires a degree of self-reflection. Regardless of the extent to which you choose to communicate your business vision, you as the business owner need to be well connected with your business 'why'.

Values and team alignment

Much of the rise in popularity of business values statements can be traced back to the publication in 1994 of *Built to Last* by Jim Collins and Jerry Porras.[7] The book analysed how well a range of the most successful corporations in the USA adhered to a set of principles called 'core values'. A reduced focus on values in management theory since that time, obscures their timeless importance to sustainable business enterprises.

Aligning values with a vision clarifies the identity of a business and serves as a rallying point for employees. Coming up with strong values — and sticking to them — requires ownership and unwavering commitment.

The key to establishing values lies in understanding that it is not a democratic process: the owners of the business vision have both the right and responsibility to set values in alignment with the vision as a means of holding the organisation to account.

The power underlying this process is the line in the sand that values create for employees. Each employee is compelled to make a choice as to whether they are a good fit based on the extent to which they're aligned with the values of the business.

Why is it up to the employee to make the call? As Shrek reveals in a key scene in his first movie, even ogres have onion-like layers. Our personal values are held deep within us, mostly kept hidden from others by the masks we wear during day-to-day interactions with the outside world. This gives rise to the key challenge associated with enabling a values-oriented business: inevitably, misalignments will show up in values-driven businesses.

A company with strong values is very appealing to new employees, especially when initial inquiries by prospective employees reveal leadership actually 'walks the talk'. Unfortunately, even the most rigorous recruitment processes have difficulty in identifying a candidate's true values. Prospective employees may not be consciously aware of their own personal core values, which can make it difficult for them to self-assess whether an organisation is a good fit, and, conversely, difficult for an organisation to truly assess a candidate's true fit with the company. This inevitably leads to misalignments for a values-driven business. Accordingly, leadership must be particularly sensitive to the fact that, when properly practiced, values create an environment where it becomes evident that some employees' behaviour is at odds with the values of the business. Even if the employee makes a significant contribution to the performance of the business in other ways, it's important for leaders to reinforce the importance of (and requirement to adhere to) the values of the business.

The feeling of cognitive dissonance created by a misalignment with the organisation's values can be what ultimately drives the employee's decision to move on. In the meantime, feelings can manifest themselves in dysfunctional behaviour such as disengagement, and the consequences of this behaviour on the wider business need to be carefully monitored and managed. Occasionally, the wider effects of the disruptive behaviour are such that nature can't be left to take its course.

Consider the challenge of making a call to move an employee on who achieves consistent results but is prepared to 'do what it takes', including setting aside the business values, in the interests of getting the job done. Sacrificing performance for alignment with values is a hard call. It's worth weighing up, though, the effects of avoiding the decision on the other employees who make up the rest of the business.

Choosing the right values

Considering the different types of values that can arise over the course of a business journey can provide a greater understanding about the additional challenges that may show up when implementing a values-based business. Some of the various values may be defined as the following.

Core values

Core values are fundamental to the ownership and culture of an organisation with Collins and Porras defining them as both inherent and sacrosanct[7]. Compromising core values is unacceptable to an organisation and must be avoided at any cost.

Aspirational values

Company ownership may identify values it may not have, but will need for future[8] success. These aspirational values may arise, for example, due to the changing nature of the industry. As explored earlier (see chapter 5) the engineering and construction industry appears to be entering a period favouring a more collaborative approach to contracting businesses may need future values associated with collaboration to improve their chances of success and longevity.

Permission-to-play values

Permission-to-play values set minimum employee expectations and are often consistent across an industry[8]. For example, inherently dangerous industries, such as engineering and construction, will have a commitment to workplace safety throughout the industry.

Inadvertent values

Inadvertent values arise spontaneously, as a reflection (good or bad) of the collective interests and personalities of the organisation's employees.[8] Inadvertent values need to be monitored as they can change as a company grows, particularly as the business takes on employees with additional skills and broader experiences. Leaders need to be particularly aware of the potential for tension to arise between 'old' and 'new' values.

Leaders should own the process of formulating business values

To reiterate, values initiatives have nothing to do with building consensus. Effective leaders need to understand the business risks inherent in consensus-driven decision-making and when the approach should (and shouldn't be) applied. For instance, taking the time to achieve consensus prior to submitting a tender is a powerful method for reducing the risks inherent in tendering for infrastructure projects, given the exposure contractors take on in participating in the game as it's currently structured. Conversely, core values are for leadership to formulate and own.

Leading and managing a values-based business is not easy. On balance though, accessing the power of aligned values can be a key element in building a sustainable business, particularly in environments where trust is in limited supply.

The three steps of the values distillation process

The following three-step process, based on a common brainstorming technique, provides an effective way of identifying your business values:

1. Find a quiet place to think about and record any words that you associate with your business. You might identify 'different', 'professional' or 'relationship' as meaningful words. And as an additional hint, the words must resonate with you personally as well as your business.

2. Take the list of words and group them into similar themes. Aim to condense the list into three categories.

3. Examine the three categories. What themes can you identify from the list of words? Aim to pinpoint three values from the lists of words that represent your business values. This is the core of your business vision.

Behavioural alignment: The fourth step

The next step to embedding the three values you've identified into your business involves agreeing on definitions and behavioural meanings for each value. This step requires engagement with your employees and starts with sharing your three values with the business.

As humans, we often make judgements about others' values based on our observations of their behaviour. Most people have an opinion regarding what is and isn't acceptable behaviour from the perspective of their personal values in a broad range of circumstances.

This widespread 'expertise' in behavioural analysis presents an opportunity that can be harnessed in gaining commitment to an organisation's values. Accordingly, the task of establishing and maintaining behaviour in alignment with the organisation's values is best achieved via consultation with employees. Asking employees what they believe would be acceptable behaviour in alignment with your business values is a powerful way of bringing the values to life. Behavioural norms, once established, are powerful drivers of conformity, enabling individuals to demonstrate their commitment to the values via their everyday behaviour.[9]

Trust: The glue binding the business together

With an aligned understanding of behavioural expectations within a business comes the opportunity to build trust between individuals, within teams and across the organisation.

Trust comprises four dimensions:

- Sincerity: is there consistency between what people say publicly and privately and their actions (are the espoused values enacted in the business)?

- Reliability: is there consistency between what people say they will do and what they produce (integrity in action)?

- Competence: do people possess the skills and ability to carry out what they say they will do?

- Involvement: are others present (as opposed to distracted) and attuned to our concerns and accepting of what is important to us?

As with most opportunities in business and in life, there are potential downsides to be managed in our efforts to build trust. Many humans, whilst tuned in to the behaviour of others, are often blissfully unaware of the way they themselves sometimes behave in public situations and the loss of trust that can transpire. The obvious way to manage this issue is for individuals to provide open, honest and actionable feedback to each other. However, many humans are also not skilled in the art and science of providing effective feedback in a business setting and require training, monitoring and ongoing support.

Effective feedback: The Johari Window

The Johari Window (see figure 7.1) is a useful framework that can be utilised to increase behavioural self-awareness and enhance communication among individuals in a group setting. American psychologists Joseph Luft and Harry Ingham developed the initial concept in 1955, drawing on University of California research into group dynamics.[10]

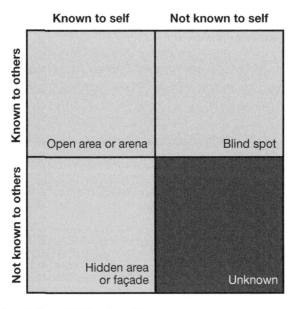

Figure 7.1: Johari Window[10]

The model is based on the premise that trust can be increased through the process of disclosing information about yourself to others, and giving and receiving feedback. Our 'self' is represented by the four quadrants of the Johari Window. Each of the quadrants signifies one of the four aspects of our personal knowledge, values, attitudes and feelings.

Open area or arena

This area signifies knowledge, values, attitudes and feelings known by the individual as well as by others. The larger this area, the more straightforward and effective communication becomes, and the greater the opportunity for establishing behavioural norms and building strong working relationships.

Blind spot

This quadrant represents information that others know about an individual, but of which the individual is unaware. Information of this nature may give rise to interpretations by others that are different to what an individual may expect, with the potential to impede effective communication. Feedback from others to the individual is how a blind spot is brought to their awareness.

Hidden area or façade

This comprises feelings, past experiences, fears, secrets and so on that are known to the individual but kept from others. Individuals are naturally reluctant to reveal information of this nature in a low-trust environment.

Unknown area

This is the information that no-one is aware of, and may include the consequences of past events or trauma that have been suppressed. This information may come to the person's awareness spontaneously or through exploration.

Feedback solicitation involves carefully listening to and actively seeking to understand feedback given by another person. This process enables an individual to increase the size of their open area, with associated benefits in terms of increased self-awareness and increased trust.

The Johari Window principles underpin formalised performance assessments such as 360-degree feedback as a means of increasing organisational self-awareness and moderating behaviour. Uncovering blind spots is a key avenue for continuous improvement and enables employees to identify and focus on developing skills in overlooked areas.

An alternative approach to feedback: Radical truth and transparency

Ray Dalio, in his 2017 publication *Principles,* outlines the approach implemented by his firm, Bridgewater Associates, in pursuing outstanding performance.[11] As Dalio proposes, by requiring colleagues to be truthful and transparent, they are forced to reveal the underlying logic of their decisions, which leads to open, robust debate. Truth allows for greater understanding, which leads to greater improvements.

Dalio's principle of organisational learning, as well as to what he terms Bridgewater's 'idea meritocracy' enables accelerated learning and regular feedback when everyone can essentially hear what everyone else is thinking.

As Dalio acknowledges, adopting the principle of radical truth and transparency in interactions between employees can create challenges, particularly for new starters unused to this very different approach to the norm in business environments. Accordingly, caution and sensitivity are required when introducing the model into a new business setting.

Building trust via integrity

Improving the performance of organisations can be a painstaking process and, as human beings, we regularly behave in ways that can thwart all efforts to build and maintain trust. One rigorous and effective method for accessing improved performance is based on the concept of integrity. The model draws on work by Werner Erhard, Michael Jensen and Steve Zaffron who created a new model of integrity outlined in their paper, 'Integrity: a positive model that incorporates the normative phenomena of morality, ethics and legality'.[12]

The stated objective of the original workshop upon which the paper is based was to provide the participants and their respective organisations with a deep understanding of the relationship between integrity and superior performance. Integrity in this context is defined as 'compete or unbroken' as opposed to a consideration of moral or ethical principles.

The concept of integrity is distinguished as a person (or an organisation) honouring their word.

As one would imagine, honouring one's word at all times creates an environment of high trust. Inevitably though, situations arise where one's word is not communicated clearly, is misunderstood by the recipient or just not kept. In these circumstances, the process for honouring one's word and restoring integrity is, at face value, deceptively simple.

Whenever your word is broken (or where it becomes apparent that you risk breaking your word), make contact as soon as possible with the recipient of your commitment and follow these steps:

- Acknowledge who came to whom with the intention of resolving the situation (ideally before the impact of the broken agreement occurs).

- Acknowledge the broken agreement.

- Recognise the impact of the broken agreement — this may involve personal as well as business impacts.

- Figure out what you will do to deal with the fall out.

- Agree on what will you put in place to avoid the situation happening in the future.

Through these simple steps, Erhard et al. maintain that integrity can be restored and trust preserved.

Brain functioning gets in the way of trust

The behavioural model and processes outlined above provide a practical and actionable means of building high-quality relationships between teams and accessing high performance. So, what else could possibly go wrong?

Dr Dean Burnett, neuroscientist and occasional comedian, focused his first book *The Idiot Brain*[13] exploring the concept that, from a rational perspective, our brains can be illogical, inefficient and sometimes just plain weird. Consider the following principles that underpin the functionality of human brains.

Our memories are unreliable

Unlike computers (with which our brain is often compared), the brain does not use logical processes for storing information. The storage method is a far more flexible and organic process and, consequently, it's a lot less fixed and reliable than one might assume. Indeed, every time a memory is retrieved, it gets tweaked or becomes corrupted in some way.

For instance, we're all familiar with the habit of embellishing a story slightly in the telling to make ourselves sound better. The effect of this is that, slowly but surely, the brain starts to remember the event differently to the reality of what happened, gradually reinforcing our version of the story. This can also happen with stored memories, which the brain might subtly edit to, say, make us feel better about ourselves.

Our brain makes us afraid

Over millions of years, the human brain has evolved to become super sensitive to danger. As you would appreciate though, the modern world isn't the same as the one faced by our prehistoric ancestors, who would have relied heavily on this threat detection system. This 'flight or fight' response is controlled by a region of the brain known as the amygdala. There are times when this ancient part of the brain is of great assistance in responding to and avoiding imminent threats, for instance, evading a motor vehicle while crossing a road. However, many of the modern threats we currently face that trigger the amygdala — such as the prospect of an impending deadline or the threat of infection due to a pandemic — require a more measured response. Unfortunately, the accumulation of these responses over time results in the sort of heightened anxiety that disrupts rational thought.

We are desperate to be liked by others

In the same way our brains have developed a sophisticated threat detection system, we've also evolved so that large portions of our brains are dedicated to engaging with others. When being part of a community is important to survival, we become very aware of how other people regard us. Our fear of criticism and need for approval means that, at times, we can be easily influenced by others. This fear extends to suppressing our opinions in public forums and can result in challenging phenomena, such as 'group think' in circumstances where diversity of opinion is necessary for achieving consensus.

Thinking fast and slow

Psychologist and economist Daniel Kahneman was awarded the 2002 Nobel Memorial Prize in Economic Sciences. His book

Thinking Fast and Slow[14] is acknowledged as a foundation piece in the field of what has become known as behavioural economics. This relatively recent school of thought takes into consideration human behaviour in predicting the economic decision-making processes of individuals and institutions.

Kahneman describes the human mind as being comprised of two 'operating systems' (again with the computer analogy!):

- system 1: operates automatically and quickly, with little or no effort and no sense of voluntary control (for example, we are born to mourn losses and are therefore programmed to avoid them if possible)

- system 2: allocates attention to the effortful mental activities that demand it (this system is often associated with the subjective experience of agency or intentional action, choice and concentration).

How the brain utilises system 1 and system 2 in making decisions gives rise to an additional issue to add to the list of irrational brain tendencies.

Our brains' 'rational' decision-making ability is unreliable

How the internal interactions between system 1 and system 2 play out is illustrated by a concept termed the 'availability heuristic'.[14] In essence, our perception of how often an event occurs is determined by the ease with which we can recall specific instances of the event happening. Let's say, for instance, we're in the middle of an argument with our business partner about who makes the greater contribution to the partnership. This conundrum could be easily solved by system 2 (firing up a spreadsheet and documenting respective tasks done over the previous month, allocating hours to each task, etc.). However, system 1 is far more likely to take over by recalling an example or two from memory and then landing on a conclusion (e.g., they cancelled last month's partnership meeting and the insurance renewal is overdue). The system 1 and system 2 that occurs when we recall information from memory can skew our view of reality. In this instance, a system 2 question (How much is my partner contributing to the partnership?) has been substituted with a system 1 question (How easily can I recall contributions that my partner has made to the partnership?).

More broadly, events that attract our attention — for instance, a recent dramatic event that has attracted lots of media coverage — will be easily retrieved from memory and can affect our decision-making. Personal experiences are also more readily available for recall than incidents that happened to others or statistics (e.g., individual partners' estimates of their respective time contributions to the partnership typically add up to more than 100 per cent of the available time!).

Furthermore, we have a tendency towards confirmation bias where we search for, recall and interpret information in a way that confirms our pre-existing beliefs or hypotheses.[14] The more emotionally charged the issue (or the greater extent to which the issue is associated with our deeply entrenched beliefs), the stronger this tendency.

So, how does all of this play out when we're in decision-making mode, particularly at times when we're under pressure? Rather than examining all the available evidence and carefully weighing it up, our system 1 thinking attempts to reinforce our existing beliefs or, in their absence, recalls the last thing we heard on the topic. This is important to keep in mind in circumstances where important decisions need to be made, particularly in team settings. Seeking consensus on a team-based decision by teasing out individuals' rationales is a great way of building trust as well as reducing the risk of 'group think'.

Conclusion

There are many ways in which internal thoughts and values systems can disrupt valid efforts to build cohesive team and organisational behaviour, commitment and high performance. This tendency can be detrimental to the personal interests of employees as well as the health of the wider organisation in a business context. One of the most effective methods of guarding against this disruption is by listening to the advice of others. Of equal importance is seeking to understand the basis for others' views, especially when undertaking essential planning and making key decisions that require consensus.

Trust is the key to effective interpersonal engagement and sustained organisational performance. High levels of trust can be built in business through behavioural alignment, commitment to truth and transparency, and diligent application of integrity. Trust, whilst hard won and more easily lost, is the organisational bedrock upon which owners can build their business vision.

Key takeaways for sustainable businesses

1   Vision as a process aligns behaviour and provides context for the business strategy and supporting management system in circumstances where the size and complexity of an organisation renders persuasive conversations insufficient. As a business owner and leader, your most fundamental role is to establish and hold a vison — the 'why' — for the business.

2   Values in alignment with the vision clarifies the identity of a business and serves as a rallying point for employees. Choosing values is not a democratic process: the owners of the business vision have both the right and responsibility to set values in alignment with the vision as a means of holding their organisation to account.

3   Conversely, consultation with employees is the most effective process for establishing behavioural expectations in alignment with the business values. Engaging with your

employees regarding what they believe is acceptable behaviour in alignment with your business values is a powerful means by which the values can be brought to life.

4 An aligned understanding of behavioural expectations creates the opportunity to build trust between individuals, within teams and across the organisation. Trust can be enhanced via effective feedback from a place of personal truth and transparency, and by a commitment to honouring one's personal word and restoring integrity in circumstances where one's word is broken.

5 Our human tendencies, particularly the ways in which brains function, create traps when seeking to build interpersonal trust, making key decisions and achieving consensus in team settings. Greater awareness and understanding of these tendencies is essential in avoiding their potentially detrimental effects on hard-won trust.

CHAPTER 8
Effective leadership

Effective leadership is a key ingredient in enacting the vision of a business and building a sustainable, high-performance enterprise. If trust is the key to effective interpersonal engagement, then it stands to reason that leadership needs to be focused on building a high level of organisational trust.

High-performance leadership is not attained by developing one skill or leadership style. It requires alignment of multiple components of a leader's abilities, strengths and self-beliefs. An effective leader needs to understand the strengths and weaknesses of the people for whom they are responsible, and how the interplay of these strengths and weaknesses effects overall performance.

Much can be learnt about leaders' key role in building sustainable businesses by considering effective leadership behaviour from a range of different perspectives. In this way, answers to the following key questions will become apparent:

- What contribution can effective leaders make to successful project outcomes?

- Is there a preferred leadership style — or set of traits — most able to galvanise outstanding organisational performance?

- What can we learn about leadership from professional services and the military?

- What contribution can the followers make to effective leadership behaviour?

Leadership's industry challenge

I've been dwelling a lot on what needs to change in the infrastructure engineering and construction industry. Three common challenges that constantly show up are the:

- capability and experience gaps in dealing with what's coming up in terms of work volume and project complexity

- appropriateness of commercial arrangements and aligned behaviour to enable more equitable outcomes for clients and contractors (in essence aligning the right contract risk allocation with the right project)

- lack of an aligned and inclusive industry culture as a fundamental requirement for attracting and retaining tomorrow's industry participants.

These are significant issues to resolve, and astute observers will note that the three challenges are interconnected. Industry leaders have a key role to play in solving these three key barriers to a better environment for all participants.

Commonality of understanding is an essential starting point in determining the path forward to a more sustainable industry. A clear and aligned understanding of *what* needs to change is a necessary pre-condition to figuring out *how* to get to where the industry needs to be. By way of example, a Grattan Institute Report highlights[1] the broad scope for improvement in the way increasingly popular mega projects are selected and delivered.

In these current circumstances (where we're seeking an outcome that looks and feels like a transformed industry), we need leaders to show up as catalysts for change. And when we think of catalysts for change, thoughts typically turn to the 'great men' who shaped the modern industry we participate in today. I believe, however, that the industry's tendency to fall back on traditional — and some would say outdated — patterns of thinking is a key element holding back progress.

While it can be confronting to step up and take ownership of change and leadership, I believe we each have an individual responsibility to take action and a personal leadership role to play (whether formal or informal).

Do leaders make a difference?

Consider, then, the issue of leadership performance from a more fundamental perspective: does effective (or ineffective) leadership actually make a difference to the performance of our private organisations and public institutions?

Our own experiences with leaders, good and bad, might intuitively lead us to the conclusion that leadership definitely does influence organisational performance. But is this a reasonable conclusion? There is an alternative position: that leadership has relatively little effect on performance. This 'contextualist' viewpoint emphasises the constraints that are placed on leaders by situational factors, in particular, firm size and the type of industry in which the firm operates.

Surprisingly, from a literature perspective, there is a real lack of consensus regarding the evidence definitively supporting or refuting the effect of leadership on performance. According to Alan Berkeley Thomas in his 1988 paper 'Does leadership make a difference to organisational performance?'[2] the contextualist argument has traditionally rested heavily on the findings of just one major study, that of Lieberson and O'Connor (1972).[3] Their findings were that leadership has a substantial effect at the level of the individual firm: however, it has little impact on performance at the aggregate level (performance between firms of varying sizes and industries).

Unsurprisingly, Lieberson and O'Connor's seemingly counter-intuitive conclusions have been the subject of substantial criticism. According to Thomas, the conclusions can be explained by recognising that while leaders can and do impact firm performance, their overall impact is insufficient to outweigh the inbuilt differences between firms that largely account for performance variation among firms.

Interestingly, the plethora of studies carried out in the nearly six decades since publication of Lieberson and O'Connor's work have apparently done little to advance the argument. Although a significant amount of empirical (observation-based) evidence has been collated regarding links between leadership and organisational performance, much of the assessment of performance has involved subjective measures, such as surveyed 'satisfaction with the leader'. This opens the work up to criticism based on attribution theory, that is, the impact of leadership on performance is no more than a social construct — people interpret it that way.

So where does this leave us?

I believe that the answer lies within the concept of what leadership actually is. Knies et al.'s article 'Leadership and organisational performance: State of the art and research agenda'[4] proposes the following based on common definitional elements used by scholars:

> ... leadership is about an influencing process, more specifically a process whereby intentional influence is exercised over other people to guide, structure and facilitate activities in groups or organisations.

So leadership does not and cannot operate in a vacuum — it's fundamentally an enabling process. In essence, leadership and employees are intrinsically linked and rely on each other to create effective performance. It stands to reason, then, that great leaders require excellent employees to achieve outstanding performance. Maybe a humbling thought for leaders who might consider their people to be expendable commodities…

The link between effective leadership and project performance

Infrastructure engineering and construction is an industry characterised by high-risk projects. It stands to reason, then, that at any given time, there will be delays and cost overruns. With distressed projects relatively commonplace in the industry, the question regarding root causes of the problems is regularly raised.

Every project, of course, has specific circumstances at play and, as with most complex problems, there is no simple answer. However, a common element that's missing in many projects is effective leadership.

In a 2017 report, 'The art of project leadership: Delivering the world's largest projects', McKinsey et al. lament the historically poor performance of large capital projects around the globe, with many examples of significant budget and time overruns. From a database of 500 global projects over US$1 billion, transport and other infrastructure projects, on average, experienced an actual versus budget cost overrun of 42 per cent and a schedule overrun of 63 per cent.[5]

Our innate tendency as humans is to focus on high-profile failures rather than unreported successes (a behaviour known as the 'availability heuristic'[6]) and, of course, there are a great many examples of successful projects. However, when large and complex capital projects fail, the cost, in terms of money, as well as suffering by the teams responsible for remedying the situation, is horrendous.

McKinsey's report explores the contribution made by the 'art' of project delivery to successful large projects, encompassing elements such as leadership, organisational culture, mindsets, and attitudes and behaviours of project owners, leaders and teams.

The authors acknowledge what is arguably the key 'scientific' contribution to successful project delivery: careful allocation of risk between owner and contractor (deliverer) and appropriate alignment of incentives. In practice, this looks like project owners thoughtfully delegating only those risks that the contractor is better positioned to manage. Sounds simple in concept, yes? Regular risk misallocations bear out the challenges in getting this right for major projects on a consistent basis.

The report focuses on exploring the extent to which the art of effective leadership contributes to successful projects, based on evidence drawn from a wide range of interviews with experienced practitioners, and established a range of best-practice leadership behaviours drawn from successful projects. With only 5 per cent of assessed projects found to have been completed within budget and on schedule, the strong indication is that the behavioural success factors are relatively thin on the ground.

What does best-practice project leadership look like?

Project owners are the people ultimately responsible for the success (or otherwise) of the project, and they must accept full ownership of project outcomes — be they good or bad. This approach sets the tone for an effective relationship between the project owner and head contractor, more akin to a business partnership with a mindset of 'we win together or lose together'. Productive contractor-owner relationships are based on mutual trust and collaboration in joint problem-solving.

Unsurprisingly, the setup phase of the project is the best opportunity to establish healthy management practices that deliver successful project outcomes. In this phase, project leadership is about articulating purpose, role modelling expected attitudes and behaviours, and nourishing the desired culture. Effective leaders also take the time to connect with team members on a personal level. These practices help create project teams with a unique and shared identity and a culture of mutual trust and collaboration.

Strong and transparent trust-based relationships with stakeholders enable prevention and rapid resolution of problems. The setup phase needs leadership with a strong focus on building constructive relationships (and particularly trust) with both internal and external stakeholders. This enables issues to be addressed early in the project timeline that would otherwise impede delivery. Building trust is also critical to productively addressing the inevitable crises that arise in projects of significant size and complexity.

Leadership: Great man versus great leader

Much of the recent history of infrastructure engineering and construction in Australia focuses on the 'great men' — and they were largely great men as the public faces of these organisations at that time — shaping their businesses off the back of nation-building infrastructure projects. Engineering and construction in Australia is built on stories of great leaders creating exceptional companies from humble beginnings.

The great man theory in engineering and construction

When transformational change is needed, the industry naturally looks to great women and men. This aligns with the school of thought (which originates in the ancient Greek and Roman times) that considers leadership to be an innate quality.[7] Great leaders are born, not made. According to the theory, leadership calls for certain qualities that one either has or does not have. People are attracted to and follow these leaders, turning to them instinctively for inspiration and support.

Neil Sarah's well-crafted article 'What's in a Name? A brief history of some of Australia's construction giants'[8] tells the stories of Bert Baulderstone of AW Baulderstone, Manuel Hornibrook of Hornibrook Constructions, Gennero Abignano of Abigroup and Les Thiess of Thiess. Common themes evident in their stories include humble beginnings and success in the face of adversity.

AW Baulderstone was incorporated in South Australia in 1946 by Bert Baulderstone, a subcontract bricklayer with ambitions to operate as a head contractor. Baulderstone survived capitalisation problems to become a national force in commercial construction and civil engineering.

Gennero (Jim) Abignano arrived in Australia in 1957 as a virtually penniless immigrant from Italy. Jim spent the next 20 years developing a successful earthmoving and civil engineering business, Abigroup.

Conversely, the salutary lesson of Transfield — once mighty, but now largely subsumed into John Holland and CIMIC — saw Italian immigrants turned business leaders Franco Belgiorno-Nettis and Carlo Saltieri become embroiled in dispute, and the business split in two.[9]

These stories live on in the psyches of many of the women and men seeking to build great and sustainable enterprises in the current era.

How does this play out?

The key implications of the theory that leaders are born and not made mean:

- not everyone can aspire to become a great leader

- inborn leadership qualities alone are necessary and sufficient for leadership success

- situational factors, such as the demands of the task and the general socio-economic environment, have relatively little influence on a leader's effectiveness; great leaders, by virtue of their sheer 'magic', bend situational factors to their advantage.

Trait theory of leadership

The trait-based theory of leadership, as a more contemporary development of the great man theory, was formalised by Thomas Carlyle in the mid-1800s. Trait theory focuses on identifying distinguishing personality qualities or characteristics linked to successful leadership across a variety of situations.

Jim Collins, in his 2001 book *Good to Great,*[10] adopts a solid research-based methodology in exploring what distinguished 11 companies with sustainable performance over a 40-year period from a sample size of 1435 publicly listed organisations in the US.

In considering the contribution of leadership to organisational performance, Collins proposed a hierarchy of leadership capabilities and traits. At the pinnacle of the hierarchy is a Level 5 leader. A Level 5 executive is defined as a leader who builds enduring greatness through a 'paradoxical blend of personal humility and professional will'. Level 5 behavioural traits are further described as follows:

- Personal humility: a Level 5 leader channels ambition into the company, not self, setting up successors for even greater success in the next generation.

- Professional will: a Level 5 leader demonstrates an unwavering resolve to do whatever must be done to produce the best long-term results, no matter how difficult.

Collins proposed specific traits associated with Level 5 leaders and identifies these leaders in a range of sustainably successful organisations. In this way, Collins makes substantial progress in refuting a key criticism levelled at trait theory, being the lack of specific, identifiable traits associated with effective leadership across a broad range of situations.[10] Of course, trait theory considers the leader alone to the exclusion of the followers, whom most would acknowledge are of great importance in enabling an effective leader.

Interestingly, by highlighting the co-existence of personal humility and professional will in Level 5 leaders, the work recognises that successful leadership traits can counteract each other. Perhaps this reflects a leader's need to regularly deal with multiple, often opposing considerations in making decisions?

Leadership lessons for professional services firms

Consider the specific leadership challenges faced by professional services firms, for instance, those who provide design services to construction contractors.

Joe Barolsky, in an article titled 'Avoiding the Bermuda Triangle of law firm management',[11] outlined the results of a study of US law firms carried out in the early 2000s by Professor Ashish Nanda of Harvard Business School. The lessons here are equally applicable to engineering firms as well as accounting and other similar professional services-based organisations.

Professor Nanda compared profit per equity partner in over 200 legal firms. The results showed that both very large firms and small boutique firms who concentrated on specific market segments generated relatively high profitability in comparison with industry benchmarks. Interestingly, mid-sized firms typically generated lower profit relative to both their smaller and larger peers. Two theories were proposed to explain this result:

- The first was that many mid-sized legal firms struggled to find a point of difference to leverage in order to gain a price premium.

- The second theory concerned management and leadership practices. Small firms, by and large, benefited from quick, informal decision-making and the ability to correct course as needed, whilst large firms had access to resources that enabled better decision-making. Medium firms were essentially stuck in a growth pain zone likened to a Bermuda Triangle.

In relation to the second theory, it is fair to say that every business with a history of growth has inevitably suffered episodes of 'growing pains' along the way. In my experience, this most clearly shows up in the spaghetti-like organisation charts that result from the reactive approach to hiring and firing that typically occurs when management time is short and the spot fires of business troubles many.

Significantly though, professional services firms face a particular leadership and management-related challenge in addition to the industry-specific issues at play. This challenge progressively manifests itself as an intrinsic consequence of the partner-as-owner model.

Professional services firms are typically established as partnerships. Over time, well-performing and like-minded staff are invited to participate as equity partners to share in the growth and success of the enterprise. The downside shows up as the number of decision-makers increases, and the decision-making process inevitably becomes more cumbersome. What this can mean day-to-day is extensive delays, compromise-based decision making or creeping decision avoidance.

Effective leadership is the most critical requirement in navigating through the Bermuda Triangle for mid-sized engineering firms. Great leaders in this space implement the right decisions quickly, building trust and acceptance among the partners and making them more comfortable with the leader's decision-making ability. Unfortunately, what leadership can look and feel like from the perspective of a managing partner — raised in a firm where technical competence is a core measure of authority — is a largely ceremonial and administrative role. This is especially prevalent in engineering services businesses, where professionals are hired for their technical competence and industry profile rather than their managerial expertise.

To some extent, the managing partner's concern is real. How, then, does an effective leader rise above the day-to-day administrative requirements of the role (which do require a certain amount of regular attention) and make a real difference to firm performance?

Here are two key challenges common to most professional services firms on which to focus.

At the core of typical professional services firms is a close (sometimes myopic) management focus on chargeable hours. Regardless of what might be discussed in management meetings about workforce training, professional skills development and work-life balance, the utilisation measure remains the key focus for senior management. This focus becomes more prevalent when times get tough (read: when the chargeable work starts to dry up).

At the end of the day, revenue and, therefore, profit in services-based businesses is fundamentally driven by chargeable hours, and whilst 'value pricing' is the holy grail of professional services, clients as a default position commonly assess the value of an assignment based on the input hours required to achieve the result.

Effective leaders of engineering services businesses have an opportunity to leverage their position and consequent access to key clients to reinforce the value-add provided by their people. Business development in professional services is often relegated to spare time when not much else is going on (an increasingly rare commodity these days in my experience). Conversations with clients and prospects are often avoided, borne of fear regarding what to talk about beyond general chit-chat. As a suggestion, a properly structured conversation with a key client about creating a partnership-based relationship (see chapter 12) has the potential to create great value for both parties.

Firms finding themselves in the Bermuda Triangle of growth could improve internal efficiency and increase client value-add by leveraging automation-based technology. By way of example, engineering firms over the last two decades have almost completely replaced manual drafting services with computer-aided design (CAD) and have moved significantly towards 3D building information modelling–based (BIM) design. Designers can improve efficiency and enhance collaboration with contractor clients by integrating the design phase with the rest of the value chain and enabling the inclusion of additional layers, such as construction schedule and cost, much earlier in the project.

Integration challenges across various design systems, documentation management platforms and communications media have so far limited further efficiency benefits in this area. However, the effects of COVID-19 are anticipated to accelerate the pace of change in this area and enable better collaboration.

On the other hand, consider what is potentially lost in the race to implement best technology? Manual drawing production and documentation reviews have been the traditional means by which junior staff learnt basic skills and developed resilience to survive and thrive in the demanding professional services environment. Juniors who are unfamiliar with hand-held calculators can lack the ability to sense-check the results of a spreadsheet. Engineering drafters, reliant on CAD-generated construction details and with scant exposure to worksites, have limited opportunity to develop a feel for the constructability issues faced by workers including restricted site access and uneven ground conditions.

Great leaders of modern engineering services businesses need to possess a deep understanding of and keen interest in building internal capability in leveraging technology such as 3D modelling, 5D information management and offshore resourcing for efficient and effective client outcomes. The need to invest in developing capable and experienced junior professional staff who can survive and thrive in a modern business environment also needs to be kept top-of-mind.

Leadership from an unstructured perspective

I've had a couple of opportunities to spend time camping on Singleton Military Area with stunning views of Brokenback Mountain range, while accompanying Barker College Cadet Unit annual cadet camps in which my son participated.

Week-long events like these expose the cadets to the army way of getting things done. Plenty of learning opportunities show up for them, as they are required to look after themselves and their mates while participating in outdoor activities like camping, hiking and abseiling.

As a parent helper, I had the privilege of getting to know a bit more about a bunch of fellow parents while cooking for the cadets and getting up to our own brand of mischief in the downtime between meals. The parents I met came with a wide range of business experiences, mostly senior and middle management, with the occasional business owner thrown in.

I came away from the camps with a few simple but powerful observations about adult leadership in action. I'm at pains to state that the camps were a fantastic experience, and the parents worked really well together for the vast majority of the time. I'm fairly sure, though, that my fellow parents won't mind me making some general observations about our occasional behaviour (and for the avoidance of doubt the observations absolutely apply to me as well):

- It's quite hard to be a follower and just do what you're told when in another, say business, life you're used to being the boss and owning decisions on a regular basis.

- It's quite possible to have far too many opinions about the best way to get something done. In this situation, having too many leaders in the discussion exacerbates the problem.

- When completing jobs that require a process to be set up and followed, it's more helpful to have one leader and lots of followers than the other way round.

- The pressure of an impending deadline is the most effective way of driving compromise in getting to a decision.

What can be drawn from these observations?

It would be clear to many, particularly those with corporate experience, that 'modern' management has moved a long way from a command-and-control style to a consultative- and participative-based approach (at least to a certain level). There are many times, however, in business life and in particular industries like engineering and construction (when a bid deadline looms, when the trucks for the concrete pour are scheduled to arrive, at 4 am when the deadline for rail track handover is approaching) where the 'old-fashioned' authoritative approach is absolutely the right and most effective way to go.

Effective leaders recognise the required leadership style to suit the situation, and either modify their own approach or enlist others with the necessary attributes to get the job done. It might seem a bit old-fashioned, but I believe the military possesses a wealth of valuable expertise and experience in getting things done when it really matters, and still has a lot to offer in this regard.

Leadership: The role of followers

There seems to be widespread, palpable disappointment and disillusionment with many of Western society's elected leaders, those responsible for leading and governing major financial institutions and even those charged with the responsibility for providing spiritual guidance to what are increasingly secular societies. This reflects a broader loss of confidence in Western leadership, with profound implications for business management and leadership.

A question that comes to mind is whether our expectations of our various leaders are too great?

Perhaps a better question to consider: if we believe effective leadership is important, then, from a self-responsibility perspective, what should we be doing about improving the performance of our leaders?

I believe that we each have three crucial roles to play in making a difference to the performance of our leaders in all spheres.

Role 1: Hold our leaders to account for the 'why'

As individuals, we can reasonably expect those in leadership positions to hold a vision or context (a 'why') that guides their own journey and points the way forward for the people whom they serve. With these expectations comes a personal responsibility to hold our leaders to account when they fail to explain a consistent 'why'.

To draw from the political sphere, the current lack of ability by our politicians to express a consistent 'why' in terms of a policy narrative, and the degeneration of political debate to positional arguments, is showing up as a major weakness in Australian politics as well as the broader Western political process.

Mark Thompson explores this issue in *Enough Said – What's gone wrong with the language of politics?*[12] Amongst other issues, Thompson considers the irony that, in our age of mass communication channels, it often seems virtually impossible for a message to be clearly and consistently conveyed.

Role 2: Have an informed opinion

We all have a right to have an opinion—and there's certainly no shortage of these expressed in cyberspace—but we also bear a responsibility to have an informed opinion. In light of the discussion above, getting to the truth of an issue requires some considerable effort in the current environment, which brings us to Role 3.

Role 3: Be engaged in the conversation

When we notice leaders speaking and behaving out of alignment with their espoused 'why', we can start to feel confused, frustrated and disconnected with the discourse. The natural and easy reaction at this point is to just disengage from the conversation. So why is this course of action problematic?

Consider the issue from a business perspective. A wide range of studies support the concept that leaders can both positively and negatively influence employees' level of engagement.[12] Research shows that employees who have trust in senior management and feel that they have a voice in the organisation, show higher levels of engagement and lower signs of withdrawal.

From a contrary point of view, what are the implications of leadership choosing to actively reduce their employees' level of engagement? This may happen for any number of reasons: reducing the level of scrutiny on senior management is one reason that might not immediately spring to mind. This might, of course, lead to a widespread uneasy feeling of mistrust — maybe with good reason!

Conclusion

The key message here is that we all have a role to play in holding our leaders to account. The challenge is to be aware of and strongly resist the easy option of disengagement as negative consequences can arise from this space.

If I reflect upon the positive attributes of the great leaders I've worked for and with over the years, the one word that regularly shows up is 'authentic'. Leaders could do worse than adopting this word as a context for building their own approach to leadership.

Key takeaways for sustainable businesses

1 Engineering and construction, being a project-based industry, requires effective project leadership as a key contributor to industry success and sustainability. Trust-based relationships between project leaders and internal and external stakeholders are critical in enabling the inevitable challenges that arise in complex projects to be managed in an effective and timely manner.

2 Leaders and employees are intrinsically linked and rely on each other to create effective performance. Great leaders require the support of excellent employees to achieve outstanding performance.

3 Effective leaders need to show up as catalysts for change in circumstances where the outcome sought is a transformed industry. Behavioural traits of personal humility and professional will are associated with sustainably successful organisations, and similar traits can also make a difference in transforming engineering and construction.

4 Effective leaders must be focused on building a high level of organisational trust. So too each and every employee has a personal leadership contribution to make by being engaged, having an informed opinion and holding the leaders to account for the business vision.

Part III
The What

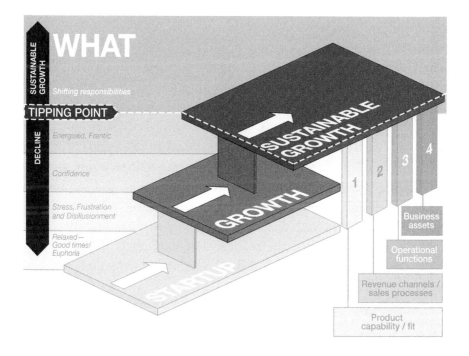

This section describes the process by which an effective strategy is formulated, taking account of the specific circumstances in which good businesses in infrastructure engineering and construction find themselves. Both design and documentation are covered, as well as the contribution made by management and governance to effective strategy formulation.

One of the hallmarks of a sustainable business is an ability to formulate and implement a strategy. This capability extends a good business, traditionally reliant upon the owner's experience and intuition, to a great business with a road-tested growth map.

Two fundamental challenges arise, though, in developing capability in strategy formulation. The first major challenge likely to show up concerns maintaining clarity regarding the fundamental difference between strategy (the 'what') and tactics (the 'how'). For this, we can turn to the military for perspective.

The Art of War was written around the fifth century BC and attributed to Chinese military strategist Sun Tzu.[1] This ancient work still influences modern military thinking as well as contemporary business tactics. Strategy, from a militaristic standpoint, is simply the art and science of options. Sun Tzu's army did not face up to an adversary with a specific plan. Rather, it relied upon an understanding of the competitive landscape upon which the battle would be fought, and the options that could potentially arise during the conflict. In this way, decisions could be made as required, in accordance with how the battle played out. Operational planning and decision-making, in turn, guided the tactical decisions made in the heat of battle. Great businesses adopt a similar approach in formulating and executing strategy.

The second major challenge appears when leaders seek to implement a strategy. This can be illustrated by considering the process of implementing strategy to be comprised of three steps:

- Step 1: formulating a strategy concept

- Step 2: developing and documenting a strategy

- Step 3: implementing a strategy.

Step 1 requires both an idea and a 'why' for the idea, providing the context for Step 2 (What are we going to do?) and Step 3 (How will we go about doing it?).

Step 2 is where the key challenges lie. In broad terms, the smaller the business, the less likely it is for the strategy to be recorded in writing prior to moving to Step 3. Small businesses typically find the process of documenting strategy to be unnecessarily slow and bureaucratic, and are tempted to skip this part of the step. Unfortunately, the decision to jump straight to Step 3 creates major consequences in circumstances where the hoped-for result is not realised. The absence of a documented strategy hampers the diagnosis of what went wrong (was the problem specifically the strategy or how well the strategy was implemented?).

The larger and more complex the business, the more likely it becomes for the business to stall at Step 2. Larger businesses often find the process of aligning stakeholders around a common path to be painful if not impossible to achieve.

Finally, it would be naïve not to recognise the contribution that luck makes to successful implementation of strategy. The key to good fortune, though, is in managing the controllable elements of business in preparation for when the luck presents itself.

CHAPTER 9
What is strategy?

When my son was a youngster at the local public school, an opportunity came up to coach his under-fives soccer team. At the time, I had no experience in playing soccer nor much exposure to the game. No matter, I thought. How hard could it be?

Let me just say, there are very few volunteer roles with more pressure than being coach of a junior sports team. What becomes apparent is that you've been entrusted with the hopes and dreams of a group of parents, most of whom are — if they're honest with themselves — impatiently waiting for their visons of sporting success to be enacted by their abundantly talented offspring (as in most fields of endeavour these days, patience is a virtue that rarely shows up). The greater the gap between expectation and reality, the greater the pressure brought to bear on the coach as the ultimate responsible party for sporting success.

What then does the coach do on match day when the parents' expectation is that they should be playing in position a-la Spanish Tiki-Taka style whilst all the kids want to do is run after the soccer ball like a busy 'bee-hive' to get a kick?

I set about coming up with a plan for success. The first step consisted of purchasing a book called *So, You Want to Be a Coach* by Les Murray (the late sports journalist and football media identity) and

Richard Alagich (a Croatian-born football coach heavily involved in Australian youth football).[1] This high-quality publication provided the basic framework for a structured learning program for small children who have just been introduced to a round soccer ball.

The next challenge to be overcome was that kids of five to seven years of age typically have limited spatial awareness and concentration, and just really want to have a kick at the ball. I recall learning this during the first couple of coaching sessions in the local park. At any time during the session, the arrival of a dog off leash would be sufficient to disrupt proceedings and result in the kids disappearing in the direction of the play equipment.

This challenge was less of an issue on game day, with the parents camped around the small-sized soccer pitch with shiny eyes and expectation in their hearts. Frustratingly, though, placing small children in typical football formation and expecting them to naturally grasp the concepts of playing like a team does not work (although that's not what the parents of the next Messi or Ronaldo would have you think).

A more effective strategy was required for the circumstances. I called the most successful approach the 'modified bee-hive' and it involved working with the all-in formation the kids naturally adopted and so enjoyed participating in. The method involved:

- getting the biggest kid to stand out front of the 'bee-hive' nearer the opponents' goal and then regularly reminding the other 'bee-hive' players to kick to the front kid whenever they see him or her

- positioning the smartest kid behind the 'bee-hive' in a centre back position near our goal, whose job it was to kick the ball back into the mix whenever it escaped.

The beauty of the strategy was two-fold. Firstly, the kids got to participate in the game and develop their tracking and kicking the ball skills. Secondly, the coach can inform the stakeholders (a.k.a. the parents) that the team is playing with 'length' (i.e., greater coverage from goal to goal), with the next aim to play with greater cross-field 'width' as the team gains further skill and experience.

Strategy: An uncomplicated answer to a complex problem

Nirvana in the strategy space is finding a simple answer to what appears to be a complex problem. The goal is to come up with a plan of action to achieve desired business outcomes for the short, medium and long term.

Good businesses in infrastructure engineering and construction have one thing in common: they've already grown against the odds despite working on high-risk, cashflow-demanding projects while balancing the increasing costs of winning highly competitive tender work.

Standing still in business is rarely an option. Businesses must grow to continue to survive in a competitive environment. All businesses need to mature and respond to changes in the industry environment in which they exist, overcoming the natural tendency to stagnate and eventually decline. The challenge is in moving through the initial stages of growth. Initial growth inevitably drives businesses to a tipping point, stagnating the organisation's ability to function effectively. What this feels like is choking operational capacity, forcing a search for new sources of higher-value revenue in an environment where there appears to be no viable alternatives.

The mistake that I most observe at this challenging time in the life of a business is borne of the assumption that the answer to the problem is one thing: a silver bullet that will resolve all the issues weighing down progress. The better answer lies in understanding that the challenge is more akin to a jigsaw, where the pieces are more than likely there but not necessarily fitting together in a way that reveals the path forward.

The good news is the tipping point is a rite of passage in disguise. Plot the course well, learn the process by which effective strategies are formulated and you'll emerge in a new phase of business called sustainable growth.

Strategy is best thought of as an excellent game. And like all excellent games, it is crucial to fully understand the rules of engagement. For this, it is useful to consider the principles underlying strategic development and operational implementation.

Strategy and operational effectiveness are both essential to superior business performance. A company can only out-perform competitors if it can establish a point of difference that it can sustain. Operational effectiveness means performing similar activities better, often but not always more efficiently, than the competition performs them. Constant improvement in operational effectiveness is necessary for maintaining the competitive position of a business. However, it is not sufficient on its own in the longer run, particularly in circumstances where competitors are able to copy what's been discovered.

In contrast, strategic positioning means performing different activities from competitors or performing similar activities in different ways. What this looks like is niche-based competition, which can be considered from the perspective of:

- variety-based positioning (choice of product or service varieties rather than customer segments)[2]

- needs-based positioning (targeting a segment of customers)

- access-based positioning (segmenting customers in different ways).

A brief history of strategy

The orthodox approach to business strategy has largely been shaped around a framework first conceived by Kenneth R. Andrews in his classic 1971 book *The Concepts of Corporate Strategy*.[3] Andrews defined strategy as the alignment between what a company can do (its strengths and weaknesses) within the universe of what it might do (its environmental opportunities and threats). As an aside, this is the basis of the SWOT (strengths, weaknesses, opportunities, threats) analysis that is commonly used in corporate business planning.[4]

Michael Porter's 1980 book *Competitive Strategy: Techniques for analysing industries and competitors*[5] provided the next important step in enabling systematic access to the concepts developed by Andrews. Porter's work focussed on the nature of competition within a given industry, setting the context for a company's strategy. Porter likened the competitive environment to a series of Five Forces impacting on the industry[6]. These forces-comprising buyer power, threat of substitutes, competitive rivalry, threat of new entrants and supplier power-impact the average profitability of industries as well as individual strategies. The challenge in maximising profitability for a given business is solved by finding a competitive position for the business to operate in.

With the understanding of the concepts of core competence and competition based on capabilities, strategic focus shifted from the external to the internal operation of the company. This model assumed that the basis of competitive advantage lay inside the organisation, with the adoption of new strategies being constrained by the company's resources. Conversely, the environment external to the business received relatively little attention.

The 1990s saw the emergence of a resource-based view of business, which has helped bridge these seemingly disparate approaches to fulfil the promise of Andrew's framework. Jay Barney's 1991 article `Firm resources and sustained competitive advantage'[7] triggered the emergence of a resource-based view of strategy, drawing together Andrew's alignment-based view of the competitive environment with Porter's industry forces framework. Barney confronted the issues raised by Collis and Montgomery,[8] whereby strategy researchers either over-emphasised the external aspects of the strategy problem or ignored the presence of internal competition when internal issues were considered.

Barney's work was founded in the importance of a company's internal resources and capabilities as potential sources of sustainable competitive advantage. For this to hold, however, three market forces need to be taken into consideration, namely the resource or capability needs to be:

- in demand: does it meet customers' needs and is it competitively superior?

- scarce: is it able to be procured or substitutable and is it durable?

- appropriability: who owns the intellectual property and, therefore, the profits?.

Game Theory

Game Theory, the mathematical analysis of competitive situations, offers a new approach to business strategy and allows for significant advances in data collection and analysis.

In the early years, the focus was on games of pure conflict (zero-sum games) or cooperation (joint-action based). Recent work has concentrated on more complex forms of interdependence, where the outcome for each participant depends upon the choices — or strategies — of all.

Game Theory was pioneered by Princeton mathematician John von Neumann. The 1944 publication *Theory of Games and Economic Behaviour* by von Neumann and economist Oskar Morgenstern was intended to correct what they saw as fundamental imprecision in the field of economics.[9]

Games involve two basic types of player strategies:

- Sequential strategies: players move one after the other, aware of their competitor's previous actions.

- Simultaneous strategies: players act simultaneously, unaware of their competitor's actions.

A sequential game comprising a finite series of moves may be resolved by looking ahead and reasoning back. In contrast, a game with simultaneous moves comprises a logical circle.

This logical circle arising from simultaneous moves may be resolved by applying a concept of equilibrium developed by another Princeton mathematician, John Nash[10]. A dominant or best game strategy can exist for a player, no matter what the other players do. Similarly, a player can adopt a dominated or bad strategy. In many situations Nash's work enables players to identify a best strategy when the other players are playing their respective best strategies. However, not all simultaneous-move-based games can be fully resolved, in that some games have many equilibria and others do not.

The following are examples of Game Theory in use.

The prisoners' dilemma

In this classic illustration of Game Theory, two prisoners suspected of a jointly committed crime are separately promised a better deal if they confess. Each faces a choice: to confess, or to keep silent in the hope their partner-in-crime will do the same, enabling both to avoid prosecution. However, keeping silent risks a confession by the other prisoner and could lead to worse treatment. The dominant strategy, the equilibrium, is for both to confess. However, both would be better off if they remained silent.

Two key lessons arise from this dilemma. The first is that a true prisoner's dilemma is played only once; with repetition, people can predict others' behaviour and learn from adverse outcomes. The second, and equally important, lesson arises from the fact that cooperation is not necessarily in one's personal best interests. The implication here from a business perspective is that cooperative behaviour between people, across teams and organisation-wide needs to be encouraged, supported and, in some cases, mandated for the greater interests of all.

Mixing moves

In this game type, rivals are required to choose moves from a finite set of options. The trap to be avoided lies in making systematic (predictable) moves which could be exploited by the other player. Mixing moves in optimal proportions keeps the other player guessing.

In business, automatically reacting to non-payment of an invoice with threatened legal action rather than exploring various options for following up on payment increases the risk of the recalcitrant debtor calling one's bluff.

The bargaining game

A generalised version of the bargaining game is one in which two or more players bargain over how to divide the gains from a trade. Each wants a larger share — implying that the players value the pie differently — and both prefer to achieve agreement sooner rather than later. Should the players disagree as to how to divide the pie and walk away from the game, each will receive their disagreement value or best alternative to negotiated agreement (BATNA).

A typical example of negotiation in a business context is Enterprise Agreements (EAs) governing workplace relationships between employers and employees across Australia. An existing EA that expires prior to finalisation of an updated EA will continue to apply after its nominal expiry date, even though the applicable rates of pay may fall below award rates. Whilst back-dated arrangements typically apply in relation to rates of pay, a better outcome may well have been achieved by both parties proactively entering into negotiations in good faith, prior to expiry of the existing EA.

Concealing and revealing information

In games where one player has access to information that others do not, it may sometimes be advantageous to conceal the information and, at other times, advantageous to reveal it. In both cases, the general principle is that actions speak louder than words. An effective tactic when concealing information involves mixing moves. When revealing information, it is best to carry out actions that would be interpreted as credible signals. As an example, quality certification and extended warranties are credible signals to clients indicating the business believes it is producing a high-quality product or service.

Threats and promises

Players can use threats and promises to influence others' behaviour, but these need to be credible to succeed and can become costly if they require significant resources to carry out. Employing a strategy of brinkmanship, to threaten a bad outcome for all if others do not act as desired, can enhance the player's credibility in this circumstance.

Limitations of Game Theory

As an illustration of the potential limitations inherent in Game Theory, let's turn briefly to the game of poker.

One of the developing areas of Game Theory is in computer-based modelling with the intention of guiding the players to maximise their chances of success. Poker has specific modelling challenges, as the computer (as player) must interpret opponents' bets despite uncertainty regarding what cards they hold. The overriding challenge inherent in predicting the outcome of a given game is the sheer volume of potential decisions involved in playing each hand of poker. For even a simplified version of Texas Hold'em played between two players and with bets fixed at a predetermined size, a full game tree contains 316 000 000 000 000 000 branches.[11]

Despite the challenge, computer scientists eventually resolved the conundrum by applying a convergence algorithm known as counterfactual regret minimisation. This involves having the programs play against themselves multiple times to reveal the least successful decisions (the 'regrets' to be avoided in future iterations). In 2015, an article in *Science* titled 'Heads-up limit Hold'em poker is solved' signalled the first time a nontrivial imperfect-information game had been resolved.[12]

Recent progress made in computer-based modelling is threatening to fundamentally alter the nature of poker tournament play, as players increasingly use computer programs to study moves and systematically improve their chances of success. Elements of tournament play remain, however, that cannot be resolved by science alone.

A common method of finishing an extended 'end game' game of poker involves a dominant player with the largest 'stack' (greatest amount of betting chips in play) betting large against the other players in a war of attrition. The object of the play is to coerce each competitor in turn to unsuccessfully bet 'all in' and be forced out of the game. Solvers can model these circumstances, but as the chip stacks get shorter relative to the size of the blind bets and antes players are required to put in the pot before each hand begins, scientific play alone offers no real insurance against what essentially becomes a game of chance.

Similar tactics that show up in a business context relate to the occasional behaviour of large contractors refuting an otherwise legitimate claim from a sub-contractor in the knowledge that the small sub-contractor does not possess the financial resources to formally pursue said claim. The threat of withholding future work is also an effective strategic move often played by contractors in this situation. Accordingly, most sub-contractors in this circumstance elect not to roll the dice and litigate.

The essence of sustainable competitive advantage: Strategic options

Let's return then to Andrews' definition of strategy, as the alignment between what a company can do within the universe of what it might do. In practice, there are two broad choices regarding how sustainable competitive advantage can be achieved and superior profits generated in comparison with industry benchmark returns:

- Cost-based competitive advantage: the product or service is undifferentiated, but the business has found some way to reduce the overall cost below that of its competitors

- Differentiation-based competitive advantage: the cost structure is on par with the competition, but the business can differentiate its product or service offering, such that its overall price is above that charged by competitors.

The prevailing view in mature, competitive industries such as engineering and construction is that competition is all about the lowest price. And this is true, to the extent that price matters when clients are making decisions — typically based on tender submissions —from a field offering essentially identical solutions. In this circumstance, price absolutely wins the race. It then becomes the ability of the business — or, more specifically, the underlying cost structure of the business — to sustainably deliver the services for the tendered price.

Just as industries exist in a dynamic environment subject to change, so do organisations. Accordingly, the extent to which the cost advantage a business has is sustainable needs to be taken into consideration.

If price-based competition is regarded as the norm in engineering and construction, then it stands to reason that differentiation, as the other side of the equation, receives less attention. Consider, though, the range of opportunities that may present themselves for competing at margins above what others are generating from the industry.

Pankaj Ghemawat has devoted much of his career to studying the principles of sustainable advantage as they apply to business. In essence, Ghemawat proposes that sustainable advantage for organisations derives from having:

- size in the target market

- proprietary access to critical inputs

- impediments to competition (contrived or otherwise).[13]

These elements can be considered from the perspective of a business seeking to enter a new industry (market) or alternatively adopting a new position in an existing market.

If a business can access economies of scale in research and development, production, distribution or other value chain–related activity, it has an opportunity to obtain and sustain a first mover advantage, particularly if the market is not large enough to support another firm operating at a similar efficient scale.

Table 9.1 provides a useful summary of the various elements upon which businesses might base a competitive advantage.

Table 9.1: Elements comprising competitive advantage[13]

Element	Basis of advantage/key considerations
Experience effects	The risk of technological redundancy must be considered.
Scope economies	Requires coordinated business activities with the actions of one part of the business working to benefit another part.
Access	Rights and/or contracts must be on better and longer terms than competitors. However, this holds the inherent risk that a changing environment could leave the business stuck with worse terms than more agile competitors.
Know-how	Better access to information may lead to a competitive advantage, but information must be kept secret in order to remain valuable.
Inputs	Obtaining exclusive/restrictive rights to supply can offer a competitive advantage. Preferred rights can also be valuable.
Markets	The opposite of Access, with advantage gained not through contracts but through mechanisms such as relationships, reputation, and the ability to switch costs as needed.
Public policy	Using patents, anti-trust laws, and other public policy mechanisms, such as regulators, to gain a competitive advantage.
Defence	Innovate by taking advantage of instances where a competitor's past investments may restrict them from innovating.
Response lags	Fast response to a dynamic market such as changing price or market position can be a significant competitive advantage. However, responses to changes requiring additional research can take longer.

The strategy of market position

Consider then, market position as a strategic concept.

Irrespective of whether a business adopts a cost-based or differentiation-based strategy, a key step in strategy formulation is to determine or evaluate an appropriate market position.

But how does position specifically relate to engineering and construction, an industry controlled by tender-based procurement and characterised by transactional, price-based relationships? It's fair to say that healthy scepticism around investment in branding makes sense in the industry (in comparison with brand-driven industries such as advertising or retail).

The key question behind any positioning strategy is 'Who are you?' In other words, do you have an understanding of the business and its capabilities? This cannot result in trying to be everything to everyone. A succinct answer to this question enables clients, customers and prospective customers to move to a contextual understanding about the business. This is the space that generates:

• fast-tracked direct sales and direct invitations to tender

• partnership (referral)–based relationships

• merger, acquisition and joint venture opportunities.

What does success in this instance look like? A successful position is determined based on what clients, prospects and competitors perceive your business to be. A successful position in the minds of your clients is a position attached to your product or service that nobody else holds. In this way, positioning provides a business with a very strong differentiator in the marketplace.

Positioning is not an image or brand, nor is it necessarily a unique selling proposition. For example, a very successful position can be built on price, by being the cheapest in the market or the most expensive — but this is not necessarily a unique position.

A primary position can be established based on one of four elements: product, price, market or service.[14] Two key strategic questions need to be answered in establishing a primary position:

- Should the business be a distribution company or product company?

- Should the business be positioned based on product, price, market or service?

The answer to the first strategic question constrains the choices in answering the second question.

Question 1: Distribution or product?

The first element of the positioning process involves choosing the contextual space in which the business sits. Is it a distribution company, a product company or both?

'Product' refers to the product or service the business offers in the marketplace. Product-oriented businesses are primarily focused on unique product research and development. To illustrate, technology suppliers such as France's Alstom and Germany's Siemens Mobility operate in the transportation product space, offering a wide range of products and services based on proprietary technology. More recent entrants, such as China's CRRC and Skoda from the Czech Republic, position against these organisations with a similar range of product offered at lower cost.

'Distribution' in this strategic context refers to how products or services are spread throughout the marketplace such that clients and customers can procure them. Distribution businesses focus on accessing and developing relationships within their chosen market-place. There is a heavy emphasis on sales and client service activities. Products and services can be externally procured or outsourced, as well as internally developed, noting that an effective means to improve profitability in a distribution business is to introduce additional products to the existing customer base. Of the many IT services providers in the engineering and construction industry, IBM Maximo is a high-profile example of an organisation distributing its industry-focused asset management solutions. By way of comparison, Oracle JD Edwards is a service-oriented business offering a 'flexible' financial management software system, which is configurable for the requirements of a wide range of customers and industries. Engineering design firms, along with accounting and legal firms, are increasingly expanding their traditional offering of professional services with aligned services, such as systems implementation partnerships with proprietary providers and software as a service offerings.

Question 2: Product/price or market/service?

Table 9.2 (overleaf) is a useful reference in determining the appropriate position for a business to adopt, based on the dominant attributes or strengths of the business. Note that product-based companies typically adopt a product or price position, whereas distribution-oriented companies choose between a market or service position.

When evaluating the appropriateness of a market position for a business, the attractiveness of the position also needs to be taken into consideration. A common process for evaluating market attractiveness is embedded within the marketing-based segmentation, targeting, positioning (S-T-P) framework illustrated in figure 9.1 (overleaf).

If the definition of an industry is a group of companies that are similar based on their primary business activities, then an industry segment can be considered as a sub-group of existing and potential customers within the industry with common attributes, including needs, wants and buying behaviour.[15] Identifying industry segments that align with the strengths of a business enables potential demand for products and services to be analysed and quantified.

Table 9.2: Determining the product/price or market/service position[15]

Business attributes	
Product strengths	**Market strengths**
• Product/service has a high profile	• Building distribution relationships and channels
• First to market with the product	• Selling second and third products
• Invests in research and development	• Building client relationships
• Draws 'me too' competitor products/services	
Price strengths	**Service strengths**
• Value pricing, undercutting competitors	• Provides client extras
• Supply chain and business model economies to enable lower margins	• Service as opposed to sales ethic
• Attractive price marketing pitched beneath market expectations	• Client relationships with company as well as salespeople

Figure 9.1: Segmentation, targeting, positioning (S-T-P) framework[16]

An additional key consideration in evaluating the attractiveness of a proposed market position concerns the number and nature of competitors. Identifying and targeting a market position with relatively low (or ideally no) competition can be fundamental to an effective differentiation strategy.

Once an attractive segment (or segments) is identified, a positioning strategy can be formulated to target the identified segment(s).

Strategic fit and sustainable competitive advantage

Michael Porter and his 1996 *Harvard Business Review* article 'What is strategy?'[2] explores the means by which a great product or service, when well positioned, can be developed into a sustainable business advantage. The key lies in paying attention to the business activities associated with the product or service.

A unique and valuable market position can be established by building and arranging a series of business activities in a different way to the competition. In this way, the concept of fit can be applied in sustaining competitive advantage. The challenge here is in selecting an arrangement sufficiently different to competitors, such that the arrangement outperforms the competition.

Porter outlines three orders of fit. To illustrate using my earlier soccer story:

- first-order fit is about simple consistency: the 'modified bee-hive' was easily adopted by the team whilst being proposed to the stakeholders (parents) as an effective way for the team to play the game

- second-order fit occurs when activities are reinforcing: the 'modified bee-hive' enabled the players to experience the game whilst developing skills and spatial awareness, under the watchful eyes of their parents

- third-order fit concerns optimisation of effort: the team naturally played like a bee-hive in the first place with no initial coaching from me!

In all three types of fit, competitive advantage can be considered to arise from the connectivity between activities. Third-order strategic fit between an entire ecosystem of activities enables sustainable competitive advantage.

To further illustrate the method, the business activity map (see figure 9.2) illustrates Serco's key source of competitive advantage. Serco was an early mover in public sector outsourcing of services to the private sector, including economic as well as social infrastructure services. The diagram shows the relationship between key activities and Serco's central business process of winning and re-securing tendered outsourcing contracts. Three key activity groups provided Serco with a sustained competitive advantage in securing and building business in the outsourced contract space:

- trouble-free business transition from government to private sector management

- strict contract cost control, implemented by managers with freedom to implement their method of choice in achieving overall financial targets

- value-adding activities associated with existing contracts, leveraging a range of internal skills and competencies that provided Serco with valuable case studies that could be utilised in positioning for re-bids.

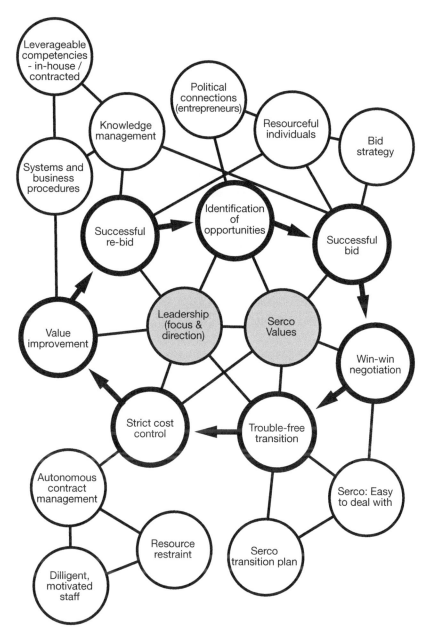

Figure 9.2: The relationship between key business activities in Serco Group.

It is harder for a competitor to match an array of interlocked activities than it is merely to, say, imitate Serco's specific approach to tender preparation.

As a footnote, Serco's early dominance of the outsourcing market in the late 1980s and through the 1990s has been steadily eroded. In Australia, for example, a wide range of organisations (CIMIC, John Holland, Downer and Veolia, to name a few) now employ sophisticated business-winning machines for multi-year outsourcing contracts of this nature. In these circumstances, activity trade-offs become key in maintaining a competitive position.

We will return to these activities later from an organisational capability perspective in chapter 14.

Conclusion

Strategy is best thought of as an excellent game. And like all excellent games, it is crucial to understand the rules of engagement, which are the principles of business strategy and operational implementation. Developing and documenting a business strategy is an effective way of dealing with the nagging suspicion that the answer to all your current business challenges, issues and problems lies with one 'silver bullet'. The better answer lies in understanding that the challenge faced by good businesses seeking to become sustainable enterprises is more akin to assembling a jigsaw, where the pieces are more than likely present in some shape or form but not necessarily fitting together in a way that enables the next phase of the journey to be undertaken.

Key takeaways for sustainable businesses

1 Standing still in business is rarely an option. Your business needs to mature and continue to develop, implement and optimise the business strategy in response to industry changes, or face stagnation and eventual decline.

2 A successful strategic position in the minds of your clients is a position attached to your product or service that nobody else holds. In this way, positioning provides your business with a strong differentiator in the marketplace.

3 A unique and valuable market position can be established by arranging your business activities in a different way to the competition. In this way, the concept of first-, second- and third-order fit can be applied in building a sustainable competitive advantage.

CHAPTER 10
The roadmap

This seems as good a place as any to consider the role of luck in business. I believe no business succeeds without a healthy dose of luck. Indeed, an essential activity in business, like many of life's challenges, is managing luck. What I'm referring to here is the behaviour of successful business owners who seek out the right business method, work hard and smart in implementing their ideas and are, consequently, well prepared for when they get lucky. Equally, successful owners prepare themselves for the arrival of their share of bad luck.

You may be interested to know that there is quite a lot of statistical probability as well as cognitive psychology embedded in this statement.

Many businesses I see in infrastructure engineering and construction are piloted by owners who are just flying by the seat of their pants, waiting for the next lucky break to come their way. Occasionally, their business has bouts of success, or at least this might appear to be the case from the perspective of an outside observer. Many more businesses have survived with just enough lucky wins along the way to balance out the tougher times. Sustainable success, though, has remained elusive.

What's missing?

Let's assume we're in an environment where business success is achievable—a reasonable assumption in my view in engineering and construction, given the sheer size and resilience of the industry as well as the lack of an obvious alternative in the foreseeable future.

For the vast majority of businesses with which I come into contact, lack of hard work is definitely not the problem: very few businesses survive for any length of time in this industry without putting in hard yards. Guess what though: it's also not all about good or bad luck!

The sustainability equation

Let me demonstrate with the help of the following equations:

Success = talent + hard work + luck

More success = more talent + lots of hard work + luck

Skills-based sports, such as golf and cricket, that generate lots of performance data, provide excellent examples proving the point.

No top golfer or cricketer rises to the top of their chosen sport without talent, nor the drive to put in the hard work to maximise their talent. And to be clear, talent in this context refers to the ability to execute the skills inherent in the sport as well as the ability to manage one's mindset whilst executing the skills under the pressure of competition. At the top of the sporting tree, however, typical sporting performances on a given day occur within a range with very few outliers (that's why they're called outliers). For instance, top cricket batsmen over time average around 50 runs per First Class innings.[1] International-standard golfers typically go around a tournament golf course at around 72 shots per round (hence 72 shots is a par[2] round for a typical golf course).

What typically happens then, after a player turns in a great performance such as a scoring a century or stringing together a series of sub-par rounds to win a tournament? The player more often than not registers a well-below average performance at their next outing. What happened here? It's highly unlikely that the player's innate talent spontaneously disappeared from one event to the next. What we are observing here is a statistical phenomenon called 'regression to the mean'. The very good result, in this circumstance, most likely reflects the results of talent plus hard work, combined with a very lucky day. Conversely, a very bad score suggests the outcome of a particularly unlucky day. Over time, the players' results will most likely tend towards an average that reflects their respective innate talent and effort expended. Indeed, on any given day, the more extreme a score, the more regression we subsequently expect.

The challenge that arises here is that our human brains invent stories (or causal links) for these variations in individual performance (they were in complete command of their game today, they must have been tired after last week's successful tournament, etc.). Our brains are wired to be very good at this, particularly in attributing good luck to high skill when all we are observing is statistical regression to the mean. Even the best sports people are occasionally guilty of falling into this trap, finding themselves questioning their technique or altering their preparation after a particularly poor performance.

From a business perspective, this phenomenon most often plays out in the aftermath of a particularly bad incident (such as a safety breach, discovery of an unanticipated job issue or loss of a must-win tender). Sadly, many managers suffer the delusion that criticism for poor performance works better than a recognition that sometimes these things just happen.

Understanding the tipping point: The revenue trap

Amongst all influences, the desire to grow revenue has perhaps the most perverse effect on strategy. As soon as a new and exciting opportunity shows up, all eyes turn to securing the work. In this way, the boom-or-bust mentality endemic in engineering and construction is difficult to break. Previously established focus areas, limits and trade-offs suddenly appear to be constraining growth. Serving one type of client or segment of customers now seems to be less about operational efficiencies and more about arbitrary limits on revenue growth.

The reality is that compromises and inconsistencies in the pursuit of sustainable growth steadily erode the competitive advantage a company had with its original capabilities, resources, product and service variety or target clients. Often, in these circumstances, competitors have a knee-jerk reaction and continue to match each other until desperation breaks the cycle, resulting, at best, in a merger or downsizing to the original positioning or, at worst, the lowest common denominator, low-margin business. This game is fine to play, as long as the business is clear about why they're playing the game and what the desired outcome looks like. Profitable growth is the only outcome truly worth aiming for.

Managing the transition through the tipping point

Our human experience of change is painful. It stands to reason, then, that transitioning through the tipping point is a painful experience. Most owners confronting the tipping point are familiar with the pain of working too hard, dealing with increasing difficulty in securing new work at an acceptable margin and taking on too much risk for the return on offer. There appears to be no clear way forward to alleviate the situation. The dynamics that have successfully generated the business of today have fundamentally altered.

The tipping point provides a context for understanding the challenges successful and sustainable businesses face at a particular phase of their growth journey. A 'second-floor' business has transitioned through the tipping point and rebuilt the 4 Pillars supporting the business for sustainable growth (see figure 10.1).

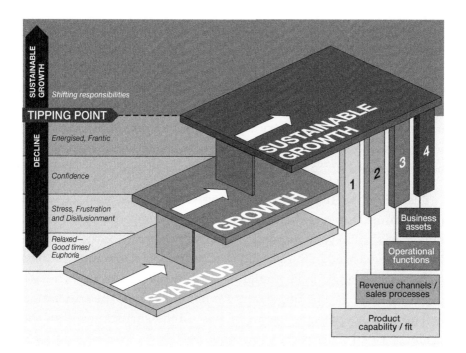

Figure 10.1: The tipping point

Good businesses go through growth stages — it's unavoidable. Even if there is no desire or plan to grow the business in size, growth is nevertheless a fact of business life. All businesses need to mature and continue to respond to changes in the industry environment in which they exist. At this stage of the journey, decision-making can become self-focused or temporarily distracted.

As a business owner, you might recall a time when you were investing a dollar in the business and making two — that euphoric feeling when it felt like you had achieved your vision for the business. You may well have bought yourself a boat or an SUV as a reward for all the hard work and sacrifice.

In business terms, you might have responded in one of two extremes: working harder to keep everything together, or hiring management and divorcing yourself completely from the business — or both! This can lead to a feeling of frustration for you and the business. Frustration for you as, in reality, even by working harder, you cannot be as fully immersed in and control every aspect of the business. And frustration for the business, as your people deal with being micro-managed or being unable to locate you when they really need you!

Businesses at this phase of growth have their own powerful momentum. However, harnessing and sustaining this momentum requires a shift in your approach and a skills upgrade for the business. Your business needs a foundation that can support additional storeys rather than a single-storey building. If those skills and the strategic priorities that become important are not addressed, the frustration will grow into a palpable feeling of stress and exhaustion within the business. Good times become 'the good old days'.

Capacity management

From time to time, I meet business owners in infrastructure engineering and construction who raise questions along the lines of: 'Why is the engineering and construction industry always either in boom or bust?' or 'Why aren't governments doing a better job at planning and coordinating projects?'

Hopefully, the assessment in Part I of this book has shed some light regarding the difficulties inherent in planning and coordinating long-lead-time infrastructure investment programmes. Likewise, there are fundamental reasons why the industry is subject to feast or famine periods that make it a particularly tough place in which to survive and thrive.

Occasionally, owners want to discuss the challenges they're encountering in running their own businesses. Most report similar issues in dealing with ups and downs in workload, job performance, business energy and a myriad of related inputs. So, as an owner of an engineering and construction business, how and where does one set an anchor in circumstances where it feels like nothing is fixed or stable?

The key to developing a sustainable business in this boom-or-bust industry is to manage growth within the bounds of the potential swings and roundabouts that are and will remain a fact of life.

Figure 10.2 (overleaf) illustrates two very different annual revenue scenarios of, in this case, a small-to-medium business in construction contracting. The dashed revenue curve illustrates what a well-planned, sustainable revenue growth profile looks like for the business. A disciplined approach to capacity management results in business revenue that looks more like the dashed profile than the grey curve of uncontrolled growth in revenue. The upwards trajectory of the grey curve (most often seen in industry boom times) is highly likely to be followed by an equally precipitous decline when industry boom turns to bust.

Effective capacity management ensures a business maximises its available output to ultimately achieve maximum profit. This requires a business to shape its growth profile within the bounds of the maximum available capacity or resource mix within the business (illustrated by the black line in figure 10.2).

The capacity of some businesses may be driven by the maximum quantity of product able to be manufactured; in others, the maximum number and size of jobs able to be delivered by project management and administrative staff or the maximum number of tenders able to be managed and responded to over a given timeframe. In each case, the limiting process or 'bottleneck' determines the maximum capacity of the business.

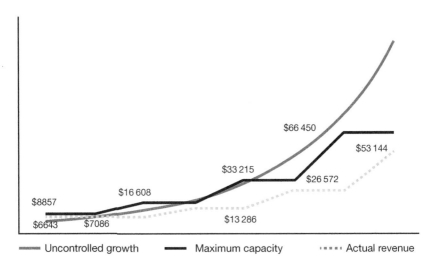

Uncontrolled growth ——— Maximum capacity ▪▪▪▪▪ Actual revenue

Figure 10.2: Theoretical growth curve

With control over the shape of the revenue curve (including the size and number of steps), owners can make effective decisions regarding:

- what size to grow the business

- profitability levels throughout the journey

- how the journey feels within the business along the way.

Designing the roadmap

In essence, the controlled revenue curve can be considered a business roadmap, a strategy that covers three essential elements:

- where the business currently is from an annual revenue perspective (Point A)

- where the business wants to get to (Point B)

- a roadmap to get from Point A to Point B.

Assuming profitable growth is the desired outcome (and why wouldn't it be?), the business can now focus on revenue as an effective monitor of desired business growth.

The two questions that define your business roadmap

A business plan is a good place to start looking for information for the business roadmap. A word of caution though: most business plans consist of 30-plus pages that can essentially be summarised in one statement: 'The business will increase revenue by [commonly 10 to 20 per cent] based on last year's performance while holding or reducing historic costs'.

An effective business plan can be useful in providing answers to two key questions:

1. Does the business have a compelling vision?

2. Does the business possess the management capability to achieve the vision?

The business roadmap defines what needs to be done to achieve the vision and, equally importantly, the order in which these things need to be done. Every builder knows that foundations need to be built in a coordinated way to enable efficient construction of the structure. Similarly, the business strategy defines the order in which each business pillar must be re-constructed/enhanced and the level of investment (in terms of time as well as money) that will be required for the elements of each pillar.

Managing revenue growth

There are two parts to each individual step that makes up the revenue roadmap:

- the vertical rise, representing periods where the focus is on maximising existing capacity by improving internal efficiencies, as well as bringing in more work to feed the current business

- the horizontal tread, where the focus is on increasing the capacity of the business to enable more output to be delivered.

Aligning business activities in this manner improves clarity, which feeds into improved confidence regarding the way forward and enables the entire business to focus on turning the roadmap into concrete outcomes.

There are many ways to drive a business up the vertical rise. For example, increasing tendering activities and post-sales service initiatives (see chapter 12 for more on Pillar 2) are two common ways of increasing the volume of work in a business. Internal efficiencies are achieved by activities associated with ensuring the right people are in the right roles and have the right skills and experience (see chapter 13 for more on Pillar 3).

However, when selecting an appropriate strategy to increase the capacity of a business, there are only the following options to choose from:

- Developing new products/services or markets (see Pillar 1: Product): this includes reducing products/services or markets to generate more focused growth. Common infrastructure engineering and construction examples of diversification, for example, could be transport industry contractors expanding into additional states across Australia and/or extending into industries requiring similar contracting services, such as water or defence. Note that opportunities to supply new product/ services to an existing client base has the added advantage of increasing customer 'stickiness'.

- Altering pricing and packaging (see Pillar 1: Product): changing product/service pricing and including/excluding components of the package (for instance, altering product warranties or service elements) increases business capacity, as removal of low value add, costly elements flows through to increased revenue and profit.

- Procuring more resources (see Pillar 3: Operations): resources typically comprise additional staff, equipment or systems for the purpose of bolstering the capacity of current business location(s) or enabling expansion into new products/services or markets. The procurement mechanism may also be via joint venture with an aligned business, merger or acquisition.

- Strategic positioning or repositioning (see Pillar 2: Revenue): applied as a diversification strategy with the intention to increase revenue as well as profit.

- Developing partnership-based relationships (see Pillar 2: Revenue): effective partnerships provide access to additional clients, resulting in increased revenue.

- Client base management (see Pillar 2: Revenue): more work with better clients results in increased revenue.

Art and science: Designing the roadmap

The art of designing an effective business roadmap lies in recognising and exploiting the interdependencies between the various strategies.

Some strategies are mutually reinforcing. Expansion into new markets will require additional resources but will naturally increase opportunities for utilising the resources. Successful repositioning will enable price increases, which create opportunities for additional high-value/low-cost elements to be added to the product/services package. Other strategies naturally follow each other. Additional staff members, once employed, need to be trained in company-specific business processes. New market development requires additional client relationships to be developed and tendering processes to be re-assessed.

The final element of key importance concerns time. The linear appearance of a business roadmap lends itself to adding time to the horizontal axis. Broadly framing the roadmap in time serves an important purpose in enabling the business roadmap to be critically evaluated: is progress being made within an acceptable timeframe or is the market signalling that the business is on the wrong track?

However, constraining the size of the individual steps in time is not the intention for two reasons.

The first reason concerns the timing of the key investment decisions that underpin the roadmap. The time to make the call regarding taking the next roadmap step (for instance, hiring additional staff and procuring equipment) is when the revenue target of the previous step has been achieved. In this way, the overall timeframe is essentially determined by the rate at which the available capacity of the business can be sustainably utilised.

The second reason concerns the size of the steps comprising the roadmap. Each step needs to be designed (and potentially re-evaluated as progress is made) taking into account key considerations, such as the financial strength of the business and anticipated market conditions.

Applying Growth Staircases to manage capacity

An additional perspective regarding the design and sequencing of the individual steps comprising a capacity roadmap is provided by a McKinsey & Co framework termed Growth Staircases.[3] McKinsey typically applies the framework when determining the steps that enable companies to edge out into new businesses in uncertain environments, emphasising learning, buying options and building capabilities.

Three considerations are applied in developing appropriate staircase architecture:

- Stretch: the distance of the step-out from the established business platform, the complexity of new capabilities targeted by a step-out, including the degree of integration required.

- Momentum: the positive effect of early success, often based on small moves, on the learning and confidence of the organisation. Momentum becomes a critical factor in markets that feature increasing returns to scale, involve de facto standard setting, or where winners take all.

- Flexibility: maintaining fluidity in the face of uncertainty has several features, including maintaining flexibility in avoiding investing in sunk assets that could later become stranded.

Effective business governance

Good businesses in infrastructure engineering and construction typically have an owner or owners regularly working in the business plying their trade whilst managing the business in their 'spare' time. This style of business management has advantages from the perspective of the owner-manager. The owner, by virtue of being fully engaged in the work, remains well connected and across what is happening on a day-to-day basis. Additionally, and equally importantly, the owner maintains a strong position to maintain credibility and authority over employees and engender respect from clients and prospects by virtue of their superior work knowledge and experience. The obvious disadvantage from the owner's perspective is the sheer amount of time required to manage a business in the industry in this manner.

What happens, though, as the business expands, and the owner's vision edges closer and closer to reality? Of course, this situation plays out as the owner becoming increasingly stretched in keeping up to speed with all that's going on.

This typical scenario is fine, if and as long as the work is being effectively managed by others. Most, if not all, owners have trusted lieutenant(s) providing expertise as well as eyes and ears on the ground. But what if, unbeknown to the owner, new job risks are being taken on? Engineering and construction is an industry full of risks just waiting to be allocated to unaware contractors. This is indeed why the saying goes: Nine projects in the industry go OK, whilst the tenth project blows the business up!

Effective governance is an essential ingredient for sustainable businesses managing the 'risk box' in which they operate. Of equal importance is the role of effective governance in enabling businesses to stay on track, particularly in the stressful times that so often characterise the industry.

Most owners I meet are also directors of their enterprise. Setting aside the legal implications of being a company director, what are the requirements and opportunities in practice of an owner implementing formalised business governance? As with management, there is both art and science involved in boards of directors providing effective business governance.

First the science. Corporations law provides many words defining and describing corporate governance requirements. We will consider here the circumstance of a business of a size justifying a formalised governance board, rather than an advisory board, which, in essence, takes on similar functions without the requisite legal exposure. The five essential functions of a governance board are:

- implementing business stewardship frameworks covering risk management, internal compliance and control, codes of conduct, legal compliance and reporting

- formulating and evaluating business goals and strategy in consultation with operational management

- monitoring organisational performance in accordance with performance measures and benchmarked against peers

- raising the external profile of the business to assist in achieving organisational growth objectives

- dealing with responsibilities in relation to shareholders and other stakeholders.

The first essential function requires further exploration. Effective business stewardship comprises the board determining the 'box' in which the business operates. This requires a board to focus on ends rather than means when formulating policies for delegated authorities for approvals, tendered contract risks, cost/benefit hurdles in relation to investments etc. What this looks like in practice, for example, is specifying financial approval limits for the levels of business management, rather than a process involving repetitive signoffs.

Through defining management limitations, a board builds an enclosure within which freedom, creativity and action are enabled and encouraged. In this way, the board defines where its role ends and where management begins. These requirements can be implemented by a managing director. As a board member, the managing director participates in the formulation and review of the enclosure, and then assumes ultimate responsibility for promulgating the requirements throughout the business. Devolution of decision-making down the organisation hierarchy enables managers to utilise their talents and develop capability as the next layer of leadership.

Per the second function (formulating and evaluating business goals and strategy in consultation with operational management), the true value of a board lies in its collective knowledge and experience and its different perspective, compared to management. Effective boards ask the right questions and offer insight into management activity or inactivity.

COVID-19, particularly, has forced separation of staff from work locations and implemented remote working, and this has highlighted the key challenges boards face in being appropriately informed regarding the activities of the business.

The art of effective board input is in being able to tap into the health of the business beyond the financial reports. This has become a much greater challenge in the current environment as restricted physical access to people results in information funnelled almost exclusively through a managing director/senior management. In these circumstances, the ability to understand and constructively challenge what's being communicated becomes critically important.

Conversely, board members have a real opportunity to bring an external perspective to management in circumstances where people may feel they have no time to lift their heads. Looking out for red flags, such as anxious behaviour, provides a great opportunity to have a conversation about what's going on out there of specific concern to the business. Certainly, this is a better use of time than generally worrying about what may or may not happen.

Conclusion

A business roadmap is a deceptively simple means by which the business strategy can be communicated to your stakeholders. One roadmap clearly illustrates current and target business revenue and a plan to get from Point A to Point B.

The ability to demonstrate the growth of your business in a series of pre-planned steps provides confidence to your staff and external investors that the business is well managed, particularly in circumstances where the wider industry is experiencing one of its regular episodes of boom or bust. A well-managed business can then demonstrate control over the shape of the revenue curve by making effective decisions regarding business size and profitability.

Key takeaways for sustainable businesses

1   There is no 'silver bullet' that will resolve all the issues weighing down progress. The better answer lies in understanding that the challenge is more akin to a jigsaw, where the pieces are more than likely there but are not necessarily fitting together in a roadmap that reveals the path forward.

2   The tipping point provides a context for understanding the challenges successful and sustainable businesses inevitably face at a particular phase of their growth journey. A 'second-floor' business has transitioned through the tipping point and rebuilt the 4 Pillars supporting the business for sustainable growth.

3   The key to developing a sustainable business in the boom-or-bust industry characteristic of engineering and construction is to manage and govern business growth within the bounds of the potential swings and roundabouts that are, and will remain, an industry fact of life.

Part IV
The How

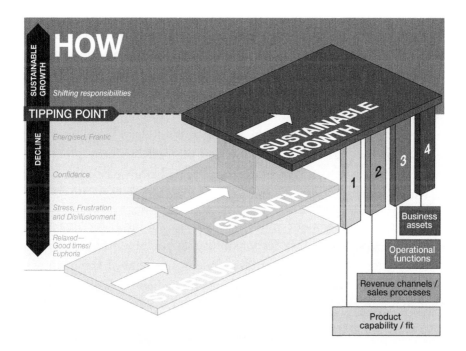

Sustainable businesses have, at their core, an effective operational management system. Part IV lays out the 4 Pillars of a business framework that, when fully implemented, forms the system that enables businesses to operate in a highly efficient manner.

The 4 Pillars framework is robust but also sufficiently flexible to enable individual skills and experiences to be harnessed when making the investments and adjustments that turn a good business into a sustainable enterprise. Sustainable businesses enable freedom within a framework, aligned with 'loose-tight' principles.

The business capability embedded within this framework has traditionally centred on:

1. having the right people

2. in the right roles

3. with the right skills and experience.

Many good business owners argue that business growth in capability is all about having the right people in the room or, alternatively, constantly upskilling and/or replacing the people in line with evolving requirements. Modern enterprises, however, can harness technology to expand capacity, improve efficiency and leverage the capability of their personnel. Accordingly, sustainable modern businesses also require fit-for-purpose technology and aligned business processes. Indeed, a key measure of business capacity and efficiency is the extent to which people, IT systems and processes are aligned.

Business management must be held accountable for operating the business system. This responsibility is fundamental to business performance. Management guides the engine room of the business, enabling organisations get things done and deliver the work for which they're remunerated.

Tension often shows up between the step-by-step logical framework that is proposed in this book and what I will refer to as a more intuitive approach to business. It's a debate that I've had more than once with coaches and advisers who ascribe to the silver bullet theory of business improvement. For a business in the start-up phase, it is quite reasonable to be looking for the one thing that is holding back growth. As a successful start-up starts to accelerate, adding or revamping a key business element may enable the business to correct course towards a better destination. For a good business seeking to mature into a sustainable business though (and this is what this book is all about), changing one thing rarely results in a fundamental shift in performance.

Aligned with the step-by-step approach to sustainable business building is the need to embed changes as they are made.

The Deming cycle is a continuous improvement model named after William Edwards Deming (1900–1993), a widely acknowledged management thinker in the field of quality.[1] Arguably, the greatest success of Deming's work is his influence on the Japanese post–World War II economic miracle, whereby Japan's industries recovered from wartime devastation and enabled transformation into the second-biggest national economy of the era.[2]

Continuous improvement is represented by a wheel being moved up an incline, driven by systematic 'plan, do, study, act' steps. Deming's original concept comprised controlled testing to evaluate a new or changed process prior to implementing a change supported by a *hadome* (brake) as the means of locking the improvement in place.

The latter part of this book deals with how a sustainable business goes about locking in and sustaining improved performance.

How to achieve sustainable growth

As a reminder of the earlier discussion in chapter 9, the essence of an effective strategy is to deliver greater value to clients and customers than competitors, create comparable value at a lower cost or do both. Delivering greater value allows a business to charge higher prices, whilst greater internal efficiency results in lower costs. Both outcomes result in increased margins.

Let's turn the focus to internal efficiency or, more broadly, the operational effectiveness of a business. Operational effectiveness means performing similar activities more efficiently and more effectively than the competition.

Continuous improvement in operational effectiveness is necessary to achieve and maintain superior profitability. However, constant improvement is not usually sufficient to maintain a competitive advantage. What typically happens in a dynamic environment is that, over time, competitors obtain direct access to best practices (say via ex-employees) or discover them based on observation and deduction. This process of competitive convergence eventually leads back to price-based wars of attrition.

The concepts of core competence and competing on capabilities emphasise the importance of the skills and collective learning embedded in an organisation. Management's ability to organise and integrate capabilities in ways that create sustainable advantage is of key importance. Capabilities and resources, then, are at the heart of a company's competitive position, subject to the interplay of the three fundamental market forces of demand, scarcity and appropriability.

Strategic fit describes how a well-positioned product or service can be developed into a sustainable business advantage. The key lies in paying attention to the inter-relationships between the business activities required to develop and deliver the product or service. With strategic fit, the whole matters more than any individual part. Competitive advantage arises from the inter-connectedness of an ecosystem of activities.

Sustainable growth can be considered as supported on what is termed the 4 Business Pillars. Like a structure with sub-standard foundations, a business without properly anchored pillars cannot be scaled without cracks starting to appear.

Sustainable growth is created as the business moves away from solely relying upon the personal resources of the business owner and towards systematised delivery of innovation and intellectual property, based on capabilities maintained within the business in the form of valuable products and services to market. Moving from a single profit-and-loss business to operating a portfolio of businesses enables access to new markets, which fuels enhanced growth and value.

Great businesses have a clear and aligned understanding across the business of exactly where marketing ends and sales begins. Partnerships ensure great businesses have a consistent flow of opportunities and revenue. Marketing and sales processes, aligned with a clear industry position, support multiple channels to clients and customers who know exactly why they procure your products and services. Efficient tender management minimises time and cost investment. And sustainable businesses share in the extra value they create for the premium service they provide to clients.

Sustainable businesses harness internal talent and capability, and focus on the right activities. A functional internal structure ensures the right people are doing the right jobs at the right time with the right skills and experience. A business with strong decision-making capabilities and an effective management framework enables leadership to invest time in strategic activities, making sure the right investment decisions are made at the right time in the right business assets.

There's an additional and powerful underlying 'why' for business innovation.

Shifting business focus from profitability only to the 'earnings multiple' variable of the business valuation equation (more on this in chapter 14) enables business owners to begin the journey towards sustainable growth with a clear end game in mind.

CHAPTER 11
Pillar 1: Product capability and fit

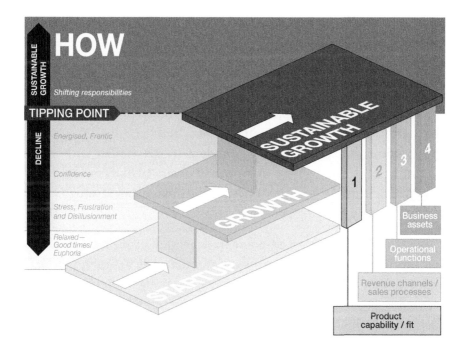

Expanding your products and services starts with defining products and services by their benefits rather than by their physical or intangible attributes. A pre-/core/post-product suite makes it easy for clients and customers to procure more than one offering from your business in different ways, with increased potential for creating client 'stickiness'.

Businesses with the best internal capabilities have a competitive advantage in the marketplace. These businesses use their capabilities to develop superior products and services for their clients and customers.

Product as the foundation of business

Product is a term drawn from the marketing discipline, which is equally applied to the tangible products or intangible services a business provides for sale. Product is most usefully thought of as the foundation of a business, being the basis of the strategic position adopted by a business in the market. In essence, without product, there is no business.

Employees in a sustainable business clearly understand the products and services the business can deliver, and continually develop and monitor the currency of the product in the market. A product portfolio enables a business to grow and diversify its client base and span multiple markets. A proactive product extension strategy is key to a sustainably growing business.

The fundamental starting point in developing your core products and services into an integrated suite of product is defining products and services by their function rather than by their physical or intangible attributes. That is, defining product by what it does for the client or customer (the benefits on offer).

A well-known example of this concept was illustrated by Theodore Levitt in his classic 1960 *Harvard Business Review* paper, 'Marketing myopia'.[1]

Railroads in America can be traced back to 1815 when Colonel John Stevens (builder of the first American steam locomotive in 1825) received the first charter in North America to build a railroad, although the physical railway was not constructed until 1832.[2] Railways rapidly expanded across the country, enabling development of vast expanses of wilderness and providing connectivity between the east and west coasts. However, following WWII and into the 1950s, railroad passenger and freight traffic was steadily eroded as the new interstate highway system took shape.

As asserted by Levitt, America's railroads did not stop growing because the need for passenger and freight transportation declined. This occurred as a result of the railroad businesses not fulfilling customers' needs. Both road and then, increasingly, air transportation took customers away from the railroads, whose operators thought of themselves as being in the railroad business rather than the transportation business.

Extending your core product

The process of generating a suite of products and services from a core product involves disassembling the core product into the following component elements:

- content: the technical description of the product

- architecture: clarifies why the client or customer needs the product

- marketability: the 'cut through' messaging or hook drawing attention to the product.

Product can be developed for client and customer purchase before or after the purchase of your core product. Figure 11.1 (overleaf) illustrates a simple pre-/core/post-product approach for a kitchen installation contractor.

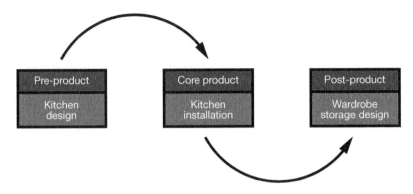

Figure 11.1: Simple pre-/core/post-product chain

A product suite based on the core product needs to be developed as a logical plan rather than random choices. This approach aligns and supports the 'cut through' marketability of the component products. A pre-/core/post-product suite makes it easy for clients and customers to procure more than one offering in different ways, with increased potential for reducing buying friction and creating client 'stickiness'. Pricing tactics can support the approach of a low-cost 'trial' pre-product to smooth the way to a core purchase, whilst post-products beneficially extend the length of client relationships.

In the kitchen contractor example above, the contractor offers a free kitchen design and quotation service (even though the business may incur costs in providing the service) to facilitate the sale of the kitchen. The core kitchen installation service could then be extended to a post-product by offering additional home storage cupboards, wardrobes etc. for which a design fee could potentially be charged.

To further illustrate, typical well-developed businesses in infrastructure engineering and construction rely upon a services suite typically comprising one or more of project construction, minor panel works and maintenance services offerings. The approach works effectively from a revenue and return perspective, as the 'peaky' construction work is balanced by typically lower, but more reliable, earnings from panel and maintenance contracts.

Most businesses in the industry will have the content element relatively well-implemented. However, for the product to be efficiently and effectively extended, all three elements, including architecture and marketability, must be fully developed.

The following two concepts may be useful in developing a product or services extension strategy:

- 'shovel' strategy: commonly described in gold rush terms, where 100 people seek to profit, 97 stake claims and excavate for gold, whilst three sell excavation equipment. On a risk versus return basis, who is likely to make the best return?

- activity chain strategy: consider the typical infrastructure project development and delivery activity chain in table 11.1. Which multiple activities might a service provider be able to participate in?

Table 11.1: Typical infrastructure project development and delivery activity chain

Project development activity step	Public sector activity	Private sector activity
Land use/planning		
Scoping		
Business case development		
Funding		
Environmental assessments		
Stakeholder consultation		
Property acquisition		
Approvals		
Financing		
Design		
Procurement		
Preliminary works		
Construction		
Maintenance		

How to find and build business capabilities

In accordance with a theory proposed by Jay Barney in his 1995 article 'Looking inside for competitive advantage',[3] a business may be thought of as a grouping of resources and capabilities brought together to produce an outcome for clients or customers. Those businesses with the best capabilities have a competitive advantage in the marketplace. So how are capabilities (a) identified and (b) built in a business?

In this sense, a resource can be considered as an input into the 'factory' of the business, whilst a capability is the capacity for the resource (or group of resources) to perform an activity. Resources and capabilities may comprise:

- financial resources (e.g., cash and financing facilities)

- physical resources (e.g., plant and equipment)

- 'invisible' resources (e.g., brand recognition and intellectual property, such as trademarks, copyrights or patents, which may not explicitly show up in financial statements)

- human resources (e.g., managerial and employee skills and experience)

- organisational resources (e.g., reputation and organisational culture)

- business management systems (e.g., IT systems and business processes).

As discussed in chapter 9, resources and capabilities can be classified in terms of the extent to which they are:

- valuable (do they help satisfy a client or customer need?)

- rare (are they possessed by none — or very few — competitors?)

- inimitable (can competitors readily replicate them?)

- appropriable (are they capable of or likely to be appropriated by suppliers?).

In this way, we can evaluate the extent to which a firm's resources and capabilities are a source of sustainable competitive advantage.

A firm's existing resources and capabilities have typically been accumulated over time, perhaps as the by-product of previous strategic decisions, such as acquisitions. Figure 11.2, adapted from Robert Grant's 1991 resource-based theory of competitive advantage,[4] outlines a process that can be applied to systematically build these business resources and capabilities. The process involves three key steps:

- Select an appropriate competitive strategy (see chapter 9).

- Identify resources and capabilities within the business and classify them as per the previous list, taking into consideration the strengths and weaknesses relative to competitors.

- Invest in upgrading/filling resource and capability gaps.

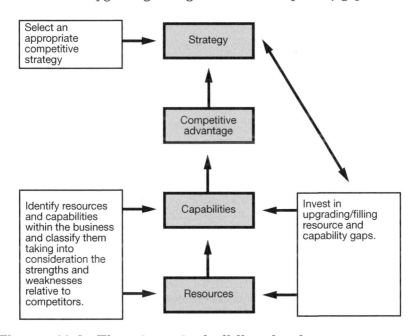

Figure 11.2: The steps to building business resources and capabilities

Source: The Resource-Based Theory of Competitive Advantage: Implications for Strategy Formulation, Robert M. Grant, Apr 1, 1991

For an organisation to achieve sustainable success, it must continually look for ways to service evolving client needs. Accordingly, a business might decide to invest in a given resource or capability. It is worth bearing in mind though, the strategic decisions that are made today will invariably influence the make up and quality of tomorrow's resources and capabilities.

Developing effective business capability

Over a 30-year career in engineering and construction, I've experienced first-hand the challenges that businesses, small and corporate, face in building effective business capability.

The circumstances may differ; for example, bids and projects are all about time pressure and having to deliver on time come what may, whereas the ebb and flow of business growth requires resilience and effective steerage. How this plays out every day, though, is pretty much the same:

- dealing with the pain of assembling a proposal whilst avoiding the descent into blind panic as the submission deadline looms

- coercing a client project submission through multiple steps and (sometimes) multiple document management systems

- chasing weekly timesheets and materials and equipment hire invoices to report on job progress

- closing out corrective actions and opportunities prior to the next quality audit.

In short, it's the little things that generate the bulk of business pain and frustration. Why is this fundamentally a business capability issue?

Before we delve into the answer to this question, it might be of interest to note that effective management capability is one of two key elements, along with vision, experienced venture capital investors look for when evaluating where to invest their money (that's right, the typical 80-page/120-slide-deck corporate business plan, in most if not all cases, supporting heroic forecasts for growth and return on investment, is given scant attention). In short, investors assess the capability of the management team to deliver the business vision.

Let's look in more depth at what comprises business capability.

Business capability has traditionally considered to be about having the right people in the room.

Gone are the days, though, when a business could just rely on great people to 'muddle through' and get the job done. The modern business environment is almost totally reliant on a plethora of IT systems to perform and enable tasks that are central to producing outputs. Increasingly, smart companies are harnessing common data platforms and process automation to optimise end-to-end business processes. What in the not-so-distant past felt like a string of disconnected systems is becoming increasingly unacceptable (and if you're still questioning whether your people are prepared to work around clunky systems, take the time to have a chat about this with some of your younger staff...).

Accordingly, effective business capability encompasses fit-for-purpose IT systems as well as aligned business processes. Just like people, though, IT systems and business processes need to be maintained, nurtured and (on occasion) transformed. Consequently, businesses require capability in effective systems implementation and associated change management skills. In my experience, it is this aspect of capability development that most challenges businesses in infrastructure engineering and construction.

What does effective IT systems management look like in practice?

Firstly, and from a strategy perspective, organisations need to know when to invest in a 'big bang' investment in upgraded IT systems, and when to adopt a more 'steady as she goes', incremental, improvement-based approach. Japanese business, having embraced the principles of continuous improvements over several decades, has bespoke names for each of these methods:

- *kaizen* refers to continuous incremental improvement

- *kaikaku,* a less-well-known term, means revolutionary change or transformation.[5]

The circumstances in which *kaizen* or *kaikaku* are employed, as well as the interaction between each methodology, needs to be carefully considered. To further explain, and as explored in Paul Stringleman's article 'From kaizen to kaikaku' in *Engineers Australia*,[5] businesses need to avoid falling into the *kaizen* versus *kaikaku* paradox trap. In essence, a business with a track record of smaller improvements may find it difficult to embrace a *kaikaku*-style leap forward on a return-on-investment basis. In this way, continuing with a series of *kaizen*-style improvements can hold an organisation back and perhaps even stifle significant development. By focusing exclusively on small improvements, the business may miss an opportunity to jump ahead of competitors and gain a significant competitive advantage. This logic can be incorporated into the formulation of a strategic business roadmap (see chapter 10).

Turning our attention to implementation, the *kaizen* and *kaikaku* approaches require different styles of project management.

Kaizen-type continuous improvement lends itself to a project management methodology known as agile. This approach uses short development cycles called 'sprints' that focus on the implementation of stand-alone system or process improvements. The agile approach was more formally codified in 2001, with the publication of the *Agile manifesto*, a 'formal proclamation of four key values and 12 principles to guide an iterative and people-centric approach to software development'.[6] Agile grew from the software-development space as an alternative to the more traditional waterfall-based (perhaps more *kaikaku*-style way of working) development model.

Infrastructure engineering and construction businesses are typically well-versed in the waterfall methodology, which is unsurprising as the waterfall methodology originated in the manufacturing and construction industries. The waterfall approach reflects a relatively linear, sequential approach to project delivery, as progress flows largely in one direction ('downwards' like a waterfall). In environments where the outputs are physically constructed assets (think engineering and construction), once construction commences, design changes become prohibitively expensive. Accordingly, typical projects have less design/procurement/delivery phase overlap and, accordingly, the methodology aligns with *kaikaku*-type business transformations.

Agile's recent emergence in infrastructure engineering and construction businesses reflects the increasing importance of minor IT systems enhancements and upgrades in maintaining the health and functionality of the business. Unsurprisingly though, agile may not always work as intended, especially if the project manager or team is unaware of the pitfalls — particularly scope management challenges — associated with the methodology.

Management's role in capability building

A 2010 McKinsey & Co Global Survey, 'Building organizational capabilities',[7] provides a range of insights into the challenges associated with business capability building. The survey explored the extent to which organisations concentrated on building capabilities deemed most critical to an organisation's business performance and why businesses focused on the capabilities they did. The survey also asked respondents how their companies created and managed training and skill-development programs, and how effective those programs were in maintaining or improving their capabilities.

Organisations typically recognised that competitive advantage may be gained through building foundational capabilities (such as lean operations, project management and leadership skills) as well as industry-specific capabilities. Notably, however, when asked why their company's focus remained on the particular capability identified as most important to business performance, the most common reason given was that the skill was embedded within the company culture, rather than reasons associated with competitive advantage. In effect, these companies were implying that their current competitive advantages in the marketplace would remain so into the future — a dangerous assumption.

Furthermore, the results indicated that companies did not typically focus on the 'nuts and bolts' activities with the potential to maintain or improve capabilities central to their business performance. For example, only 41 per cent of survey respondents whose companies focused on supply chain management spent time defining roles and responsibilities for key supply chain management positions, and just 39 per cent set targets and tracked metrics.

The results highlighted the fact that companies whose training programs were effective in maintaining or improving the drivers of business performance paid more attention to tools that support or enable capability building, such as standard operating procedures, IT systems and target monitoring. In essence, strengthening an organisation's business management systems was widely recognised as a key source of capability.

However, companies typically struggled to measure the impact of training on business performance. Of the respondents, 50 per cent said their companies kept track of direct feedback, and, at best, 30 per cent used another kind of metric. In addition, a third of respondents didn't know the return on their companies' training investment. In effect, these organisations weren't measuring what they were managing — a fundamental business mistake.

Despite widespread recognition of the importance of capability building, executives' responses indicated that they weren't good at executing. Only about a quarter of the respondents thought their companies' training programs were 'extremely effective' or 'very effective' in preparing various employee groups to drive business performance or improve the overall performance of their companies. Further responses indicated a potential explanation: respondents felt the training programs were misaligned with what was thought to be the most important capability to a company's business performance. Only 33 per cent of respondents said their training and skill-development programs focused on developing their companies' most important capability. Anecdotal feedback across the industry indicates that not much has changed since the 2010 survey in this regard.

To summarise, management can make a telling contribution to the health and sustainability of a great business by developing competence in:

- identifying and building capabilities that are clearly linked with improved business performance

- delving into the 'nuts and bolts' of competence in the tools that support enhanced capabilities

- focusing internal training on activities directly associated with capability improvement.

Harvard Business School Professor Clayton M. Christensen proposes three central choices when seeking innovative ways to grow business:

- chasing new business

- extending products

- driving business efficiency and effectiveness.

A great deal of modern business innovation concerns technology enablement. Christensen, in partnership with Bower, published a well-recognised article in *Harvard Business Review*[8] exploring two types of technology-based innovation: those associated with sustaining technologies and those technologies that disrupt an established industry, causing new industry leaders to emerge and previously dominant players to decline and potentially even disappear.

Christensen and Bower differentiate between these two types of innovation using the concept of performance trajectories. A performance trajectory is the rate at which the performance of a product has improved and is expected to improve over time. Almost every industry has a critical performance trajectory.

Sustaining technology-based innovations tends to maintain the industry rate of improvement along the performance trajectory; that is, they give customers something more or better in the attributes they already value.

On the other hand, the technological innovations that disrupt existing industries have two important characteristics:

- they typically present a different package of performance attributes — ones that, at least at the outset, are not valued by existing customers

- the performance attributes that existing customers do value improve at such a rapid rate that the new technology becomes relevant to existing customers.

Disruptive technologies introduce a very different package of attributes from the one typical clients or customers historically value. Indeed, they often perform far worse along one or two dimensions that are particularly important to those customers. As a rule, mainstream customers are unwilling to use a disruptive product in applications they know and understand. At first, then, disruptive technologies tend to be used and valued only in new markets or new applications; in fact, they generally make possible the emergence of new markets.

So where and how should businesses seek to innovate? The answer to this question could lie in any aspect of the business and may cover the full spectrum of strategies including:

- outsourcing a 'non-core' activity

- strengthening a weakness

- building an industry-leading business asset.

Managerial talent is a key ingredient in driving and enabling innovation. Sustainable businesses require key people with the ability to manage others in executing the following activities:

- identifying a market opportunity or direction

- selecting the right products and/or services to meet the anticipated demand

- organising the business (such as securing investment) to chase and secure the identified opportunities

- managing successful delivery.

In this way, senior management in the business perform the role of business 'shapers', supporting the efforts of leadership who, in turn, are responsible for the vision, setting direction and governing the business. Business shapers are characterised by a desire to create and the ability to make decisions in the face of ambiguity and change. They require autonomy and permission to build from more senior leadership.

Shapers are best fostered by devolving decision-making down the organisation hierarchy. A business unit managed by a shaper, with operational performance responsibility for generating and implementing new ideas, is more likely to own their outcomes and strive to make them happen. Within this unit, operators with industry expertise and experience can flourish, bringing their energy and drive to deliver on plans and meet targets.

As a final observation, and with the abrupt shift in working arrangements experienced by most organisations since COVID-19, new questions are being asked of management regarding their role in effective business performance.

For instance:

- How do supervisors/middle managers develop their more junior home-based staff beyond monitoring that they're spending the requisite amount of time on a computer?

- What happens to organisational cohesion when businesses operate with two classes of people: those who work remotely and those who turn up on the premises?

- How do new remote workers in a business get to know the 'way things are done around here' in the absence of behavioural cues?

Clearly, these questions relate more to staff able to utilise remote working technology than the 'hands-on' workers who have no option but to show up at the job site. With the broad trend towards greater digitisation of work, managers and leaders will increasingly need to have credible answers to these questions.

Product and fit

Returning then to strategic fit, being the means by which well-positioned product of value to clients or customers is developed into sustainable business advantage. As noted in chapter 9, the key to achieving fit and consequential competitive advantage lies in paying attention to the inter-relationships between the internal business activities required to develop and deliver the product or service.

Consider a business comprised of a range of products and services that relate in a logical way to each other, all drawn from the same well of business capability. With the presence of simple consistency—first-order fit—across the product suite, the opportunity arises for the business to develop common supporting business activities that reinforce each other (the subject of Pillars 2–4 in chapters 12–14) and thus create second-order fit. Accordingly, the organisational challenge of optimising overall effort can also be addressed, pursuing third-order fit in an environment where a logical product suite addresses client and customer needs. Pre-, core and post-products not only reinforce each other in improving and extending client and customer relationships, they are more easily supported by the business in effective and efficient ways.

Conclusion

A key business challenge to be addressed concerns the degree of focus to apply in providing products and services to clients and customers. The question is this: do we offer more products and services in the hope of appealing to a wider audience? Or do we concentrate on what our business is capable of delivering? From a product perspective, the answer lies in creating a logical suite of products and services meeting the needs of your client base.

Key takeaways for sustainable businesses

1 Products and services are better defined by the benefits they offer clients and customers than their physical or intangible attributes. This approach unlocks opportunities to build a product portfolio, enabling your business to develop a product extension strategy to diversify the client base and span multiple markets.

2 Resources are inputs to the 'factory' of your business, whilst capabilities are the capacity of your business to perform activities. Both resources and capabilities can be a source of sustainable competitive advantage, so long as they are valuable, rare and able to be protected from being appropriated or copied by competitors.

3 For an organisation to achieve sustainable success, it must continually look for ways to service evolving client needs. This need should drive investment decisions and influence the make up and quality of tomorrow's resources and capabilities.

4 Business capability building requires the right people in the right roles with the right skills and experience, supported by fit-for-purpose IT systems and aligned business processes. Modern businesses increasingly require capability in effective IT systems implementation and associated change management skills.

5 Your senior management can make a telling contribution to the health and sustainability of your business by immersing themselves in the nuts and bolts of business capability building. Focused effort on improving the effectiveness and efficiency of the business activities underpinning your portfolio of products and services is the means by which your competitive advantage is sustained.

CHAPTER 12
Pillar 2: Revenue channels and sales processes

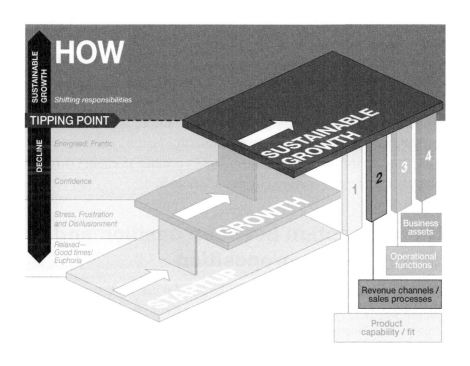

Sales, and to a lesser extent marketing, are not words commonly associated with infrastructure engineering and construction. For instance, sales personnel are more likely to be labelled 'business development' representatives. Of course, the use of the term business development reflects the industry's reality of securing work, which, in most circumstances, occurs via complex tender-based processes and procedures. However, a broad and deep understanding of the principles underlying the disciplines of both sales and marketing, as well as judicious application of the principles, underlies sustainable businesses in the industry.

What does a sustainable business look like in the discipline of sales and marketing? Great businesses have a clear and aligned understanding across the business regarding exactly where marketing ends (creating the opportunity) and where sales begins (securing the opportunity). Multiple routes to market via distribution channels ensure great businesses have a consistent flow of opportunities and revenue. Marketing and sales processes aligned with a clear industry position support multiple channels to clients and customers who know exactly why they procure your products and services. A tender win rate closer to one in two than one in 10 minimises the time and cost investment in tendering. And sustainable businesses share in the value they create via the extra service they provide to clients through the positive energy generated by the relationships.

The connection between position and unique selling proposition

Clients (like all of us) want to feel like they're receiving a product or service that's been specifically designed for them, from someone who knows what they want and need.

As covered in chapter 9, an effective market position translates to clients knowing exactly why they procure from a business. A business position sets the business apart from competitors in the mind of the client as the best option to satisfy their requirements.

Business owners often fall into the common trap of expanding the range of products or services in the hope of capturing more attractive business. This approach-apart from eroding profitability-commonly generates less attractive clients and customers. Why? Prospects and clients are attracted to businesses who understand and focus on their needs and wants. Businesses that set out to be everything to everyone can easily fall into the trap of becoming nothing to no-one.

The business needs absolute clarity regarding the primary position adopted in the market based on product, price, market or service. The key then is in investigating what your ideal clients or customers really want and making that a niche market.

Emotions play a huge role in the buying decisions of prospects as wants are inherently emotion-based. Needs are logic-based, and this is how prospects justify buying decisions once the decision has been made. When the product or service matches what prospects want, the business begins to attract ideal prospects. Nirvana consists of ideal prospects procuring from you and you alone. They're loyal and will think long and hard before leaving the business. They will send referrals and provide (sometimes unsolicited) testimonials.

A niche business position provides the basis for developing a unique selling proposition (USP) that can be pitched to potential clients and customers in capability statements and other marketing collateral, as well as used in conversations. The USP must ideally:

- make a proposition to the client or customer (e.g., buy this product or service for this specific benefit or outcome)

- be a unique offer that the competition can't match

- be strong enough to attract new prospects.

The most powerful pitch is the owner's 'why', the vision for the business.

Conversely, lack of alignment between the business position and USP results in mixed messages and confusion, externally to clients and prospects as well as within the business. This, at worst, can result in pricing inconsistencies with the potential for ad hoc service delivery in the absence of clear indications regarding the relative importance of prospects to the business. As an example, tendering a low-ball price to a key client prepared to accept a premium price results in a lower target profit, which will be further eroded if the premium service the client is used to is provided. A classic no-win situation.

Partnerships: Sourcing new revenue and higher-value business

How many industry networking events have you or your key client-facing staff attended in the last 12 months? How many conferences have you sat (and hopefully not just eaten your way) through? How many new and interesting people have you met at these events? And how many of these people are you still in contact with or, more to the point, doing business with? How would it feel if there was actually an overarching context for all of this activity?

It's worth reflecting on the typical experience of introductory meetings at these networking-style events. As humans we don't consciously set out to offend people we've just met, and an exchange of business cards and a vague 'we must catch up for coffee sometime' most times gets us off the hook. On occasion, though, we might be motivated to seek or accept a follow-up meeting, which could lead to an exchange of brochures or (on the odd occasion) result in an initial referral.

A referral in these circumstances, however, is likely to be a low-value test case offered by a traditional referrer, who is looking to see what type of job you do at looking after this client. It may well be that normally you wouldn't take on this type of client. If you refuse, the referrer may decide not to refer any further potential clients and you lose. If you take on the work and it requires more effort than you would normally have to provide to your existing client base, again, you lose — there are no winners in using the traditional approach.

The concept of partnerships concerns creating mutually beneficial relationships that generate referrals and enable transactions to occur. These relationships act as channels to market, providing pre-sold referrals that create and maintain a steady flow of opportunities, replacing the peaks and troughs many businesses experience. Less time is required to position your business to pre-sold clients as they are already ready to buy. They know who you are, and they want to do business with your business.

Building effective business relationships

At the core of the gap between traditional networking and partnerships is abundance versus scarcity (sometimes referred to as the 'givers get' principle).

What does an abundant business relationship look like? It involves plenty of revenue, client loyalty and referrals. In my experience, however, many businesses struggle to make referrals, even when they're aware of the benefits that flow from applying the 'givers get' principle. Of course, many businesses would much rather just receive referrals.

Most people accept that giving referrals is a virtuous activity, particularly if they're truly focused on delivering the services their clients need. But is there actually any truth to the maxim 'givers get'? Let's consider the argument Professor Adam Grant of Wharton University, Pennsylvania, puts forward in his book *Give and Take: A revolutionary approach to success*.[1]

Grant approaches the argument from the perspective of behavioural psychology. According to conventional wisdom, success involves a combination of hard work, talent and luck. Grant proposes that success also depends on how we behave with others: in essence, do we give or do we take? It turns out that people typically display one of three distinctive styles: Takers, Givers or Matchers.

Takers like to get more than they give, whereas Givers pay more attention to what other people need from them. In business, however, few of us are purely Givers or Takers — rather, we become Matchers, trying to preserve an equal balance of giving and getting and exchanging favours on this basis.

So which behaviour gets the best results in business? The answer seems at first unfortunate: research demonstrates that Givers sink to the bottom of the business success ladder.

If Givers are at the bottom, though, then who's on top: Takers or Matchers? As it turns out, neither! Grant's data showed that Givers can be both the worst and the best performers, with Takers and Matchers more likely to land in the middle. The reason for this lies less with raw talent or aptitude, and more about the strategies Givers use and the choices they make. Successful Givers are every bit as ambitious as Takers and Matchers; they simply have a different way of pursuing their goals. And guess what else shows up? When Givers succeed, they create a ripple effect, enhancing the success of people around them.

The conclusion? Great businesses apply Giver-based behaviour in creating effective partnerships.

Many in infrastructure engineering and construction might struggle to identify current industry examples of Giver-based behaviour. It's fair to say that this current era is heavily transaction focused, noting, for example, the prevalence of joint ventures of convenience for major projects. In the not-too-distant past, however, there were industry relationships between consultants and contractors that stood the test of time and generated benefits for all parties.

As an example, in the early 2000s Leightons (now CIMIC) and Maunsell Australia (now part of AECOM) established a strong, multiple-project relationship in the major roads design and construction space, which, despite much effort, competing consultants were unable to break apart. The relationship was greatly assisted by the parties' respective Queensland corporate offices being located adjacent to each other in Fortitude Valley.

In another example in the engineering contracting space, for over two decades, the Transfield Worley joint venture provided engineering, project management, procurement, construction, maintenance and shut-down services for multiple power plants, prior to Worley fully acquiring the entity in 2020. The incorporated joint venture, whilst 50-50, was characterised by a mismatch of resources involvement between the two parties across each project. To illustrate, a handful of Worley personnel managed construction of a project, while potentially hundreds of Transfield maintenance and shut-down personnel were involved during the project's operational phase. Allocation of project returns on a 50-50 basis in these circumstances can become problematic when issues of perceived fairness are raised. From time to time, when this issue was raised, the governance board provided a valuable service by reminding the parties regarding the 'why' for the joint venture, in that neither party alone could secure and deliver a project in the first place.

What, then, is the source of reluctance to commit to abundant behaviour?

Creating effective partnerships

Another way of expressing scarcity is fear, and fear prevents either party from fully engaging in a partnership. The best way to deal with fear is to address it.

Figure 12.1 illustrates a simple four-step process designed to create effective partnerships, enabling Giver-based behaviour to create benefits for both parties in the partnership.

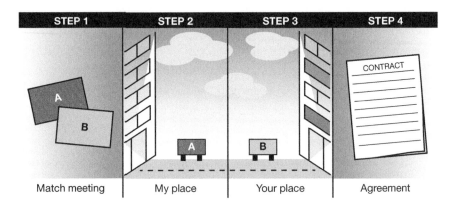

Figure 12.1: Simple four-step process: partnership relationship establishment

Step 1: Match meeting: this is about finding out whether there's potential compatibility between the parties, as well as complementary offerings. Note that people typically only do business with those they know and like.

Step 2: My place: this involves an invitation for the potential partner to visit your business premises. The potential partner will be curious about what your place looks and feels like to confirm (or otherwise) whether it aligns with expectations.

Step 3: Your place: a return invitation is a good indication that Step 2 has been successful and provides an opportunity to satisfy your own curiosity.

Step 4: Agreement: this is about acknowledging the 'fears' and explicitly documenting expectations between the parties.

Each step in the process of building a relationship provides an opportunity to explicitly acknowledge and address any fears either party may retain. Step 4 in particular involves documenting agreed actions that will be taken, or exclusions that will be respected by both parties. The following fears, left unresolved, will guarantee eventual failure of the partnership:

- Trust and credibility: will this business treat our clients like we do?

- Loss of control: will we lose control of the relationship with my client?

- Quality: will the quality of service/advice match our client's expectations?

- Consistency: will the client experience match what we offer?

- Time: do we have the time to devote to this relationship?

The final step in embedding effective partnership relationships within a business is to establish a governance process covering:

- management and monitoring of client and prospect relationships

- regular partnership contact activities

- monitoring the health of the relationship.

The ongoing commitment of both parties to this process goes a long way towards addressing concerns either party may still harbour regarding time commitment to the relationship.

Business opportunities pipeline management: What shape is the funnel?

What is the current shape of your business opportunities pipeline? Is it wide and squat like an exhaust stack or elegantly tapered like a martini glass?

What, indeed, is an opportunities pipeline? Imagine a visual representation of the individual steps marketing, business development and sales take in identifying the 'universe' of potential opportunities accessible to the business, initially engaging with a potential opportunity, to qualifying the 'suspect' to a prospect, to further validating the prospect as a 'real' opportunity, followed by engagement, tendering or direct negotiation and finally securing a job. The width of each step, arranged top to bottom, typically falls within a range defined by the two shapes in figure 12.2.

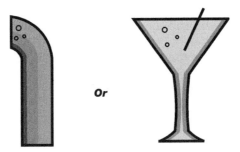

Figure 12.2: What shape is your business opportunities pipeline?

The method of determining the shape of the business opportunities pipeline consists of listing all current opportunities, then visually capturing the quantity of opportunities at each stage from the top to the bottom of the pipeline. See table 12.1 for typical progress stages associated with a tender-driven opportunities pipeline.

Table 12.1: Stages of the business opportunity pipeline

Stage	Description
Lead (unqualified)	Initial information obtained; yet to qualify suitability/interest
Opportunity (qualified)	Opportunity aligns with business capability and interest
EOI	Expression of interest issued by client
Short-listed	Short-listed for request for tender (FRT) stage
RFT	RFT issued by client

Many business owners are likely to respond at this point to this call to action with 'we have a customer relationship management (CRM) system that does this for us'. Certainly, an up-to-date CRM system with the right reports keeping the business regularly informed, and enabling the right management intervention at the right time, is absolutely the right answer here. For those who have yet to invest in an appropriate pipeline management system, however, a spreadsheet is a serviceable place in which to start.

Effective sales pipeline management enables a sustainable business to optimise sales efficiency while reducing costs, minimising wasted time spent on those opportunities that, in reality, the business is highly unlikely to secure. The best way to turn an exhaust stack into a martini glass is to cull opportunities labelled 'strategic', 'let's give it a go as we have some spare time at the moment' or 'it's been a while since we've heard anything, but we're still in with a chance' regularly and ruthlessly by getting to 'no'. An unmanaged opportunity pipeline spells danger for businesses, especially contractors who face each reporting year without a full order book and rely on 'winning and doing' work within a given financial year to meet budget targets. A poorly culled pipeline results in unrealistic expectations for new work.

Of course, like all well-designed exhaust stacks, the length and flow rate of the sales pipeline needs to match the requirements of the business. Sometimes a business needs to secure work at an acceptable margin to make sure administrative overheads are covered. At other times, the capacity of the business is fully committed, and additional opportunities are best pushed away. What, then, should be assessed when the pipeline flow rate isn't serving current needs?

An overly short sales pipeline may not match clients' buying behaviour. So, too, an overly complicated sales process may be preventing the pipeline from flowing freely, and may even obscure prospects that would otherwise have paid off.

The trick to maintaining optimal pipeline operation is to remove redundant steps and processes while still retaining the necessary steps to enable systematic progression of opportunities. Don't unnecessarily draw the process out by attempting to build awareness in prospects for whom the first contact has already been made. Clients should either be flowing steadily towards the completed deal, or 'leaking' out of the sides of the pipeline to enable the right opportunities to continue forward unimpeded.

Sales: Successful tender submissions

As a business owner, have you recently participated in a final tender review meeting and heard the comment: 'it's all about price'? Variations on the theme include 'the lowest tender always wins' and 'money is the only language clients understand'.

In a perfect world, and following a fair evaluation between tenders, with parties all assessed as being equally capable of delivering the job in accordance with a clear scope of work, the lowest tendered price should, and will, in all likelihood, be awarded the job.

In reality, harassed client representatives under time pressure make decisions based on their best judgement and with their own masters to keep happy (and if you think that you're tendering for a job for which your business is not going to be fairly considered for, then you're better off saving your efforts for a better opportunity).

The submitted tender needs to provide the assessors and decision-makers the evidence and assistance they need to make the right decision. Winning tender submissions achieve this by clearly communicating 'win themes'.

What's a win theme? It's a topic that (a) really matters to the prospective client and (b) the business can demonstrably deliver on. What if nothing of this nature easily comes to mind? What if the business is unable to consult with the client regarding what they really want? In my experience, this is a strong sign that the job is the wrong one on which to expend precious resources.

Persuasion can make the difference, especially if it comes down to two similar submissions that are competitively priced. Just don't waste time reminding the client what your business as well as everyone else is good at! Here are some win theme concepts to help the process along:

1. What does your business do well that enables it to stand apart from competitors?

2. What key aspects of the job does your business understand better than the competitors?

3. How does your business understand the client better than anyone else?

Consider, too, that the best win themes are high in the 'FUD factor', namely they create fear, uncertainty and doubt in the mind of the decision-makers when they're contemplating deciding in favour of the competition.

As a particular industry example of an effective win theme, the practice of outsourcing government services to the private sector in the late 1980s and 1990s was accompanied by a great deal of uncertainly on the public sector side. This uncertainty was twofold: firstly, scepticism regarding the private sector's ability and motives in delivering the services, and, secondly, the lack of confidence in the public sector's internal ability to effectively manage (and police where necessary) the outsourced arrangements. The concept of a 'safe pair of hands' became a popular submission win theme during these times.

Deepening client relationships

Have you ever had the experience of delivering a job for a client where everything went pretty much according to plan, so much so that legitimate claims submitted for variations were accepted and paid without the business needing to chase them up and argue the position? The client was most probably satisfied with the overall result, particularly given there was none of the typical haggling around claims (although you secretly believed they should have been more impressed or at least grateful for the claims you left on the table and did not pursue). On the next job, with the same client, the business is back to the same old story of fighting over variations, with apparently no recognition of the great service delivered last time around.

There's a behavioural element behind this phenomenon. When the client is excited the first time, they're aware they've received something positive and unexpected, and they perceive this as an extra service. But, once the client expects delivery of the same service every time, the 'extra' service is then thought of as part of the standard package. And there's worse news. Clients must be explicitly informed each time an extra activity or item is provided, otherwise, the client may not even register they're received something extra.

In the infrastructure engineering and construction industry, unclaimed variations typically fall into this category. An important lesson for all businesses to absorb is that there is no value to either party in leaving legitimate variations unclaimed. In these circumstances, service providers are not compensated for work legitimately performed and clients are misled as to the actual value of work provided.

A business built on a standard service alone is eventually likely to encounter problems with client relationships. An approach based on explicitly differentiating between a standard service and extras provides a means by which businesses can effectively manage the energy associated with their client relationships.

A client relationship based on the provision of a standard service is likely to involve neutral energy at best. Any deviation from the standard service will start to tip the relationship into negative energy. Conversely, the basis of a great client relationship with positive energy is a clear understanding of what the standard service is and what constitutes an extra service. The business can then manage the energy of the relationship by choosing where or when to inject an extra service into the package.

Clarifying standard service versus optional extras is a concept with broad application to a host of other relationship-based circumstances including staff, say as part of performance reviews, and partnerships.

Conclusion

Marketing activities involve a fair degree of creativity, sales is often referred to as an art rather than a science and client relationships are typically relegated to rare occasions when not much else is happening. Sustainable businesses underpin marketing, sales and client relationship management activities with systematic processes, transforming these often-uncoordinated efforts into a revenue-generating machine with measurable inputs and predictable outcomes.

Key takeaways for sustainable businesses

1　A strategic market position aligned with a unique selling proposition results in clients and customers knowing exactly why they procure from your business, setting it apart from competitors as the only option that can truly satisfy their requirements.

2　Partnerships are mutually beneficial relationships acting as channels to market, providing pre-sold referrals that create and maintain a steady flow of opportunities. Abundant behaviour is at the core of an effective partnership, and fear (as the blocker of abundant behaviour) can be explicitly addressed using a simple four-step process for creating effective partnership relationships.

3　Monitoring the shape of your business pipeline is an effective way of optimising sales and tendering efficiency while reducing costs. Getting to your No's quickly is key in minimising wasted time spent on those opportunities that the business is unlikely to secure.

4　Winning tenders, apart from being in the frame on price, provide (via win themes) the evidence assessors and decision-makers need in making the right decision. Even better, win themes are high in FUD factor, creating fear, uncertainty and doubt when the decision-makers are leaning towards your competition.

5   Unacknowledged extra services, such as unclaimed legitimate variations, benefit neither party. In these circumstances, your business is not compensated for work legitimately performed, clients are misled as to the actual value of work provided and the energy of the relationship between both parties will be neutral at best.

CHAPTER 13
Pillar 3: Operational functions

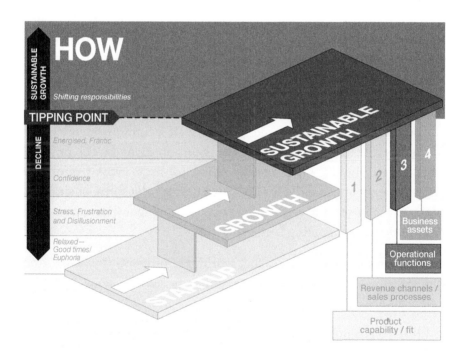

Sustainable businesses harness internal talent and capability by focusing on the right activities. A functional internal structure ensures the right people are doing the right jobs at the right time with the right skills and experience. In this way the business implements the strategic concepts of first-, second- and third-order fit (see chapter 9). In each of the three types of fit, the whole matters more than any individual part. Competitive advantage arises from the interconnectedness of the entire ecosystem of activities. Strategic fit, when enacted, enables sustainable advantage.

When considering making improvements to the efficiency and effectiveness of a business (be they incremental or transformational in nature), one typically begins with the organisation chart and the underlying individual roles, responsibilities and reporting connections. Increasingly, however, businesses need to take primary consideration of the strategic IT architecture underpinning the business. And with improvements (be they minor or transformational) comes the need to manage and mitigate the negative and unintentional consequences of change when they arise.

In looking more closely at workforce productivity, and particularly the productivity of office-based support staff, it is of prime relevance in disruptive times to assess the contribution made by the physical work environment. The recent shift towards work-from-home arrangements appears likely to assist, but not fully solve, businesses' need to achieve the right mix between collaborative space and environments supporting focused work.

At the same time as assessing workforce productivity, it is often illuminating to take the opportunity to assess your personal performance.

Whilst it is tempting to consider the business as a machine operating in accordance with pre-defined processes and transactional rules, this does not absolve great businesses from accessing and harnessing talent to drive the organisation forward. Talented people, though, do not necessarily arrive with all the skills and answers. Ongoing training and development in core business skills, such as design thinking, and the ability to define and solve complex problems, builds internal capability in confronting challenges as they arise.

Finally, an operational management system supporting a sustainable business enterprise is not complete without an effective framework for measuring and managing performance. A business with strong decision-making capabilities and an effective operating framework enables leadership to invest time in working on the business and in particular monitoring progress and critically reviewing the strategic roadmap (as outlined in chapter 10).

Efficiency, effectiveness and fit

Intense competitive pressure has been a fact of life in the engineering and construction industry, particularly over the course of the growth cycle since the early 2000s. This period has seen a shift from alliance-based relationships to design and construction, and operations and maintenance tenders and subcontracts forming the basis of public-private partnerships. Hard dollar pricing with tight margins highlight the need for organisations to focus on being cost-competitive in their submissions and to be super-efficient in delivering their services. Over the more recent past, and with the rise in 'mega projects' since 2015, the level of competition in subcontracting to major and mega project contractors has, if anything, been even more intense. Businesses large and small have responded by looking hard at their cost structures and 'right-sizing' administrative overhead, deferring capital expenditure, as well as identifying and removing superfluous people and discretionary activities.

As explored in chapter 2, the industry typically moves in cycles, and the prevailing methodology of project delivery is no different in this regard. The next cycle is likely to see a re-emergence of collaborative contracting, more in the form of hybrid arrangements such as early contractor involvement–style contracts. How well businesses have managed and responded to margin pressure in an environment with a large (and tempting) volume of work on offer will largely determine how well placed they will be to take advantage of new opportunities as they begin to emerge.

Business efficiency, as ever, is important in engineering and construction. Of greater importance, however, in this next phase will be business effectiveness.

In this instance, I am drawing a distinction between efficiency and effectiveness. Efficiency in this context is the ability to produce maximum output with a given set of resources. Conversely, effectiveness considers the intended outcome. Effectiveness considers the relationship between the means and ends.

An observation, borne of many years working with a wide array of businesses in the industry, is that less overhead (i.e., fewer support people) may flow through to greater efficiency; however, the reduction does not automatically equate to greater organisational effectiveness. The question that regularly springs to mind when observing the fallout from 'right-sizing' activities is: has the business (a) spent sufficient time and effort in developing a *deep* understanding of how their business previously operated (or did not operate) prior to making changes, and (b) made changes in such a way that the new and improved organisation is more effective as well as more efficient than before? In many cases the evidence suggests a negative answer to both questions. Only from a position of deep organisational knowledge can the challenge of strategic fit be solved and sustainable advantage achieved.

A deep understanding of organisational process capability enables businesses to have confidence in committing to health and safety, environmental and quality compliance as well as delivery outcomes at tender time. This capability comes to the fore when clients procure under collaborative arrangements, weighting capability as well as price when assessing tender submissions. As an added advantage, businesses who clearly understand their strengths — and their gaps — will be better able to respond to opportunities as they arise and augment their businesses with the skills they need.

Business organisational architecture

Business improvement projects or programs, whether specific process updates or involving broader organisational transformation, typically start with a review of the company's organisation chart. Understanding people's titles and reporting lines is a good starting place for assessing how the business currently operates. Greater insight can then be obtained by delving further into people's functional responsibilities, specific tasks and the processes that connect the business activities.

Increasingly, however, the structure or architecture of the business IT systems is a more effective access point for analysing the operations of a modern organisation. An IT architecture map (such as the example in figure 13.1, overleaf) provides an end-to-end roadmap of the IT systems supporting people and processes, indicating data inputs, internal flow between the various systems elements, storage repositories and extraction points. A business supported by one end-to-end system is a relatively easy candidate for an IT architecture map. Most businesses in the current environment, though, are somewhere along the journey towards full process digitisation. Business processes in these organisations are typically supported by multiple systems, stitched together with a combination of manual (Excel spreadsheet–based) data transfers and more automated application programming interfaces (APIs).

Process bottlenecks in a paper-based business were traditionally identified by inspecting the premises and looking for the highest in-tray stacks. Some contemporary organisations still lend themselves to this style of analysis. However, with progressive digitisation of information, an architecture map is a valuable tool in identifying and reorganising the range of process inefficiencies that typically show up including (but definitely not limited to) multiple entry requirements for the same data, redundant storage, offline spreadsheets for manual data validation and multiple layers of transaction approval.

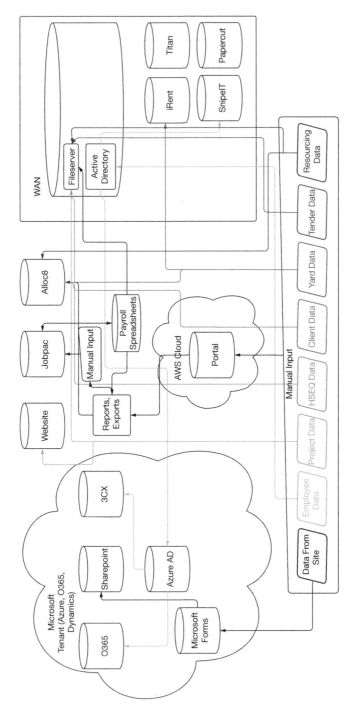

Figure 13.1: Sample: Business systems architecture map

Managing the organisation

Organisation charts for small businesses are typically oriented around the key individuals. An example of what this commonly looks like is shown in figure 13.2, with a relatively straightforward functional structure with key people reporting to the owners and responsible for the various groups comprising the organisation.

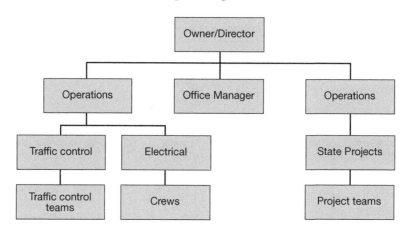

Figure 13.2: Sample organisation chart: Early phase functional structure

As businesses become more complex, the workable organisation structure often morphs into an arrangement more akin to a spiderweb, with confusing reporting relationships that only make real sense to the individuals involved. A merger or an acquisition or two may well add to the complexity. Accordingly, the need arises for reorganisation and realignment. There are several means to reorganise a business at this point; for instance, aligning the various parts of the business with specific markets, geographical locations or services groupings. Identifying and defining discrete groups or units within the business is an effective way of improving employee clarity around responsibility levels and reporting relationships.

An added benefit in moving to a group- or unit-based business is that it creates the opportunity to apply different approaches in managing the individual groups. Just as a business progresses through the various phases of maturity, the various groups comprising the business (be they operational or support) also move through similar phases. Separating and then defining discrete groupings (often termed 'business units' or 'divisions') creates the opportunity to manage the units in different ways, aligning the approach with the specific needs of each respective group's phase of development. Figure 13.3 is typical of a business organised along divisional lines.

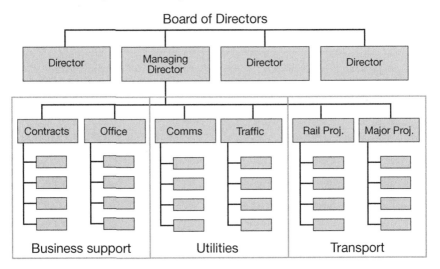

Figure 13.3: Sample organisation chart: divisional structure

Aligning performance targets throughout the business is an effective way to align organisational energy and capacity for a small business. A more complex organisation, however, requires management to differentiate performance metrics to reflect the specific needs of individual business units.

To illustrate, using the revenue-generating business groups, three fundamental challenges arise in managing performance:

1. fixing performance problems

2. driving profitability

3. growing revenue.

Looking at these three areas, it's apparent that it rarely makes sense to grow unprofitable businesses. Accordingly, groups with performance problems do not require a focus on top-line growth, but on fixing fundamentals.

A mature business group, performing profitably, needs to be managed with a focus on bottom-line results and cash flow. Typical measures include profit, return-on-invested capital, costs, productivity and efficiency.

On the other hand, the success of an emerging business group depends on how quickly it establishes its product or service as attractive to clients, and how rapidly and effectively it expands. The aim is not so much to achieve profitability as soon as possible, but rather to prove the business model and beat competitors to capture a desired market position. Top-line growth is the focus. Accordingly, new client acquisition, revenue growth, gross or operating margins, market share and the efficiency of capital investments are more relevant performance metrics for an emerging business group. These measures provide management with visibility regarding the growth potential of the group. Profit expectations should be realistic, with other measures applied as primary assessors of performance.

Whilst the foregoing outline applies specifically to revenue-generating groups, a proxy approach can be adopted in managing the performance of the various support groups, such as business development, finance, IT, administration etc. In these cases, as non-revenue-generating groups, revenue/profitability targets need to be substituted with targets that reflect the efficiency and effectiveness of the services provided by each support group to the revenue-generating units. Beware though: the larger the business, the more tempting it becomes to fall into a bureaucratic trap of spending more time on capturing the cost of the groups internally transacting with each other than focusing on delivering the products and services for which the business is being renumerated. The answer to this conundrum lies in judicious application of business KPIs (more on this later in the chapter).

Managing change

Good businesses in engineering and construction are familiar with the effects of constant change. Great businesses accept the inevitability of change and understand its relationship with organisational psychology, organisational development, culture, mindsets and leadership.

Businesses must be committed to effective management of change, particularly the potentially disruptive effects of process changes, however minor proposed changes may initially appear. Gone are the days when people were able to carry on with their work during a systems outage, and there is nothing more destabilising to business confidence than constant disruptions to the basics, such as email and the internet.

There are a host of reasons why process change programs fail including an unclear 'future state', lack of leadership alignment, ineffective engagement and communication, and/or passive or active resistance. My anecdotal evidence indicates the main driver of failure, by far, to be serious underestimation of the impacts of the proposed changes on the people tasked with implementing the new arrangements. It stands to reason then, that the people need to be actively engaged with before, during and after the changes occur.

Disciplined change management of a process upgrade begins with clear definition of the current or 'as is' state and the 'to be' end point. Regardless of whether the type of change intervention is a transformational process or a more flexible agile activity, managing change still requires planning, analysis and good execution in accordance with *kaizen* or *kaikaku* principles as appropriate (see chapter 11).

Productivity and COVID-19 learnings

Another fundamental topic in the genre of business effectiveness concerns the productivity of those managing and supporting the operations, works site or factory-based revenue-generating areas of the business. Employee productivity was a hot topic during the COVID-19 pandemic, centring on two environmental issues: the impact of anxiety, and workplace configuration on employee performance.

A range of studies, including 'Beginning of the pandemic: COVID-19-elicited anxiety as a predictor of working memory performance' by Fellman et al.,[1] indicates a correlation between pandemic-related anxiety and decreased working memory performance. Our working memory (or 'system 2' as referred to by Kahneman; chapter 7), which we use for effortful mental activities, can be depleted or even overwhelmed by the effects of anxiety. There may be several different mechanisms for how anxiety, pandemic-related or otherwise, interrupts cognitive function. However, when apparently straightforward cognitive processes, such as making a daily to-do list, require additional brainpower (and potentially different tactics), the relationship certainly appears plausible. The flow-on effects in terms of personal productivity are obvious.

Turning to the working environment, the productivity of knowledge workers has been an area of focus for some time.[2] The trend towards open-plan offices has attracted scrutiny, encompassing hot-desking or a virtual office where employees don't have a permanent desk at all, but are allocated a space when they turn up to work. Reducing office space yields cost savings; however, these savings may represent false economy when the effect on staff productivity is taken into consideration.

Researchers have identified the importance of individual focused work in enabling knowledge workers to be effective in a workplace environment. The typical open-plan workplaces and the like (intended to facilitate collaborative behaviour) make life difficult for those who wish to indulge in individual focused work.

Susan Cain's book, *Quiet: The power of introverts in a world that can't stop talking*,[3] provides an in-depth analysis of how the 'extraversion' versus 'introversion' preference manifests itself. The following extract from Cain's 2012 TED talk illuminates the preference for introversion:

Introversion is [more] about, how do you respond to stimulation, including social stimulation. So, extroverts really crave large amounts of stimulation, whereas introverts feel at their most alive and their most switched-on and their most capable when they're in quieter, more low-key environments.

Cain's central argument is that the key to maximising individual talent is for individuals to be put in the right zone of stimulation. Cain contends that workplaces (as well as schools and other learning institutions, particularly in the US where she hails from) are typically designed for extroverts and for extroverts' need for stimulation. This places introverts at risk of over-stimulation and, therefore, at a systematic disadvantage to their extroverted colleagues.

What are the real benefits for people associated with working in an office? In the wake of COVID-19, people appear to be expressing a reluctance to return to the office environment on a full-time basis. Work from anywhere, enabled by constantly improving communications technology, is now an established element of most businesses. A certain amount of quiet time, wherever this may be, is beneficial for most people when completing tasks that require concentration and focused effort. However, the psychological benefits of being physically engaged with what's happening at work, as well as the prospects associated with being present when the boss is around, will also figure heavily in the new norm as this becomes apparent.

Business owners should be aware of the workability — or otherwise — of their existing workplace arrangements. A formal assessment of the current physical workplace environment and how well — or otherwise — it serves the needs of the workforce can be a good place to start. This can be achieved via a workplace survey, but beware, surveys raise expectations that something will be done about the issues raised, so be prepared to act! Also to be considered is whether a sustainable business can afford to sacrifice workforce productivity by catering for the needs of some staff but not others.

Breaking the cycle: The power of focus

Before embarking upon a workforce productivity improvement project, it might be illuminating to consider the subject of personal productivity.

Many smaller business owners I consult with assume chronic busyness to be the exclusive domain of small business. It might be illuminating to note then an observation from Pricewaterhouse-Coopers' 25th Annual Global CEO Survey: 'Reimagining the outcomes that matter'.[4] The PWC survey raises a long list of important and urgent issues of concern for CEOs of major corporations, including:

1. redefining the balance between short- and long-term profitable growth

2. recalibrating organisational skills

3. reframing the environmental, social and governance conversation into realistic trade-offs with near-term financial goals to bring investors and stakeholders along on the journey

4. reappraising succession and rethinking incentives

5. reimagining collaboration with government/policymakers, other business leaders and investors.

Amidst all of this appears an open acknowledgement of how full the inboxes of CEOs have become.

It's often said that what shows up for us is a direct reflection of how we show up in the world. Like most business owners, on average, 20 per cent of what you do every day in your business is directly contributing to 80 per cent of your business results.[5] That also means that 80 per cent of your daily activities produce only 20 per cent of your results.

A great place to start in figuring out whether this is true for you is to determine exactly where all the time goes in your typical day:

1. Note down your daily process or routine and the time spent on each element.

2. Measure your daily outcomes (tasks completed, tasks not completed, issues resolved/unresolved).

3. Review and consider adjusting your tactics.

Remember, you can't manage what you don't measure. Transparency is key here. You might find processes, results and activity in your business lacking in transparency — in some cases staff might be actively keeping information hidden.

So, where should you be spending more of your time?

The better question is: where should you be *investing* more of your time?

You might discover that you're spending most of your time responding to emails, answering the phone, approving expenditure invoices, surfing the internet … these are *not* high income–producing activities.

How would you feel if you were investing your time, say in Pillar 2 income-producing activities, such as improving your current service, developing joint venture relationships, innovating your product or service so that it makes your business unique and superior, or acquiring various elements of proof to use in your marketing, such as testimonials or research? Or investing time in having conversations with your people about 'the way things are done around here' (refer to chapter 7). In short, working on the business rather than in the business.

This is where you need to shift your energy and where your focus needs to be. Some of these areas you may be good at; your unique abilities lend themselves to these specific types of activities. Others, you're not so good at — so consider delegating them! You need to leverage your time to work on higher-value activities.

Key organisational skills: Problem-solving

Talented people are the lifeblood of a sustainable business. Not only do they make things happen without needing to be micro-managed, high-performing people, through their achievements and reputations, attract additional high-performing people to the business and assist in retaining other capable staff.

Consider, then, what great businesses truly want from their talented employees. I would argue that the most important skillset of all in business is the ability to solve problems.

In engineering and construction, the vocational training, with its emphasis on mathematics and physical science and the application of these disciplines to the world of structures, electrical, mechanical and computer systems, teaches students how to solve complex problems. However, the typical training engineers and construction professionals receive does not devote nearly as much time to the world of problems involving the grey area of human interactions.

The core elements involved in leading and managing people as they relate to engineering and construction businesses have been dealt with in chapter 8. Let's now take a closer look at the process of problem-solving and some of the challenges from an engineering perspective as they apply to the key processes of problem identification, data analysis and negotiation.

The current era, which has seen the invention of the Google search engine in 1998, seems to be increasingly characterised by an overwhelming preference for a quick answer. This shows up across the entire spectrum from 'thought shower' problem-solving popularised in business to the relatively more disciplined minimum viable product methodology commonly applied to IT product development. When faced, though, with truly complex challenges, the ability to systematically work through a problem and come to a well-reasoned answer remains a valuable business skill.

Design thinking

How do professional problem-solvers, such as designers, engineers and management consultants, specifically go about their craft?

The answer lies in the concept of 'design thinking': a paradigm for dealing with the complex problems that increasingly challenge businesses with expanding interactions with clients and customers, suppliers, competitors, stakeholders and regulators. We can gain some insight into the core of what is itself a rich and complex process with the help of *The core of 'design thinking' and its application* by Kees Dorst.[6]

In gaining an understanding of the application of design thinking for complex problem-solving, consider three basic ways in which reasoning is applied in logical thought: deductive, inductive and abductive reasoning.

Deductive reasoning

Consider the following simple equation:

$$What + How = Result$$

If we know the 'what' (for instance an object such as a soccer ball) and the 'how' (external energy is required to make it move in a certain direction), we can predict the 'result' when we kick the ball in the right direction (it will end up in the goal!). This thinking process is known as 'deduction'.

Inductive reasoning

Alternatively, 'inductive' reasoning applies when we know the 'what' and the 'result' in our equation but not the 'how'. In the case of our soccer example, by observing and experimenting, we can determine the process by which the soccer ball might be kicked to end up in the goal.

In more scientific language, we apply inductive reasoning in the discovery phase when developing a hypothesis for the 'result' (soccer ball in the goal), and deductive reasoning in the justification phase by subjecting the hypothesis to critical tests (such as propelling the soccer ball in the general direction of the goal multiple times) with a view to disproving the hypothesis if possible (perhaps external factors, such as the wind and the goalkeeper's efforts, need to be taken into account?).

Abductive reasoning

Consider what happens when we change the outcome of our simple equation from a result to the more generalised outcome of value:

$$What + How = Value$$

In this circumstance a reasoning pattern known as 'abduction' (loosely defined as inference) comes into play. Abduction involves forming a conclusion from known information. Abductive reasoning is applicable in simple as well as more complex circumstances.

With simple abduction (as is typically the case with problems routinely solved by designers and engineers) the 'how' (the working principle) associated with the problem is understood and the 'value' is well defined. To illustrate, an experienced player is hired for an elite soccer team, based on the potential 'value' brought to the team by the new player (more wins), but without knowing exactly how the recruit might gel in the team environment to achieve the desired outcome.

Complex problem-solving

But what if the 'what' and the 'how' are unknown, and we only loosely know the desired outcome in terms of 'value'? This is where more complex abduction applies.

One key creative activity out of a wide array of design practices associated with complex abduction is known as 'framing'. In essence, the encountered problem is considered from a specific viewpoint whilst adopting a given working principle in determining whether the result generates the desired 'value'.

Framing itself becomes more complex when faced with paradoxical, conflicting requirements. However, judicious application of framing enables systematic analysis of a problem and identification of a range of potentially satisfactory or — better — innovative solutions.

Once a potential solution has been determined via complex abduction, deductive thinking is applied in qualifying/proving the potential approach.

Relatively inexperienced designers and problem-solvers are tempted to apply adduction in a random manner. More experienced practitioners apply a logical methodology and can draw upon a wider body of experience in identifying potential options that might solve the problem at hand.

Problem definition

Another key element in complex problem-solving concerns problem definition.

McKinsey alumni Charles Conn and Robert McLean's *Bulletproof problem-solving*[7] explores the standardised methodology by which McKinsey & Co, as the go-to organisation for high-end management consulting services, approaches complex problem-solving for its clients. Problem-solvers and businesses in general can significantly improve their problem-solving capability just by adopting a more rigorous approach to defining the problem needing to be solved. Step 1 of the McKinsey problem-solving methodology involves defining the problem in terms of the following aspects:

1. decision-maker(s)

2. key forces acting on decision-makers

3. boundaries/constraints

4. criteria/measures for successful effort

5. time frame for resolution

6. level of accuracy needed.

This one step mitigates the natural tendency of designers, engineers and others with logically oriented thought processes to dive into problem-solving mode prior to fully understanding the nature of the problem at hand.

I'll further illustrate with an example taken from long-ago personal experience. As a not-long-graduated depot mechanical engineer at Flemington Maintenance Centre, my electrical engineer colleague was faced with an unusual problem: a Tangara Passenger train, not long released from the workshop after an overhaul, was reported to be unable to accelerate properly from a standing start. As an electrically powered vehicle with an Intel 80486 microprocessor controller (dwarfed today by the processing power of the average smart phone) and relatively complex electromechanical and regenerative braking systems, there were many potential sources of the problem.

Prior to launching into exhaustive inspections of the various train systems for potential faults, my wise colleague (as was his way) spent time analysing and clearly understanding the specific nature of the problem at hand. Repeated testing in the depot revealed that the vehicle would repeatedly accelerate to a velocity of 10 km/h, whereupon the power would ramp down and the vehicle slow to a virtual stop.

It took quite some time to identify the root cause of the problem. While initial observations pointed to a likely problem with 'wheel slip', my colleague used his deductive reasoning to conclude this was not the case, nor, with further exploration, was the system being 'tricked' into recognising wheel slip behaviour. Steel wheels running on steel rails wear over time, requiring re-machining to restore the shape of the contact area between wheel and rail to a design 'profile', and enable the wheel to continue to roll over the track efficiently and effectively. The depot's re-profiling machine had been recently taken offline for maintenance. A check of the machine revealed that it had been incorrectly recalibrated, resulting in recent wheelsets being re-machined with different wheel diameters.

In this circumstance, systematic problem analysis resulted in (a not immediately clear) identification of a root cause that, undetected, could have resulted in (at best) excessive railcar wheel wear and consequential rectification costs to (at worst) a heightened risk of train derailments. My colleague's swift but considered approach mitigated the consequences of the issue, which was then addressed by inspecting all recently maintained wheelsets and replacing faulty components.

Quantitative analysis applied to project estimation

Another key area often neglected in the problem analysis space concerns the judicious application of quantitative methodologies in project estimation.

As discussed in chapter 5, an enormous amount of industry time and effort has been expended in analysing the reasons for project delays and cost blow-outs in comparison with the baselines established at project commencement. One problem that often shows up in engineering and construction projects concerns the extent to which the judgement and experience of individuals is invisibly embedded within the time and cost assumptions comprising the baseline project estimate.

A properly defined project comprises a scope of work, cost estimate and a work schedule. For discussion purposes, we will assume the scope of the project and the applicable engineering and health, safety, environmental and quality standards are fully known. Similarly, input cost escalation and the potential for project task re-sequencing is set aside. (At this point it is worth acknowledging that we're well away from the reality of a typical project.) On this basis, then, the assumed timelines within the cost estimate and schedule drive the extent to which the estimate will align with the actual project cost and time outcomes.

From where, then, are these task durations sourced?

Input task durations are typically based on estimates provided by experienced project people. The question being raised here, however, is not about the validity of these assumptions. The issue concerns how these assumptions are interpreted when they are incorporated into the cost estimate and work schedule. In many cases, in my experience, it is unclear on what basis the assumptions have been made. In essence, is the task duration a 'most likely' assumption or something different?

To illustrate using a fictional example: a cost estimator compiling an estimate assumes (based on experienced input) the task of laying X sq m of a 300 mm–thick concrete slab to require one eight-hour shift for an average six-person crew to complete. Rather than go down the rabbit-hole of potential crew efficiencies etc., let's consider the range of potential task outcomes from a behavioural perspective. If the crew knows they have an eight-hour shift in which to complete the slab, it's highly likely the crew will use up the allotted time. However, any overtime on offer will significantly increase the chances of an increase in the duration of slab laying. Conversely, putting the owner-builder (who has committed to a fixed price for the slab) in charge of the crew would be highly likely to result in a quicker job!

In this example, the cost estimator appears to have done the right thing by inputting the 'most likely' duration into the cost estimate. However, what if the project is driven by time? Alternatively, what if the project is plagued by delays? Or something in between?

For relatively simple job estimates, an assessment of job duration can be made at tender review time. Adjustments can then be considered based on experienced judgement regarding how the job is likely to play out. For more complex projects, however, this process can be fraught with danger due to lack of insight regarding the basis upon which the cost and time estimates have been compiled.

A better answer

Valuable insight can be gained from a systematic assessment of the potential variability of the time-based input assumptions, and a summation of these inputs as a total consolidated estimate with an associated range of accuracy (or error bounds). This analysis can be undertaken with the help of a Monte Carlo simulation,[8] which can be used to model a range of possible results by substituting a range of potential input values (a probability distribution) for any factor with inherent uncertainty. The output of the simulation is a range of possible outcomes for the consolidated estimate with associated confidence limits.

If we link total project (critical path) duration with the time-related (say, site overhead) costs associated with managing and delivering a project, we're then able to quantitatively estimate the probability of the occurrence of a range of cost outcomes. Or put another way, statistical analysis can provide insight into how confident we should be in achieving a given project duration and consolidated project cost. To reiterate, though, the key to success is not in the number crunching. The value is generated via the process by which the potential variability of the input assumptions is systematically captured and evaluated.

Of course, the exercise proposed above is not put forward as an alternative to tender reviews by experienced personnel. However, informed scrutiny of the results of a probability-based (or stochastic) assessment of cost and time estimates will add value to the review process.

Using negotiation as a problem-solving tactic

At some point in a typical engineer's career, it becomes apparent that winning an argument is not always about being right. This realisation marks the beginning of an understanding of the importance of negotiation in problem-solving.

The key point to consider is that not all situations require negotiation to resolve the issue at hand. With the benefit of authority, knowledge and logical arguments, most engineers are adept at influencing and persuading others to agree with their point of view. However, the ability to negotiate an effective outcome requires the ability and preparedness to put yourself in another's shoes to truly understand what the other party wants and needs.

A wide range of research supports the view that a cooperative rather than competitive nature makes for a more effective negotiator.[9] This view aligns with one key indicator of a potentially successful negotiation, which is how much you know about what the other side needs and wants. The best negotiators are curious collaborators who spend more time listening than talking. It is through this tactic that they gain coveted information about what the other side wants and needs.

A second key indicator of a successful negotiation outcome concerns the amount of homework done, and the consequent level of preparedness, prior to commencing a negotiation.[9] Establishing a goal for the negotiation is critical during the preparation phase. An effective goal is one that matters to the negotiator. What is the difference? The main difference is in one's attitude.

There are compelling psychological reasons to set goals and expectations.[10] Studies indicate that once a goal is set, people tend to believe that anything outside the goal has already been forfeited, which can aid focus. Also, it's been shown that humans exhibit 'striving mechanisms' and focus their actions and behaviours on something once it's been stated or formally recorded (as the action of recording a goal is interpreted as making it real). For this reason, it's essential to focus on setting challenging but realistic goals and expectations, rather than aiming for the bottom line.

Establishing which party has greater leverage prior to a negotiation is also of prime importance. Generally, the side most comfortable with the status quo is likely to be able to exert the most leverage.

They have the least to lose if the deal falls through. Accordingly, establishing a personal 'best alternative to no agreement' (BATNA) is key in maintaining perspective in a negotiating position and avoiding being pressured into a win-lose outcome.

Understanding one's personal bargaining style is also a crucial element in being prepared. Table 13.1 describes the range of default individual bargaining styles.

Table 13.1: Bargaining styles[9]

Bargaining style	Description
Avoidant	Refuses to participate in a negotiation; prefers the status quo
Compromising	Ready to equally split costs or benefits
Accommodating	Willing to bow to the other's demands or preferences
Competitive	Possesses drive to obtain more for one's own side
Collaborative	Seeks mutually beneficial solutions

The key is in understanding the circumstances in which the range of different bargaining styles are best suited. This involves modifying your style as needed to align with the importance of the relationship with the other party and the level of conflict anticipated with the impending negotiation. To illustrate:

- An accommodating style works well when conflict is low. However, problem-solving works much better as the level of conflict rises and where preserving the relationship is important.

- Competitive behaviour, or even 'take it or leave it' avoidant behaviour, is worth risking when the importance of the relationship is low.

- Compromise as a 'circuit-breaker' is an option in all negotiating circumstances.

- Collaboration is the behaviour to strive for when the relationship is important and conflict is likely to be high.

One useful alternative to altering one's personal style to suit the requirements of a given negotiation may be to enlist the assistance of others with different bargaining styles and align tactics to achieve an overall outcome.

Once a negotiation has commenced, discovering what the other side wants provides the basis for a potential agreement to be reached. Why is this typically so difficult to determine? First, most people suffer from confirmation bias.[11] We assume, based on our initial assumptions, that others have the same outlook as us or we think we have someone figured out. It becomes hard to see beyond our initial assumptions, and we close off other — sometimes contradictory — ways of interpreting words and behaviour. The result is that it becomes more difficult, if not impossible, to accurately read subtle signals received from the other side.

Another negotiating trap is referred to by psychologists as a 'fixed pie bias'.[12] Under this assumption, we get drawn into a win-loss mentality and, consequently, fight for every morsel. Thinking this way creates blindness to potentially mutually beneficial options for both parties. Perhaps there is something you're willing to give up in exchange for something the other side would be prepared to concede?

KPIs: Measuring the management system

'You cannot manage what you aren't measuring' is one of a great many truisms in business.

Key performance indicators (KPIs) are typically used to measure business performance and can be powerful drivers of behaviour, especially when used to assess and reward employee performance. KPIs as a clear and succinct form of communication are highly likely to be acted upon. The main caveat, then, in designing and implementing a KPI regime is that perverse behaviour may result. Business leaders need to remain vigilant for signs of unintended outcomes (for instance, incentivised managers maximising their own personal KPI performance to the detriment of broader business performance) and be prepared to make swift adjustments as needed. So, too, once a KPI has outlived its usefulness, leaders shouldn't hesitate to replace it with a measure that better aligns with the underlying business objectives.

When developing a strategy for formulating KPIs, the team should start with the basics, which means understanding what the organisational objectives are, how these objectives will be achieved, and who can act on this information. This needs to be an iterative process that involves feedback from staff and management.

Defining KPIs

The operative word in KPI is 'key' because every KPI should relate to a specific business outcome with a performance measure. Each KPI should have clear answers to the following four questions:

1. What is the desired outcome?

2. Why does this outcome matter?

3. How and how often is progress to be measured?

4. Who can influence the outcome and how?

The SMART (specific, measurable, attainable, relevant, time-bound) criteria are an effective means of evaluating the practicality of a performance indicator. In other words:

1. Is the objective *specific*?

2. Can progress be *measured* towards the goal?

3. Is the goal realistically *attainable*?

4. How *relevant* is the goal to the organisation?

5. What is the *timeframe* for achieving the goal?

Incorporating KPIs as part of individual performance management frameworks

Performance measurement based on 'hard' metrics is only one of a range of feedback mechanisms that can be harnessed in aligning individual and business performance. The challenge arising in relying on hard metrics only, is those other elements (such as job competency in accordance with the role description, and positive behavioural attributes, such as teamwork and alignment with business values) are not taken into consideration. On this basis, personal performance frameworks need to be carefully designed to take account of (on a weighted basis) subjective as well as objective performance elements. More rounded and, therefore, more effective assessments can be developed by including elements such as:

1. project outcomes, for projects in which the individual has participated as part of the team

2. job functional competency, assessed against a job description

3. behavioural attributes, for instance leadership behaviour (see chapter 8).

Continuous improvement: Applying the kaizen *approach*

Sustainable improvement in business efficiency and effectiveness requires a means of locking in improvements. Returning to the *kaizen* methodology for achieving continuous improvement from chapter 11, I will draw on the work of James Clear and his article titled, 'This coach improved every tiny thing by 1 percent and here's what happened',[13] which illustrates what can be achieved with focused, incremental change. He cites the example of Dave Brailsford, who, as general manager and performance director for British professional cycling Team Sky, led a performance-improvement process based on the concept of 'aggregation of marginal gains'. By optimising many things, in areas one might expect a professional cycling team to address as well as in areas overlooked by almost everyone else, the team implemented a five-year plan to conquer the Tour de France, the premier race on the professional cycling calendar.

The team began by focusing on training, nutrition, bicycle ergonomics and weight. They then moved on to 'one-percenters' that others overlooked, including pillows offering the best sleep and good hygiene habits to ward off sickness.

For those unfamiliar with cycling, Bradley Wiggins' victory for Team Sky in 2012 was the first by a rider from the United Kingdom, a mere three years after Brailsford commenced the incremental improvement process. Team Sky went on to dominate the sport for over a decade.

The principle of 'aggregation of marginal gains' demonstrates that incremental changes, when added together over time, can result in major shifts in overall outcomes.

The process implemented at Team Sky also echoes the *kaizen* approach, which goes beyond simple productivity improvement. It is also a process that, when implemented correctly, humanises the workplace, eliminates *muri* (or overly hard work) and teaches individuals how to perform experiments on their work using the scientific method and eliminate waste in business processes.

Kaizen has historically yielded transformational outcomes in the form of compound productivity improvement. *Kaizen* methodology includes making small, experimental changes and monitoring results prior to locking in changes (the plan-do-check-act process commonly associated with total quality management).[12] Large-scale pre-planning and extensive project scheduling are replaced with smaller experiments, which can be rapidly adapted as new improvements are suggested. The principles of *kaizen* continue to form the basis of contemporary lean improvement programs.

The Team Sky story also reminds us of our individual tendency to overestimate the importance of one defining moment and underestimate the value of making better daily decisions. Almost every habit we have—good or bad—is the result of many small decisions over time. And yet, we easily forget this principle when we seek to shift business performance. *Kaizen* represents the Japanese method of mitigating this tendency in a business environment, generating sustained business success in highly competitive global industries, such as automotive manufacture, over decades.

Both *kaizen* and the approach implemented at Team Sky have one key prerequisite: a willingness to spend time and effort in developing a deep understanding of how an existing process works—or does not work—prior to making changes. This understanding enables changes to be made in such a way that the new and improved process works—and can be measured and, therefore, objectively verified to work—more efficiently and effectively than what has been done before.

Conclusion

The essence of this pillar concerns taking on board tried-and-tested frameworks and methodologies in addressing the common operational issues that show up during the key transition phase from a good to sustainable business enterprise.

In essence, similar problems show up at similar times as small businesses grow into larger and more complex entities. In a similar vein to revenue-related challenges associated with Pillar 2, when a familiar operational problem shows up, the challenge is in recognising the probability that the same problem must be solved in a different way so as to mitigate the effects of your more complex business circumstances.

Key takeaways for sustainable businesses

1 First-, second- and third-order operational fit comes to life when businesses analyse, adjust and optimise the people, processes and IT systems underpinning the organisation to better meet the needs of their clients and customers. The whole matters more than the individual parts, with competitive advantage arising from the interconnectedness of the entire ecosystem of activities.

2 The best starting point for analysing your operations is the structure or architecture of your IT systems. An IT architecture map with an end-to-end roadmap of the key systems supporting your people and processes is a valuable tool in identifying and reorganising process inefficiencies.

3 The effects of environment on employee productivity is a topic demanding management attention. Don't neglect an assessment of your personal productivity, though, as it is likely to have a far more fundamental impact on the efficiency and effectiveness of your management team and the rest of the organisation.

4 Talented people are the lifeblood of a sustainable business. Training and development in the problem-solving skills of complex problem assessment, quantitative analysis and negotiation will enable your business to reap the benefits of your talented employees more fully.

5 Sustained business growth requires management ability in applying different performance methodologies reflecting the specific needs of individual business units. To do their job, your management team requires both an effective KPI regime and a means for locking in incremental business improvements.

CHAPTER 14

Pillar 4:
Business assets

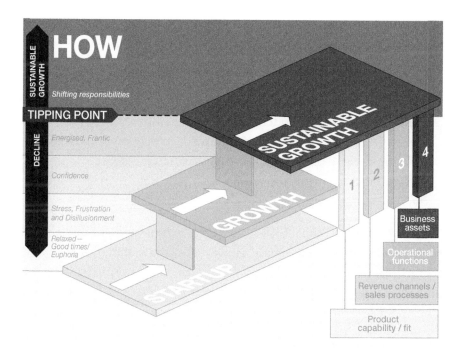

Pillar 1 is about identifying and building business resources and capabilities for the purpose of producing better outcomes for clients and customers. Pillar 4, then, is about taking a closer look at your resources and capabilities and identifying the source(s) of your business assets. Why? Because assets represent business value that can be monetised via a business transaction.

A range of capabilities are potentially valuable to your enterprise, including those operational functions covered in Pillar 3. The most valuable organisational capability in engineering and construction — as with many other, if not all, industries — is an ability to innovate to respond to changing customer needs. Innovation creates management opportunities to sustain enterprise growth and maintain a continuous pipeline of business-building initiatives.

People as assets

Referring to the work of Smallwood and Ulrich in a 1984 *Harvard Business Review* paper 'Capitalising on capabilities',[1] the collective skills, abilities and expertise of an organisation are the outcome of investments in people, including their training and skills development. The ways in which people and other resources are brought together to accomplish work form the identity and personality of the organisation. Culture creates stability over time and is much more difficult for competitors to replicate than, say, financial resources, physical resources (such as plant and equipment), business management (IT) systems or even product strategies.

Organisational capabilities are the combined abilities and competencies of its individuals. However, a single employee who may be technically brilliant or demonstrate leadership proficiency is not enough; the broader business must embody the strengths for it to be a business capability.

Leveraging your 'secret sauce'

As a smaller player in a mature industry, like engineering and construction, with established players controlling most of the market, opportunities are limited to leverage capabilities and resources to create sustainable advantage. Exploitation of Ghemawat's proposed sources of competitive advantage (size, impediments to competition and, to a lesser extent, proprietary access to critical inputs; see chapter 9) is, realistically, the domain of the dominant industry players.

The vast majority of good small businesses, having survived the initial journey from start-up, possess more than a dash of 'secret sauce', something the industry really needs and which the business does as well or better than others. This capability can form the basis of a business asset. It might be useful at this point to refer to table 9.1 in chapter 9, which summarises a broad range of elements upon which businesses might base such a competitive advantage.

Great and sustainable businesses possess the organisational ability to optimise what they're capable at, coming up with new ideas and ways of offering the secret sauce to their clients and customers.

Most owners consider their business to be all about the products and services they provide. And they're right: no product or service, no business! Moreover, and as explored in chapter 11, the right pre-/core/post-product strategy can transform long and complex sales processes into client and customer relationships involving a regular flow of jobs and revenue.

However, the real source of a sustainably successful enterprise is the asset on which the business is built. This secret sauce enables the business to expand the range of strategic options for selling their products and services, between pursuing a cost-based strategy (having found a way to reduce overall cost below that of competitors) and a differentiation-based strategy (enabling a higher price to be charged than that charged by competitors) or any combination of the two.

Consider then, business 'know-how' as a potential asset. It's one thing to know, for example, various road or bridge building methods better than anyone else. It's an entirely different proposition, though, if your business can invent new and better ways of delivering roads and bridges (or even delivering alternatives to roads and bridges if, say, traffic diversion or temporary alternative transportation is required whilst the road or bridge is under construction). This is the definition of innovation.

Innovation, then, implies that the business is good at developing and implementing something new, be it in content, process or a combination of the two. Celebrating the innovative nature of an organisation has an added benefit of energising internal and external stakeholders alike.

Innovation in infrastructure engineering and construction

Disruptive innovation is not traditionally associated with engineering and construction. The situation is inevitably changing, however, as the forces of industry consolidation (see chapter 3) create opportunities (particularly in relation to mega projects) for mandating standardised systems and processes and streamlining interfaces, enabling innovations to be easily and seamlessly incorporated into the design and construction process. Intense competition and margin pressure on businesses, large and small, continue to drive the need for change and improvement. So, too, the sheer size of the industry globally continues to attract outside attention from a new breed of corporation armed with disruptive business models.

In the meantime, developments in the construction technology space have given rise to a plethora of scheduling and construction project management, work scheduling, documentation control and variations management solutions. Progress has also been made in the digital twin space, with device communications propelled by Internet of Things technology enabling capture and analysis of vast reams of data for asset construction and management purposes.

These recent developments have been somewhat overshadowed internationally by the high-profile collapse of Katerra in mid-2021. Katerra was an American enterprise founded in 2015 by former Tesla interim CEO Michael Marks and the executive chair of real estate investment house The Wolff Company, Fritz Wolff. Katerra sought to disrupt the housing construction industry by scaling production of prefabricated materials for on-site assembly. Katerra developed expertise in mass timber manufacture comprising glued and cross-laminated products. In 2018 it acquired MGA, a leading architectural firm in the field of tall wood buildings and mass timber construction. By the end of 2018, Katerra had over 700 projects under way across several states in the USA. Despite reportedly receiving over $US2 billion of funding from Japanese Softbank Vision Fund, including bailout support in December 2020, Katerra filed for bankruptcy in June 2021.[2]

This case study highlights the challenges involved in standardising physically constructed buildings, which involve many different parts that vary enormously across different building types. Instead of concentrating on perfecting standardised manufacturing for one particular type of building (such as apartments), Katerra expanded its range of product well beyond the company's ability to manage, and ultimately failed. The experience further highlights the broader issues in the non-standardised environment characteristic of the infrastructure elements of engineering and construction.

One key to understanding where this industry might shift is to consider what aspects of the industry can, and therefore might, change quickly versus what might be more difficult to shift. As a simple example, consider the humble 240V electrical plug. It is a large device for reasons of socket configuration, electrical safety etc. and is therefore the bulkiest item in many low-amperage applications, such as mobile phones. Consider, though, all the electrical infrastructure that would need to be changed should a different type of interface be dreamt up between fixed outlets and electric powered devices. On the other hand, what if wireless charging of small electronic devices went 'mainstream'? Get the idea?

What to innovate

The most effective way to sustainably improve business costs and, consequently, the competitive position of a business is by leveraging innovation-based product or productivity improvements. Many would say mature industry competition is all about defending margins: dealing with client pressure to reduce quotes and tendered prices while managing rising input costs. The best way to shift the competitive position of your business, and therefore your negotiating power, is to find and implement ways to:

1. reduce the input costs of your product or service

2. improve the quality of the output

3. shift the speed with which you can deliver it.

As a starting point, you might like to consider whether re-jigging the time/cost/quality mix of your product or service would better align it with what your clients actually want.

As the forces of disruption move through the industry, accelerated by the post–COVID-19 'new normal', opportunities will arise for companies who have invested in capability and learnt the skills of innovation to chase and gain market share.

There is no shortage of opportunities for innovation in engineering and construction. You might like to explore areas likely to be at the forefront of industry disruption:

1. improvements to the maintainability/durability/reliability/ sustainability of existing products and services

2. application of alternative materials with superior attributes/ reduced cost/reduced environmental footprint, taking disposal into account

3. application of modular or off-site construction techniques for permanent structures as well as temporary formwork — for

instance using 3-D printing techniques to create wax moulds for pre-cast concrete

4. application of technology for data collation and sharing, project and process management, trend analysis and reporting

5. 5-D building information management: linking 3-D information models to scheduled time (4-D) and cost (5-D) to drive process digitisation and data integration

6. higher-definition surveying and geo-location, supporting site management and progress tracking

7. digital collaboration and mobility supported by widespread use of handheld devices

8. the Internet of Things and advanced analytics, enabled through adoption of smart design principles at the front end of developments, driving product digitisation

9. future-proof-based and resilient design and construction.

When targeting potential innovative products or processes for development, however, one needs to be mindful of the interplay of three fundamental market forces:

1. demand: does the innovation meet customers' needs and is it competitively superior?

2. scarcity: is the innovation substitutable and durable?

3. appropriability: who owns the intellectual property and, therefore, the profits?

How to innovate

What if, like most entrepreneurial owners, you want your business to be outstanding in the field? In short, you will need to find an unsolved problem in the market and solve it, whilst managing the risks associated with your solution better than your competitors.

From a practical perspective, then, how should owners and leadership go about generating innovative business thinking? Here's a few tips to get started:

1. There needs to be sufficient time regularly allocated to innovative activities — it just won't happen if it's at the bottom of everyone's 35-item daily to-do list.

2. There must be pressing problems or challenges identified to be solved. Sitting around dreaming up ideas (or even having an off-site strategy day, which conversely can be a great idea with focus and specific outcomes to be achieved) is unlikely to generate useful ideas on its own.

3. Regular conversations with suppliers, sub-contractors and partners, both inside and outside of the industry, are an excellent source of new ideas.

4. Finally, there is always a risk of failure when implementing a business innovation. The key is in adopting a minimum viable product–based (MVP) approach (popularised in the software industry) to trying something new, and if you must fail, fail fast!

A final perspective regarding innovation was provided by Vivek Ranadivé, who was widely credited with digitising Wall Street in the 1980s with his first company, Teknekron Software Systems. His thoughts, expressed in 2018, outline the necessary pre-conditions for innovative ideas:

> I believe innovation comes from hunger ... You can't innovate for the sake of innovation. It has to be genuine, not phony or insincere ... The most innovative ideas come from hiring really smart people and challenging them, not coddling them ... [3]

A note on external facilitation

External facilitation is often required to remove blockages that typically constrain our ability to think creatively. Typical blockages include:

1. The thinking process: we naturally solve a problem in two stages: the first stage, or lateral thinking, where we define the problem, followed by the second stage, or vertical thinking, where we solve the problem. The longer we spend in first-stage thinking about the problem, the more likely we are to fully understand the problem and recognise the full range of possible solutions. As explored in chapter 13, those of an engineering bent are particularly susceptible to jumping early into problem-solving mode.

2. Patterning systems: we need to be aware of how our mind seeks patterns that relate to our store of experience and how it applies these tried-and-tested patterns in solving the problem at hand. Disrupting these thinking patterns creates the opportunity to come up with truly different answers.

3. Mindset: we need to be aware of how our minds 'self-constrain' based on the nature of the problem and/or the way the problem is defined or expressed. Changing the problem definition creates opportunities to think outside the square.

Management strategies for innovation

Consider, then, the management challenge of sustaining growth and the requirement for businesses to maintain a continuous pipeline of business-building initiatives.

3 Horizons

The 3 Horizons concept is drawn from *The Alchemy of Growth* by David White, Mehrdad Baghai and Steve Coley.[4] The underpinning framework provides a means of categorising business units in terms of the required management approach to support their respective phase of growth (see figure 14.1).

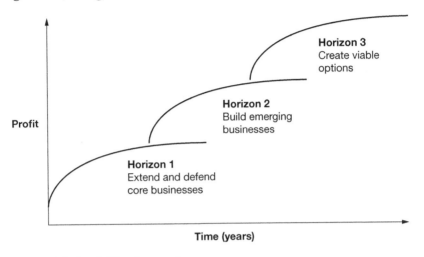

Figure 14.1: 3 Horizons[4]

The model provides useful insight in circumstances where management is preoccupied with driving profitability from their current enterprise. Businesses often lack a means of assessing and monitoring current businesses, new enterprises coming on stream and future opportunities in a conscious way. To sustain growth, however, there must be a regular pipeline of new business representing new sources of profit. Sustainable business enterprises constantly seek ways to innovate in their core businesses, whilst simultaneously building out new opportunities. What mastery looks like is reenergising the pipeline at just the right time.

Growth share matrix (GSM)

The 3 Horizons framework, in turn, aligns with the growth share matrix concept published in 1968 by Bruce Henderson, founder of Boston Consulting Group.[4] Each quadrant of the four-quadrant matrix in figure 14.2 represents a specific combination of relative market share and growth, in which each business element of a portfolio can be mapped.

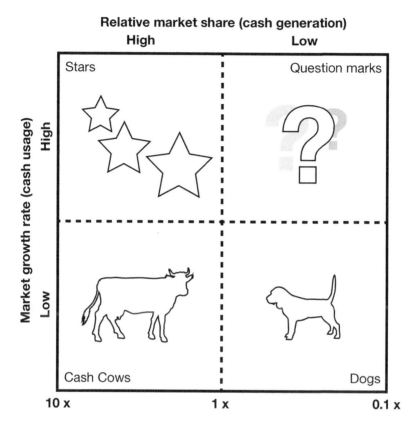

Figure 14.2: Growth share matrix[5]

Source: Animal illustrations: © Igor Djurovic/iStockphoto

- Low growth/high share: businesses should milk these 'cash cows' for cash to reinvest.

- High growth/high share: businesses should invest in these 'stars' as they have future potential.

- High growth/low share: businesses should invest in or discard these 'question marks' depending on their chances of becoming stars.

- Low share/low growth: businesses should liquidate, divest or reposition these 'dogs'.

Managing the business portfolio

Regardless of the choice to apply the 3 Horizons or growth share matrix in managing your business portfolio, each horizon/quadrant represents a different stage in the development of a given business unit and each poses a different management challenge.

- *Horizon 1: Cash cows:* mature business units generating profits and cash flow are critical to the current performance of the enterprise as they generate the funding for the rest of the enterprise. Mature businesses can be incrementally extended via continued innovation in product and process. Management focus on structure, productivity enhancement and cost management will assist in maintaining healthy performance for as long as possible. Setting clear expectations and holding these mature businesses to account in relation to profitability will ensure sufficient cash is generated to fund additional business expansion via Horizon 2 and 3.

- *Horizon 2: Stars:* this business sector is where the concept is taking root or growth is accelerating. These units could transform the enterprise, but not without considerable investment in cash and time. Typical business units have customers, revenue and may already generate some profit, and management needs to maintain a single-minded drive to increase revenue and market share. These businesses need to be in play concurrently, with each requiring sufficient management time and attention to enable and guide their journey towards reliable profitability.

- *Horizon 3: Question marks or Dogs:* these embryonic business activities may include research pilots or projects as well as minority investment and strategic partnerships. The primary goal with these initiatives is not profit, although a pathway to profit is a key consideration in the ultimate selection of an initiative for additional investment. Moving an initiative from Horizon 3 to Horizon 2 'Star' status is the next step towards the goal of an actual business, whilst an unsuccessful venture means relegation to 'dog' status. The question mark quadrant requires judicious investment in capital and management time, as over-investment in this horizon/quadrant will negatively affect both the health and return on investment of the consolidated business.

Building business valuation and enabling succession

There's an additional and powerful underlying 'why' for business innovation.

Most entrepreneurs have a reasonably good concept of the business problem they want to solve in the marketplace. Not as many entrepreneurs know how best to solve client and customer problems while developing and delivering the answers in a way that maximises the value of their business.

Consider the following standard formula for business valuation:

$$V = P \times M$$

The value or Valuation (V) of a business equals Profit (P) multiplied by a Multiple (M) of earnings. Reliable 'profit' is the starting point of any form of reasonable 'valuation'. However, shifting the 'valuation' of a business by sustainably improving 'profit' is a difficult proposition (as many business owners in the construction contracting game would no doubt agree). Without going into finer details, the magic of 'valuation' is not in the 'profit' element of the equation. Shifts in the earnings 'multiple' are what drive increases in 'valuation' of a business.

From where, then, is the earnings 'multiple' for a business derived?

Tangible assets are things you can touch, like premises, plant and equipment. They exist on a company's balance sheet as a capital item and are treated as assets for accounting purposes.

Intangible assets in an accounting sense are things that can't be touched, but are nevertheless an asset to the company, such as patents, trademarks and goodwill (being the summation of harder-to-value elements, such as a company's brand name, solid customer base, good customer and stakeholder relations, proprietary technology and know-how). Notwithstanding the fact that these can be the most valuable assets a company holds, the investment allocated to these is treated as a company expense. Incurred expenses reduces reported profits, which (all other things being equal) reduces earnings per share. However, there's a bigger picture at play here.

The building blocks to managing business assets

Figure 14.3 describes a business in possession of several discrete and valuable assets.

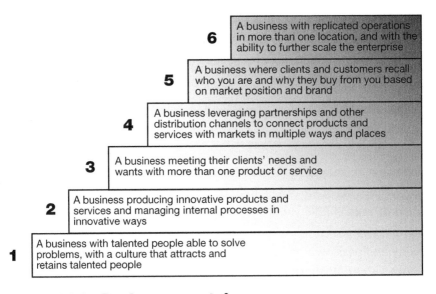

6 A business with replicated operations in more than one location, and with the ability to further scale the enterprise

5 A business where clients and customers recall who you are and why they buy from you based on market position and brand

4 A business leveraging partnerships and other distribution channels to connect products and services with markets in multiple ways and places

3 A business meeting their clients' needs and wants with more than one product or service

2 A business producing innovative products and services and managing internal processes in innovative ways

1 A business with talented people able to solve problems, with a culture that attracts and retains talented people

Figure 14.3: Business assets[6]

Consider, by way of explanation, asset 2 on the list concerning innovation. Access to a reliable stream of talented people (asset 1 in figure 14.3) is a prerequisite for developing innovation as a business asset. Innovation, in turn, enables a business to develop and deploy a product or service strategy as outlined by asset 3. In this way, each asset is a prerequisite for the next one in the chain, resulting in increased business value and, therefore, increased implied earnings 'multiple' as each successive capability is developed within the business.

Rule-of-thumb estimates are available for the specific earnings 'multiples' associated with each of the listed business assets. The key to remember is that the higher the asset number, the higher the associated earnings 'multiple' and associated business 'valuation'. A business with the ability to scale across multiple locations (asset 6) is worth inherently more than a business with the ability to attract and retain talented people (asset 1).

It is worth reflecting for a moment on how this concept plays out for technology-based companies, in particular, stock market–listed technology companies trading on what appears to be outlandish price/earning ratios when earnings look more like losses. At the end of the day, what matters most is how much cash a company produces, not earnings. However, what the market is reflecting in these circumstances is the perception of how much cash a company's intangible assets are likely to generate in the future. What actually matters when it comes to business 'valuation' is how long it takes for the invested capital in a business to generate earnings, enabling an investor to recover their money.

Monetising asset value

Having a business with a high earnings 'multiple' is one thing, but how do you, as the owner, monetise this value?

The ultimate answer to this question is that the 'valuation' of a business as an ongoing concern is determined as the outcome of a transaction between buyer and seller. The transaction may take one of several forms. It may occur as an internal arrangement (e.g., transfer of business equity to employees) or as an external event (e.g., a sale, merger or external investment that enables a rearrangement of the business capital structure). By enabling others to increase their interest in your business, you, as owner, can release part or all of your equity tied up in the business for other purposes.

The key to your successful transition, though, is the successful entry of the other parties. This is achieved through (a) understanding the interests of *all* parties involved in the transaction from an income versus equity versus control perspective, and (b) designing the transaction to align the parties' interests. What are these three interests?

1. Income is typically comprised of salary and dividends.

2. Equity is typically ownership of shares in the company.

3. Control is considered from both a business operations (day-to-day decision-making) and a board (voting rights) perspective.

A workable transaction needs to be designed to recognise and explicitly deal with these three interests as they show up for the individual parties to the transaction. This approach acknowledges the individual expectations the separate parties have of the business — be it income, equity and/or control — with a view to aligning these different interests.

What might this exercise result in? You might just transform your existing business with new blood, who are incentivised to drive the enterprise to the next phase and beyond. Your business might be supported by an injection of funds, with you as founder having the freedom to pursue other interests whilst maintaining engagement with the enterprise.

So, if you agree that business is all about identifying risk, managing it better than your competitors and making money out of the game, you might consider that business is also about beginning with the end game in mind!

Conclusion

Building a sustainable business in infrastructure engineering and construction remains a challenging activity, not the least because the long-term rewards on offer do not compensate for the risks typically accepted in delivering the work in accordance with client expectations. One approach to dealing with this conundrum is to 'ride the boom times' and cash in before the inevitable 'bust' arrives. This gambler's approach to business requires both skill and a great deal of luck, particularly in precisely identifying the time when boom is about to turn to bust. A measured approach to business investment management, guided by the owner's end game (i.e., building business value with the outcome in mind) is an approach that places your business destiny firmly in your hands and shifts the odds of ultimate success in your favour.

Key takeaways for sustainable businesses

1 There's more than likely a dash of 'secret sauce' in your business that can form the basis of an asset. Business assets enable your business to out-compete rivals by adopt a cost-based or differentiation-based strategy or any combination of the two.

2 Innovation as a capability, matched with know-how, is a valuable business asset. Sustainable business enterprises constantly seek new ways to innovate core products or services.

3 Innovation must be effectively managed. Managers of sustainable business enterprises develop the pipeline such that fading sources of growth are replenished at exactly the right time.

4 Capable business entrepreneurs know how to solve their clients' and customers' problems, while developing and delivering the answers in a way that maximises the value of their business enterprise.

5 Building business value with an end game in mind provides you with an access to monetising your business asset.

Conclusion
Embedding business improvement

If finding the one thing that kick-starts growth is the goal for start-up businesses, and implementing strategy is what intermediate businesses require, then organisational mindset is the key to advanced business success.

Successful business founders are already in possession of the entrepreneurial mindset. The ability to step outside one's comfort zone, face your fears and access curiosity is the antidote to existing in a state of inaction constrained by fear. Harnessing passion and tenacity provides the energy source to focus on the drivers of business success for longer than most others are prepared to.

Entrepreneurs also have potential sources of weakness that must be confronted. There is immense pressure for external validation, be it from winning, making money, achieving social or corporate status. The focus on what is outside our control can lead to stress and anxiety.

Focusing attention on what is controllable (such as who we want to be) enables us to step away from external distractions. In this way, we create the headspace to better understand the difference between happiness and satisfaction, and how this understanding can be harnessed to create deeper meaning in your enterprise.

After finding a business that aligns with your background, knowledge and interests, the most important skill for an entrepreneur to develop is inspiring those you hire into your business

You will have noted a few sporting analogies in this book. As Simon Sinek describes in *The Infinite Game*,[1] finite games like golf, cricket, soccer or Texas Hold'em poker involve known players, fixed rules and have clear winners and losers.

In an infinite game like business, the players come and go, the rules are changeable, and there is no defined endpoint. There are no winners or losers in an infinite game; there is only ahead and behind.

Business owners who fall in love with the game of business, particularly the game played in engineering and construction, and are prepared to teach their organisations how to play the game, are maximising their chances of success in this industry.

Why business coaching?

Coaching in 2019 was estimated to be a $US2.8 billion global industry characterised by rapid growth, as evidenced by a dramatic increase in coaches, professional coaching organisations and coaching-related research.[2]

Although business coaching is a relatively new phenomenon, coaching as a profession in the sporting arena has a long history.

In my experience, the core value brought by a coach/adviser to a business is the ability to ask the right questions. Asking questions from a space of genuine curiosity focuses attention, elicits new ideas and enables commitment.

Other reasonable expectations of a capable coach/adviser include:

1. access to domain-specific knowledge (e.g., business knowledge for a business coach), enabling clients to shorten their learning curve

2. the ability to identify where clients need to improve and where they cannot

3. honesty in calling a situation or weakness for what it is

4. goal-setting guidance to stimulate personal and professional growth

5. discipline and encouragement in the right measure, creating necessary boundaries clients cannot set for themselves

6. acting as a sounding board for an unfiltered opinion

7. being a trusted adviser and connector.

Tools and frameworks for better communication

Business advisory and coaching work involves lots of time communicating with people. This also provides plenty of opportunities to observe how people communicate with each other in a business context. I can assure you, the key to improving the way we communicate with those around us is to improve our personal awareness and understanding of what makes us feel like we're being heard as individuals. From this position comes the opportunity to branch out and seek to better understand the needs of others.

Fortunately, there are a wide range of tools available to assist in this process. Here are a few examples I've found to be useful in a wide range of business circumstances.

Think/Feel/Know (TFK)

Think/Feel/Know (TFK)[3] is a contextual tool based on our individual preferences for a particular style of communication. The model recognises three primary communication styles:

1. Think: based on data with information processed in the head

2. Feel: based on energy with 'the vibe' processed in the heart

3. Know: based on intuition with 'the answer' processed in the gut.

Individuals process information in different ways, and typically have a preference for a particular style of communication. Although we can use all three styles, individuals usually have a primary and a secondary communication preference. TFK enables individuals to better understand how they prefer to process information (verbal, visual or written), how they prefer to communicate and how they prefer to learn. This simple but effective tool can be absorbed quickly and applied in a wide range of situations, with immediate benefits in terms of improved communications.

DiSC

DiSC is a behavioural assessment tool based on the theory of Swiss psychiatrist Carl G. Jung and American psychologist William Moulton Marston, which centres on four personality traits: dominance (D), inducement (I), submission (S) and compliance (C). This theory was developed into a self-assessment tool by industrial psychologist Walter Vernon Clarke.[4]

Marston published his findings in his 1928 book *Emotions of Normal People*[5] in which he contended that people illustrate their emotions using the four DiSC behavioural types. His argument centred on the contention that these behavioural types arose from an individual's sense of self as well their interaction with the environment. He proposed two dimensions that influenced people's emotional behaviour:

1. whether a person views the environment as favourable or unfavourable

2. whether a person perceives themself as having control or lack of control over the environment.

The primary relationships between sense of self, perceived power over the environment and perception of the environment are illustrated in figure B.

Dominance Perceives oneself as more powerful than the environment and perceives the environment as unfavourable.	**Inducement** Perceives oneself as more powerful than the environment and perceives the environment as favourable.
Submission Perceives oneself as less powerful than the environment and perceives the environment as favourable.	**Compliance** Perceives oneself as less powerful than the environment and perceives the environment as unfavourable.

Figure B: DiSC personality types

A range of DiSC-style assessment tools are available, accompanied with instructions regarding how to interpret the results, including the following caveats:

1. All DiSC traits are equally valuable, with individuals exhibiting a blend of all four behavioural traits.

2. An individual's approach in a work setting is influenced by other factors, including life experiences, education and maturity.

Learning about one's personal DiSC behavioural style, as well as the styles of others, can greatly assist when faced with challenging circumstances, where our default communication style (or lack of communication) is more likely to be employed, often without thought to how another personality type may react, and sometimes with undesirable consequences.

Myers-Briggs Type Indicator

The Myers-Briggs Type Indicator (MBTI) assessment was developed by Isabel Briggs Myers and Katharine Cook Briggs based on psychiatrist Carl Jung's work in his 1921 book *Psychological Types*.[6] Jung proposed a psychological typology based on his theories of cognitive function developed via clinical observations.

MBTI proposes typologies based on the following dimensions. How individuals:

1. focus their attention or source their energy (extraversion (E) or introversion (I))

2. perceive or absorb information (sensing (S) or intuition (N))

3. prefer to make decisions (thinking (T) or feeling (F))

4. orient themselves with respect to the external world (judgement (J) or perception (P)).

Individuals exhibit a psychological type based on an underlying personality pattern arising from the dynamic interaction between their four preferences in conjunction with environmental influences and their own individual tendencies. Sixteen different outcomes are possible, each identified by its own four-letter code comprising the first letters of the component typologies (N is used for iNtuition, since I is used for Introversion). Myers and Briggs state that individuals are likely to develop behaviours, skills and attitudes based on their MBTI type. Each personality type is associated with both strengths and weaknesses, with insights arising from the assessment providing opportunities for personal growth.

Coaching techniques: Asking the right questions[1]

Facts and feelings

What it is:

A contextual tool based on our individual preferences for a particular style of communication.

When to use it:

When diagnosing a situation/problem/issue of which someone has knowledge and experience.

How to use it:

1. Start in *think*: ask about a topic, explore it, categorise it, play with it, ask what they mean to get a conversation going.

2. Then switch to *feel*: ask how they feel about this topic; they start to describe the energy and use verbs.

3. Listen for the level of engagement in each space; people interact differently at different stages.

4. Once you've done feel, you can go down to *know* and ask what they believe using closed questions to elicit a yes or no answer.

5. Then move back to *think* to determine how they are going to implement their conclusion.

Choices

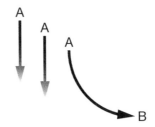

What it is:

- A technique that elicits a response from a deep feeling space.

- Use the technique by *fully* taking a response away or giving it back. An energy shift occurs by saying 'No, that's not it'.

When to use it:

To assist someone experiencing difficulties in choosing between multiple options.

How to use it:

1. Ask a question, listen to the answer, and say 'No, that's not it, what is it?'

2. If you get an answer, the first one wasn't it.

3. And if you say again, 'No, that's not it either', eventually you get to a point where they say, 'Actually, that is it'.

Options

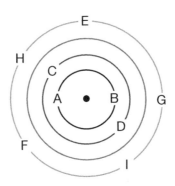

What it is:

A technique to assist in choosing between options.

When to use it:

To assist someone experiencing difficulties in choosing between two specific options.

How to use it:

1. When someone is stuck in the middle and they say they don't know, give them two options.

2. If the options are fairly narrow, and they can't choose between them, extend the options out.

3. If that doesn't work, extend the options as far as you can and then work back in towards the innermost option pair.

4. Finally work your way in until you get a specific answer.

Third Party/Me

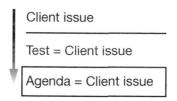

What it is:

- A technique to confirm that the coach is working to the client's agenda.

- The concept of third-party language comprises direct language vs third-party language, and involves listening for sentences that people use.

- The underlying assumption here is that, as humans, we can only see something in the world if we have experienced it (e.g., How do you know someone is angry? Because you have experienced the feeling of being angry).

When to use it:

Whenever confirming an agenda.

How to use it:

1. Listen for third-party language, such as 'everyone seems angry at the moment!'

2. Apply this in identifying the client's agenda, such as 'Anger management [in the business]'.

3. Test your assumptions by asking 'Could the angry person be you?'

Serve

What it is:

- A technique for shifting a situation from a negative context to a positive context or vice versa.

- When someone can't see the consequences of something (for instance a recurring behavioural pattern) that may or may not be serving them, 'flip the coin' and show them how it is or isn't serving them.

- This creates a shift in the client's perception.

When to use it:

When apparently dysfunctional behaviour shows up, this technique reveals the cause of the behaviour.

How to use it:

As an example, rephrase the sentence, by taking the word *not* out and replying, 'But it is serving you'. Work through the conversation along the lines of 'I appreciate that you can see how that's not serving you, but if that's your behaviour pattern, then at some level it must be serving you'.

Anchoring

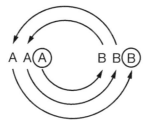

What it is:

A learning technique in a coaching environment.

When to use it:

To embed and reinforce key learnings.

How to use it:

1. Anchoring may be achieved by repeating the same phrase (e.g., is this useful?) to confirm continued engagement with the conversation. The repetition aligns client behaviour, facilitates recall and reinforces learning.

2. A physical 'anchor' can also be created by associating a specific location in a room with a specific subject or behaviour (e.g., a location where the past is always explored, a 'teaching spot' etc.)

Open Loop

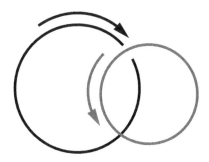

What it is:

A technique that elicits a deep *feeling* response.

When to use it:

To embed and reinforce key learnings.

How to use it:

1. An open loop is created by carrying out a controversial action (e.g., passing judgement on a client's activity, dismissing an opinion, having a 'confidential' conversation with a participant in a group session without explaining why).

2. The 'open loop' creates an (unspoken) response and puts the client (session participants) into a deep *feeling* state.

3. 'Closing the loop' occurs by exploring (with the client) the source of the client's reaction to the 'open loop' and creates a learning opportunity.

The power
of action

Realising your business vision is within your capability, but only if you dare to do the things others will only contemplate, plan for and talk about.

To borrow a phrase that resonated with me during a Landmark course I experienced some years ago, there are always plenty of people 'in the stands' watching the game and just waiting for an opportunity to offer their opinion. Far fewer people are 'on the court' playing the game

Business owners are on the court. They are very familiar with the fear of business failure showing up at 4 am. They are the ones prepared to confront the fear and even make friends with it (!) in return for the opportunity to realise their outcomes.

On 23 April, 1910, Theodore Roosevelt gave what would become one of the most widely quoted speeches of his career. The former US president (having left office in 1909) embarked on a tour of Northern Africa and Europe. Upon arrival at the Sorbonne in Paris' Latin Quarter, and before an audience of two thousand ticket holders, Roosevelt delivered a speech called 'Citizenship in a republic', which became more widely known as 'The man in the arena'.

The speech contained the following message:

> *It is not the critic who counts; not the man who points out how the strong man stumbles, or where the doer of deeds could have done them better. The credit belongs to the man who is actually in the arena, whose face is marred by dust and sweat and blood; who strives valiantly; who errs, who comes short again and again, because there is no effort without error and shortcoming; but who does actually strive to do the deeds; who knows great enthusiasms, the great devotions; who spends himself in a worthy cause; who at the best knows, in the end, the triumph of high achievement, and who at the worst, if he fails, at least fails while daring greatly, so that his place shall never be with those cold and timid souls who neither know victory nor defeat.*

Those who dare, earn the right to win.

References

Introduction

1. Australian Building and Construction Commission (ABCC) n.d., *Overview*, Australian Government, viewed 6/4/2022, https://www.abcc.gov.au/about/who-we-are/overview.
2. Mates in Construction n.d., *Why Mates exists: The problem*, viewed 6/4/2022 https://mates.org.au/the-problem.
3. Infrastructure Australia 2021, *Infrastructure market capacity*, Australian Government, viewed 6/4/2022, https://www.infrastructureaustralia.gov.au/sites/default/files/2022-02/Infrastructure%20Market%20Capacity%20report%2020220201.pdf.
4. Grattan Institute 2021, *Towards net zero: Practical policies to reduce transport emissions*, viewed 6/4/2022, https://grattan.edu.au/wp-content/uploads/2021/04/Towards-net-zero-Practical-policies-to-reduce-transport-emissions-Grattan-Report.pdf.
5. Macquarie Dictionary n.d., *Context, Macquarie Dictionary*, viewed 6/4/2022 https://www.macquariedictionary.com.au/features/word/search/?search_word_type=Dictionary&word=context&fuzzy=on.

Part 1

1. Australian Constructors Association & BIS Oxford Economics 2020, *Sustaining the infrastructure industry: Challenges, solutions and case studies,* Australian Constructors Association, viewed 9/4/2022, https://www.constructors.com.au/wp-content/uploads/2020/09/ACA-IA-Response-Final-Version.pdf.
2. The New Daily 2018, *Major transport infrastructure projects – Australia [map],* The New Daily, viewed 16/4/2022, https://thenewdaily.com.au/wp-content/uploads/2018/10/15391 52595-major-transport-projects-macromonitor.png.
3. Infrastructure Partnerships Australia n.d., *Chart centre: Pipeline forecast by expenditure,* Infrastructure Partnerships Australia, viewed 16/4/2022, https://infrastructure.org.au/chart-centre/.
4. As an example refer to: Centre for International Economics (Australia) 2006, *Building wealth through infrastructure setting priorities and valuing gains in New South Wales,* Centre for International Economics, viewed 9/4/2022, https://www.vgls.vic.gov.au/client/en_AU/VGLS-public/search/detailnonmodal/ent:$002f$002fSD_ILS$002f0$002fSD_ILS:311601/ada?qu=Property+investments.&d=ent%3A%2F%2FSD_ILS%2F0%2FSD_ILS%3A311601%7EILS%7E37&ic=true&ps=300&h=8.
5. Terrill, M., Emslie, O., Moran, G. 2020, *The rise of megaprojects: Counting the costs,* Grattan Institute, viewed 9/4/2022, https://grattan.edu.au/report/the-rise-of-megaprojects-counting-the-costs/.

Chapter 1

1. Department of Agriculture, Water and the Environment n.d., *Outback Australia – the rangelands,* Australian Government, viewed 8/4/2022, https://www.awe.gov.au/agriculture-land/land/rangelands#:~:text=Australia%20is%20the%20driest%20inhabited,average%20rainfall%20between%20250%2D350mm.

2. World Population Review 2022, *Australia Population Density Map 2022*, World Population Review, viewed 9/4/2022, https://worldpopulationreview.com/countries/australia-population.

3. Australian Bureau of Statistics 2019, *Historical population 2016*, ABS, viewed 18/4/2019, https://www.abs.gov.au/statistics/people/population/historical-population/latest-release.

4. Australian Bureau of Statistics 2014, *Talkin' 'bout our generation: Where are Australia's baby boomers, generation X & Y and igeneration?* ABS, viewed 9/4/2022, https://www.abs.gov.au/ausstats/abs@.nsf/products/630A9E938550C1C8CA257EA4001C1D1C?OpenDocument.

5. National Museum Australia 2022, *Postwar immigration drive*, National Museum Australia, viewed 9/4/2022, https://www.nma.gov.au/defining-moments/resources/postwar-immigration-drive.

6. Based on the cost of a 1953 Holden FJ in Stahl, M. 2017, Retro: 1953 Holden FJ – Fundamental as anything, *Wheels*, 6 November 2017, viewed 9/4/2022, https://www.whichcar.com.au/features/classic-wheels/retro-1953-holden-fj.

7. Roe, I. 2018, Brisbane trams: *Why we no longer take them to work, and where to go for a ride today*, ABC News, 21 March, viewed 9/4/2022, https://www.abc.net.au/news/2018-03-21/brisbanes-trams-what-happened-to-them-curious-brisbane/9555274; Ticher, M. 2019, Erased from history: how Sydney destroyed its trams for love of the car, *The Guardian*, 28 July, viewed 5/5/2021, https://www.theguardian.com/australia-news/2019/jul/28/erased-from-history-how-sydney-destroyed-its-trams-for-love-of-the-car.

8. Melbourne Transportation Freeway Network Image, viewed 9/4/2022, http://3.bp.blogspot.com/_AfZBOmqon4I/Sj4m7Pwys6I/AAAAAAAAG9U/ZdtJyNOEHNU/s1600-h/0604-freeway plan-large.jpg.

9. Wikipedia n.d., *Sydney Orbital Network*, Wikipedia, viewed 9/4/2022, https://en.wikipedia.org/wiki/Sydney_Orbital_Network.

10. Dictionary of Sydney 2008, *County of Cumberland Planning Scheme*, Dictionary of Sydney, viewed 9/4/2022, https:// dictionaryofsydney.org/entry/county_of_cumberland_ planning_scheme.

11. Krosch, A. 2011, *Part 2 – History of Brisbane's major arterial roads*, Queensland Roads, viewed 9/4/2022, https://documents .parliament.qld.gov.au/tableoffice/tabledpapers/2011/ 5311t5272.pdf.

12. Stephenson, G., Hepburn, J.A. 1955, *Plan for the metropolitan region Perth and Fremantle Western Australia*, National Library Australia, viewed 9/4/2022, https://nla.gov.au/nla.obj-745050840/view?sectionId=nla.obj-745860121&partId=nla. obj-745052780#page/n11/mode/1up.

13. For example: AECOM 2011, *High speed rail study – Phase 1*, Department of Infrastructure and Transport, viewed 9/4/2022, https://www.infrastructure.gov.au/sites/default/files/migrated/ rail/publications/high-speed-rail-study-reports/files/HSR_ Phase1_Report_Executive_summary.pdf; and Williams, P. 1998, *Australian very fast trains – A chronology*, Background Paper 16, Parliament of Australia, viewed 9/4/2022, https://www .aph.gov.au/About_Parliament/Parliamentary_Departments/ Parliamentary_Library/Publications_Archive/Background_ Papers/bp9798/98bp16.

14. Hewett, J. 2022, The little known revolution taking place in Australian freight, *Financial Review*, 8 April, viewed 8/4/2022, https://www.afr.com/companies/infrastructure/revolution-in-freight-finally-on-track-20220407-p5abnhce=2022-04-08-06-00-AEST&jobid=29376844.

15. Wood, T., Reeve, A., Ha, J. 2021, *Towards net zero: Practical policies to reduce transport emissions*, Grattan Institute, viewed 9/4/2022, https://grattan.edu.au/report/towards-net-zero-practical-policies-to-reduce-transport-emissions/.

16. Climate Policy Watcher, 2022, *Stringent Vehicle Emissions Standards*, Climate Policy Watcher, viewed 2/7/2022, https:// www.climate-policy-watcher.org/power-generation/stringent-vehicle-emissions-standards.html.

17. Bureau of Meteorology 2015, *Recent rainfall, drought and southern Australia's long-term rainfall decline*, Australian Government, viewed 9/4/2022, http://www.bom.gov.au/climate/updates/articles/a010-southern-rainfall-decline.shtml.

18. Ho, K. 2020, Desalination plant to reach full capacity amidst critical works, *Utility*, 21 July, viewed 9/4/2022, https://utilitymagazine.com.au/desalination-plant-to-reach-full-capacity-amidst-critical-works/.

19. Melbourne Water 2021, *History of sewerage*, Melbourne Water, viewed 9/4/2022, https://www.melbournewater.com.au/water-data-and-education/water-facts-and-history/history-and-heritage/history-sewerage.

20. Sydney Water n.d., *Upper South Creek Advanced Water Recycling Centre*, Sydney Water, viewed 9/4/2022, https://www.sydneywatertalk.com.au/uppersouthcreek.

21. Hurlimann, A., Dolnicar, S. 2010, *When public opposition defeats alternative water projects – The case of Toowoomba Australia*, University of Wollongong, viewed 9/4/2022, https://ro.uow.edu.au/cgi/viewcontent.cgi?article=1752&context=commpapers.

22. WaterWorld 2019, *Construction completed on Australia's largest recycled water project*, WaterWorld, viewed 9/4/2022, https://www.waterworld.com/international/article/16216644/construction-completed-on-australias-largest-recycled-water-project; Caldwell, F. 2021, Get them drinking is the thinking as recycled water scheme stalls, *Brisbane Times*, 23 August, viewed 9/4/2022, https://www.brisbanetimes.com.au/politics/queensland/get-them-drinking-is-the-thinking-as-recycled-water-scheme-stalls-20210818-p58jtk.html.

23. Government of Western Australia Department of Health 2020, *Water Corporation groundwater replenishment scheme*, viewed 9/4/2022, https://ww2.health.wa.gov.au/Articles/F_I/Groundwater-replenishment-scheme Viewed 9/4/2022.

24. Australian Energy Market Commission n.d. *National electricity market*, AEMC, viewed 9/4/2022, https://www.aemc.gov.au/ energy-system/electricity/electricity-system/NEM.

25. Wilkinson, M. 2021, *The carbon club: How a network of influential climate sceptics, politicians and business leaders fought to control Australia's climate policy*, Allen & Unwin.

26. Taylor, A. 2021, *Joint Press Release, The Hon Angus Taylor MP 'Australia's plan to reach our net zero target by 2050'*, viewed 9/4/ 2022, https://www.minister.industry.gov.au/ministers/taylor/ media-releases/australias-plan-reach-our-net-zero-target-2050.

27. Energy Networks Australia 2022, *Transmission the backbone of our energy grid*, Energy Networks Australia, viewed 9/4/2022, https://www.energynetworks.com.au/news/energy- insider/2022-energy-insider/transmission-the-backbone- of-our-energy-grid/; Comley, B. 2022, Net zero electricity sector will be five times bigger than today, *Financial Review*, 26 January 2022, viewed 26/1/2022, https://www.afr.com/ policy/energy-and-climate/net-zero-electricity-sector-will-be- five-times-bigger-than-today-20220126-p59ra3.

28. Elkington, P.A. 1987, The Roma to Brisbane pipeline – meeting an expanding market, *The APPEA Journal*, vol. 27, no. 1, pp. 331-4.

29. Government of Western Australia, 2022, *Dampier to Bunbury pipeline*, viewed 2/6/2022, https://www.wa.gov. au/government/document-collections/dampier-bunbury- pipeline#:~:text=The%20Dampier%20to%20Bunbury%20 Natural,and%20homes%20within%20Western%20Australia.

30. APGA, 2022, *Goldfields Gas Pipeline*, viewed 2/6/2022, https:// www.apga.org.au/goldfields-gas-pipeline

31. AMEC, 2022, *WA: Pilbara Pipeline System*, viewed 2/6/2022, https://www.aemc.gov.au/energy-rules/national-gas-rules/ gas-scheme-register/wa-pilbara-pipeline-system

32. Langenbrunner , B., Joly, J., Aitken, G. 2011, *Pipe dreams: Stranded assets and magical thinking in the proposed global gas pipeline buildout*, Global Energy Monitor, viewed 9/4/2022,

https://globalenergymonitor.org/wp-content/uploads/2022/02/
GEM_GasPipelineReport2022_r7.pdf.

33. Tabuchi, H. 2021, For many, hydrogen is the fuel of the future.
New research raises doubts, *New York Times*, 12 August,
viewed 9/4/2022, https://www.nytimes.com/2021/08/12/
climate/hydrogen-fuel-natural-gas-pollution.html.

Chapter 2

1. Berman, J., Pfleeger, J. 1997, Cyclical sensitivity: Which
industries are sensitive to business cycles? *Monthly Labor
Review*, February, viewed 10/4/2022, https://www.bls.gov/
mlr/1997/02/art2full.pdf.

2. Robertson, H. 2021, Ray Dalio's Bridgewater lost $12.1 billion in
2020 – But he's still the best-performing hedge fund manager of
all time, *Business Insider*, 25 January, viewed 10/4/2022, https://
markets.businessinsider.com/news/stocks/ray-dalio-bridge
water-hedge-fund-lost-12-billion-2020-2021-1-1029998262.

3. Hargreaves, R. 2019, *Graham's weighing machine and time
arbitrage*, GuruFocus, 7 March, viewed 10/4/2022, https://www
.gurufocus.com/news/829158/grahams-weighing-machine-
and-time-arbitrage- Viewed 10/4/22; Buffett, W.E. 1989, *To
the shareholders of Berkshire Hathaway Inc.*, Berkshire Hathaway
Inc., viewed 10/4/2022, https://www.berkshirehathaway.com/
letters/1987.html.

4. For further details: Caplinger, D. 2022, *What is a stock market
index? The Motely Fool*, viewed 10/4/2022, https://www.fool.
com/investing/stock-market/indexes/.

5. Westpac, n.d., *Australian Economic Reports: Westpac-Melbourne
Institute Index of Consumer Sentiment*, Westpac, viewed
4/5/2022, https://www.westpac.com.au/about-westpac/media/
reports/australian-economic-reports/.

6. Google Finance, n.d., *XJO index: S&P/ASX 2000*, Viewed
4/5/2022, https://www.google.com/finance/quote/XJO:INDEX
ASX?sa=X&ved=2ahUKEwiOydChisT3AhXZxTgGHX8WCWcQ3
ecFegQIJxAY&window=MAX.

7. World Bank n.d., *GDP Australia (image)*, World Bank, viewed 10/4/2022, https://data.worldbank.org/indicator/NY.GDP.MK TP.CD.
8. Bourse Communications 2020, *The investment clock, Bourse Communications*, viewed 10/4/2022, https://boursecommunica tions.com.au/the-investment-clock/.

Chapter 3

1. Georgiou n.d., *About us*, viewed 11/4/2022, https://www .georgiou.com.au/about-us/.
2. IBISWorld 2021, *Contract mining services in Australia – Market size 2007–2028*, viewed 14/4/2022, https://www.ibisworld.com/ au/market-size/contract-mining-services/.
3. Delisted Australia n.d., *Delisted Australia*, viewed 10/4/2022, https://www.delisted.com.au/company/costain-australia-limited/.
4. Wiggins, J. 2019, 'We're not about growth': Balfour Beatty shuns risky bids *Financial Review*, 2 October, viewed 10/4/2022, https://www.afr.com/companies/infrastructure/ we-re-not-about-growth-balfour-beatty-shuns-risky-bids-20191001-p52whc.
5. Australia Business Directory n.d., *Citra Constructions*, viewed 10/4/2022, https://www.aus61business.com/company/ Citra-Constructions-Ltd.
6. Vinci Construction n.d., *Our history*, Vinci Construction, viewed 10/4/2022, https://www.vinci-construction-projets.com/en/the-company/our-history/.
7. Bouygues n.d., *Discover the history of the Bouygues Group*, viewed 10/4/2022, http://www.bouygues.com/upload/pdf/discover historybouygues%20group.pdf; Roads and Infrastructure 2018, *Bouygues Construction announces Australian acquisition*, Roads Online, 6 June 2018, viewed 10/4/2022, https:// roadsonline.com.au/bouygues-construction-announces-australian-acquisition/.

8. Transfield n.d., *The Melbourne CityLink*, viewed 11/4/2022, http://www.transfield.com.au/THfirst60years/16-the-melbourne-citylink; Cranston, M. 2016, Japan's Obayashi to help Built take on the big players, *Australian Financial Review*, 16 November, viewed 10/4/2022, https://www.afr.com/property/japans-obayashi-to-help-built-take-on-the-big-players-20161115-gspyk1; Allen, L. 1997, Kumagai Gumi to rebuild in Australia, *Australian Financial Review*, 22 October 1997, viewed 11/4/2022, https://www.afr.com/property/kumagai-gumi-to-rebuild-in-australia-19971022-k7phr.

9. Australian Government Department of Infrastructure, Transport, Regional Development and Communications 2020, *WestConnex*, Australian Government, viewed 10/4/2022, https://investment.infrastructure.gov.au/projects/ProjectDetails.aspx?Project_id=048726-12NSW-NP.

10. Tyndall, F., Skulley, M. 2005, Construction collapse hits major projects *Australian Financial Review*, 3 February, viewed 11/4/2022, https://www.afr.com/politics/construction-collapse-hits-major-projects-20050203-jldfz.

11. Zublin Strabag n.d., *Australia and New Zealand*, viewed 11/4/2022, https://www.strabag.com.au/databases/internet/_public/content30.nsf/web30?Openagent&id=EN_STRABAGAUSTRALIA_COM_australia.html&men1=2&sid=260.

12. Evans, R. 2003, Forging Australians a place in a hard-rock industry, *Sydney Morning Herald*, 5 June, viewed 11/4/2022, https://www.smh.com.au/national/forging-australians-a-place-in-a-hard-rock-industry-20030605-gdgvmd.html.

13. Road Traffic Technology 2014, *Australia selects contractor for WestConnex project*, Road Traffic Technology, viewed 11/4/2022, https://www.roadtraffic-technology.com/news/newsaustralia-selects-contractor-for-westconnex-project-4462334/.

14. NSW Government 2022, *Sydney Metro West tunnelling contract awarded*, 1 March, viewed 11/4/2022, https://www.nsw.gov.au/media-releases/sydney-metro-west-contract.

15. OHLA Group 2017, *OHL completes a section of its second project on the Pacific Highway, one of Australia's most important highways*, 7 November, viewed 11/4/2022, https://ohla-group.com/en/ohl-completes-a-section-of-its-second-project-on-the-pacific-highway-one-of-the-australias-most-important-highways/.

16. Wiggins, J. 2020, CIMIC tests regulators with Broadspectrum deal, *Financial Review*, 8 January, Viewed 11/4/2022, https://www.afr.com/companies/infrastructure/cimic-tests-regulators-with-broadspectrum-deal-20200106-p53p8z.

17. Carballo-Cruz, F. 2011, *Causes and consequences of the Spanish Economic Crisis: Why the recovery is taken so long?*, University of Minho, viewed 11/4/2022, https://www.researchgate.net/publication/227639627_Causes_and_Consequences_of_the_Spanish_Economic_Crisis_Why_the_Recovery_is_Taken_so_Long.

18. European Stability Mechanism n.d., *Spain*, viewed 11/4/2022, https://www.esm.europa.eu/assistance/spain.

19. Ferguson, A. 2014, How Leighton was lost, *Sydney Morning Herald,* 15 March, viewed 11/4/2022, https://www.smh.com.au/business/how-leighton-was-lost-20140314-34sdv.html#:~:text=Leighton's%20share%20price%20lost%20more,string%20of%20experienced%20senior%20managers.

20. Acciona n.d., *Projects*, Acciona, viewed 11/4/2022, https://www.acciona.com.au/projects/?_adin=02021864894.

21. Wiggins, J. 2017, Spain's Acciona doubles Australian business with Geotech acquisition, *Financial Review*, 9 March, viewed 11/4/2022, https://www.afr.com/companies/infrastructure/spains-acciona-doubles-australian-business-with-geotech-acquisition-20170309-guu2as.

22. Wiggins, J. 2019, Lendlease stuck with losers after engineering sale to Acciona, *Financial Review*, 19 December, viewed 11/4/2022, https://www.afr.com/companies/infrastructure/acciona-builds-in-oz-with-180m-lendlease-buy-20191219-p53lfx.

23. John Holland 2022, *John Holland acquisition finalised*, John Holland, viewed 11/4/2022, https://www.johnholland.com.au/who-we-are/latest-news/john-holland-acquisition-finalised/.

24. Rogers, D. 2020, John Holland announces job cuts and restructuring after $40m loss, *Global Construction Review*, 15 June, viewed 11/4/22, https://www.globalconstructionreview.com/john-holland-announces-job-cuts-and-restructuring/.

25. Market Screener 2013, *Impregilo SpA : Deed of merger by incorporation of Salini S.P.A. into Impregilo S.P.A. The name of the new company will be "Salini Impregilo S.P.A."*, Market Screener, 26 November, viewed 11/4/2022, https://www.marketscreener.com/quote/stock/WEBUILD-S-P-A-160071/news/Impregilo-SpA-Deed-of-merger-by-incorporation-of-Salini-S-P-A-into-Impregilo-S-P-A-The-name-of-t-17531635/.

26. Webuild n.d., *Progetto Italia: an operation that will consolidate Italy's construction sector*, Webuild, viewed 11/4/2022, https://www.webuildgroup.com/en/investor-relations/strategy/progetto-italia.

27. Webuild 2021, *Webuild Consortium selected as preferred bidder for North East Link project in Melbourne*, WeBuild, 25 June, viewed 11/4/2022, https://www.webuildgroup.com/en/media/press-releases/webuild-consortium-selected-as-preferred-bidder-for-north-east-link-project-in-melbourne.

28. NSW 10-year civil infrastructure forecast reports, 2020, 2021, 2022, *Civil Contractors Association & BIS Oxford Economics*, Civil Contractors Federation NSW.

29. Infrastructure Australia n.d., *Infrastructure pipeline by project status*, Infrastructure Australia, viewed 12/4/2022, https://infrastructurepipeline.org/charts/status-location.

30. McBride, J., Siripurapu, A. 2021, *The state of US infrastructure*, Council on Foreign Relations, 8 November, viewed 11/4/2022, https://www.cfr.org/backgrounder/state-us-infrastructure.

31. Vartabedian, R. 2022, Costs of California's troubled bullet train rise again, by an estimated $5 billion, *Los Angeles Times*, 8 February, Viewed 11/4/2022, https://www.latimes.com/

california/story/2022-02-08/california-bullet-train-costs-rise-roughly-5-billion.

32. Jones, S. 2020, Socialists and Podemos to rule together in Spanish coalition, *The Guardian*, 8 January, viewed 11/4/2022, https://www.theguardian.com/world/2020/jan/07/pedro-sanchez-spain-pm-government-vote-parliament.

33. Hakiman, R. 2021, Integrated rail plan 'worrying' cuts for Northern Powerhouse Rail', *New Civil Engineer*, 18 November, viewed 11/4/2022, https://www.newcivilengineer.com/latest/integrated-rail-plan-worrying-cuts-for-northern-powerhouse-rail-18-11-2021/.

34. Yusof, A. 2022, *Work on JB-Singapore RTS Link almost 10% completed, says Malaysia's transport minister*, Channel News Asia, 14 March, viewed 11/4/2022, https://www.channelnewsasia.com/asia/work-jb-singapore-rts-link-almost-10-completed-says-malaysias-transport-minister-2563321.

35. Foxman, S. 2021, Qatar sees $20 billion bump to economy from Soccer World Cup, *Bloomberg*, 18 June, viewed 11/4/2022, https://www.bloombergquint.com/global-economics/qatar-sees-20-billion-bump-to-economy-from-soccer-world-cup.

36. Porter, M.E. 1979, How competitive forces shape strategy, *Harvard Business Review*, March–April, viewed 11/4/2022, https://www.hbs.edu/faculty/Pages/item.aspx?num=10692.

37. Australian Constructors Association & BIS Oxford Economics 2020, *Sustaining the infrastructure industry: Challenges, solutions and case studies*, Australian Constructors Association, viewed 9/4/2022, https://www.constructors.com.au/wp-content/uploads/2020/09/ACA-IA-Response-Final-Version.pdf.

38. Terrill, M., Emslie, O., Fox, L. 2021, *Megabang for megabucks: Driving a harder bargain on megaprojects*, Grattan Institute, viewed 12/4/2022, https://grattan.edu.au/report/megabang-for-megabucks/.

39. NSW Government Department of Premier & Cabinet 2021, *M2021-10 Procurement for large, complex infrastructure projects*, viewed 12/4/2022, https://arp.nsw.gov.au/m2021-10-procurement-for-large-complex-infrastructure-projects/.

40. Infrastructure NSW 2021, *Framework for establishing effective project procurement for the NSW Infrastructure Program*, viewed 12/4/2022, https://www.infrastructure.nsw.gov.au/media/2944/procurement-framework_3-june-21_final.pdf.

41. Gameng, M. 2020, *Preferred builder announced for $852m Bunbury Outer Ring Road WA*, Felix Vendor Marketplace, viewed 12/4/2022, https://www.felix.net/project-news/preferred-builder-announced-for-852m-bunbury-outer-ring-road-wa.

42. Bulmer, M. n.d., *Pacific Highway upgrade Woolgoolga to Ballina Project*, Infrastructure Australia, viewed 12/4/2022, https://www.constructors.com.au/wp-content/uploads/2020/11/ACA-IA-Response-Pacific-Highway-W2B.pdf.

43. The Star, Gamuda Australia and Laing O'Rourke Consortium awarded major Sydney Metro Tunnelling package, *The Star*, 1 March, viewed 14/4/2022, https://www.thestar.com.my/business/business-news/2022/03/01/gamuda-australia-and-laing-orourke-consortium-awarded-major-sydney-metro-tunnelling-package.

44. Australia New Zealand Infrastructure Pipeline n.d., *Suburban Rail Loop*, Australia New Zealand Infrastructure Pipeline, viewed 12/4/2022, https://infrastructurepipeline.org/project/suburban-rail-loop.

45. Wikipedia n.d., *Comeng (train)*, viewed 12/4/2022, https://en.wikipedia.org/wiki/Comeng_(train).

46. Wikipedia n.d., *UGL Rail*, viewed 12/4/2022, https://en.wikipedia.org/wiki/UGL_Rail

47. Wikipedia n.d., *Clyde Engineering*, viewed 12/4/2022, https://en.wikipedia.org/wiki/Clyde_Engineering.

48. Reliance Rail n.d., *The journey*, viewed 13/4/2022, https://www.reliancerail.com.au/project-timeline; Smith, K. 2012, NSW Government bails out Reliance Rail PPP, *International Rail Journal*, 24 February, viewed 13/4/2022, https://www.railjournal.com/in_depth/nsw-government-bails-out-reliance-rail-ppp/.

49. Hamid, T. 2021, *Downer rolls out the last of the Waratah Series 2 passenger trains*, Roads & Infrastructure, 8 July, viewed 13/4/

2022, https://roadsonline.com.au/downer-rolls-out-the-last-of-the-waratah-series-2-passenger-trains/

50. Railway Technology 2019, Hyundai Rotem delivers first batch of electric trains to Australia, *Railway Technology*, 3 December, Viewed 13/4/2022, https://www.railway-technology.com/news/hyundai-rotem-electric-trains-australia/.

51. Victoria Department of Transport n.d., *High Capacity Metro Trains Project*, viewed 13/4/2022, https://transport.vic.gov.au/our-transport-future/our-projects/high-capacity-metro-trains

52. Metronet n.d., *WA Railcar Program*, Metronet, Viewed 13/4/2022, https://www.metronet.wa.gov.au/projects/wa-railcar-program

Chapter 4

1. Puentes, R. 2015, *Why infrastructure matters: Rotten roads, bum economy*, Brookings 20 January, viewed 15/4/2022, https://www.brookings.edu/opinions/why-infrastructure-matters-rotten-roads-bum-economy/.

2. Kent, C. 2016, *After the boom, Speech by Christopher Kent*, Reserve Bank of Australia, 13 September, viewed 16/6/2022, https://www.rba.gov.au/speeches/2016/sp-ag-2016-09-13.html.

3. The New Daily 2018, *Major transport infrastructure projects – Australia [map]*, The New Daily, viewed 16/6/2022, https://thenewdaily.com.au/wp-content/uploads/2018/10/1539152595-major-transport-projects-macromonitor.png.

4. Infrastructure Partnerships Australia n.d., *Chart centre: Pipeline forecast by expenditure*, Infrastructure Partnerships Australia, viewed 16/4/2022, https://infrastructure.org.au/chart-centre/.

5. Infrastructure Australia 2021, *Infrastructure market capacity report*, Infrastructure Australia October, viewed 16/4/2022, https://www.infrastructureaustralia.gov.au/sites/default/files/2022-02/Infrastructure%20Market%20Capacity%20report%2020220201.pdf; Wiggins, J., Thomson, J. 2019, Cracks appear in infrastructure boom, *Financial Review*, 14 June, viewed 16/4/2022, https://www.afr.com/companies/

infrastructure/cracks-appear-in-infrastructure-boom-2019
0614-p51xpg.

6. WA.gov.au 2020, *WA recovery: Developing Industry*, WA.gov.au,
    viewed 16/4/2022, https://www.wa.gov.au/government/covid-
    19-coronavirus/wa-recovery-developing-industry.

7. Queensland Reconstruction Authority n.d., *Homepage*,
    Queensland Government, viewed 16/4/2022, https://www.qra
    .qld.gov.au/.

8. Infrastructure New South Wales n.d., *Restart NSW*, Infra-
    structure NSW, viewed 16/4/2022, https://www.infrastructure
    .nsw.gov.au/restart-nsw/.

9. Nangia, I., Brinded, T., Tilahun, L., Trueman, P., Watson, B., Joseph,
    S., Sahulhameed, R. 2019, *Australia's infrastructure innovation
    imperative*, McKinsey & Company, viewed 16/4/2022, https://www
    .mckinsey.com/~/media/mckinsey/featured%20insights/asia%20
    pacific/australias%20infrastructure%20innovation%20imperative/
    australias-infrastructure-innovation-imperative-final.pdf.

10. Saville, M. 2021, *'When it's a byelection you're only focusing on that
    seat': Berejiklian tells ICAC funding projects for political reasons was
    not unusual*, Crikey 1 November, viewed 15/4/2022, https://
    www.crikey.com.au/2021/11/01/berejiklian-tells-icac-political-
    funding-not-unusual/; refers to ICAC Operation Keppel
    transcript 01-11-2021 p.72.

11. Australian Government Department of Infrastructure,
    Transport, Regional Development and Communications 2014,
    Information Sheet 55: Infrastructure, transport and productivity,
    2 July, viewed 16/4/2022, https://www.bitre.gov.au/sites/
    default/files/is_055.pdf.

12. Adapted from Dalio, R. 2013, *How the economic machine works*,
    YouTube, 23 September , viewed 4/5/2022.

13. NSW Government n.d., *Productivity Commission green paper:
    Continuing the productivity conversation*, viewed 16/4/2022,
    https://www.productivity.nsw.gov.au/sites/default/files/2020-
    08/Productivity_Commission_Green%20Paper_FINAL.pdf.

14. Gruen, D. 2012, *The importance of productivity, Productivity Commission-Australia Bureau of Statistics Productivity Perspectives Conference*, viewed 16/4/2022, https://www.pc.gov.au/research/supporting/productivity-perspectives-2012/01-productivity-perspectives-2012-gruen.pdf.

15. Aust Govt Department of Infrastructure and Regional Development n.d., *Infrastructure, transport and productivity*, Australian Government, viewed 4/5/2022, https://www.bitre.gov.au/sites/default/files/is_055.pdf.

16. Australian Bureau of Statistics 2021, *Estimates of industry multifactor productivity*, ABS, viewed 4/5/2022, https://www.abs.gov.au/statistics/industry/industry-overview/estimates-industry-multifactor-productivity/latest-release.

17. Aust Govt Department of Infrastructure and Regional Development n.d., *Infrastructure, transport and productivity*, Australian Government, viewed 4/5/2022, https://www.bitre.gov.au/sites/default/files/is_055.pdf.

18. Australian Government investments in rail and road, 1988–89 to 2012–13 "Infrastructure, Transport and Productivity" Aust Govt Department of Infrastructure and Regional Development Information Sheet 55 https://www.bitre.gov.au/sites/default/files/is_055.pdf Viewed 4/5/2022

19. Generated via CEIC, *Australia private new capital expenditure: Actual: Transport, postal & warehousing*, CEIC, viewed 16/4/2022, https://www.ceicdata.com/en/australia/private-new-capital-expenditure-actual/private-new-capital-expenditure-actual-transport-postal-warehousing.

20. Reserve Bank of Australia 2021, *Statement on monetary policy May 2021, Graph C1: Resident population growth*, viewed 16/4/2022, https://www.rba.gov.au/publications/smp/2021/may/box-c-international-border-closures-slower-population-growth-and-the-australian-economy.html.

21. Terrill, M., Emslie, O., Moran, G. 2020, *The rise of megaprojects: Counting the costs, Grattan Institute*, viewed 9/4/2022, https://grattan.edu.au/report/the-rise-of-megaprojects-counting-the-costs/.

22. Transport for NSW n.d., *Easing Sydney's Congestion Program Office, Transport for NSW*, viewed 16/4/2022, https://roads-waterways .transport.nsw.gov.au/projects/easing-sydneys-congestion/ index.html

23. Victorian Government Level Crossing Removal Project 2022, *Featured information*, viewed 16/4/2022, https://levelcrossings .vic.gov.au/.

24. Australian Government Department of Infrastructure, Transport, Regional Development & Communications 2022, *Urban Congestion Fund Queensland*, viewed 16/4/2022, https:// investment.infrastructure.gov.au/about/national-initiatives/ urban-congestion-fund.aspx#qld.

25. Gittins, R. 2014, How the econocrats can lift their game, *Sydney Morning Herald*, 31 August, viewed 16/4/2022, https://www .smh.com.au/business/how-the-econocrats-can-lift-their-game-20140830-10ad5c.html.

26. NSW Government n.d., *SCATS*, NSW Government, viewed 16/4/2022, https://www.scats.nsw.gov.au/.

27. NSW Government 2021, *A 20-year economic vision for regional NSW, February*, NSW Government, viewed 16/4/2022, https:// www.nsw.gov.au/sites/default/files/2021-02/20%20Year%20 Vision%20for%20RNSW_0.pdf.

28. NSW Government Department of Industry 2020, *Making it happen in the regions: Regional Development Framework*, NSW Government, viewed 16/4/2022, https://www.nsw.gov.au/sites/ default/files/2020-11/making-it-happen-in-the-regions-regional-development-framework.pdf

29. Vue, T. 2019, Committee 4 Wagga seminar to give residents chance to work on 20-year vision for city, *The Daily Advertiser*, 21 June, viewed 16/4/2022, https://www.dailyadvertiser.com .au/story/6234269/seminar-to-give-residents-chance-to-work-on-20-year-vision-for-city/

30. Howe, N. 2016, Millennials are so happy (living and working) together, *Forbes*, 14 July, viewed 16/4/2022, https://www.forbes .com/sites/neilhowe/2016/07/14/millennials-are-so-happy-living-and-working-together/?sh=72e942df4fb4.

31. Brotherhood of St Lawrence 2019, *Smashing the avocado debate: Australia's youth unemployment hotspots*, Brotherhood of St Lawrence, viewed 16/4/2022, https://library.bsl.org.au/bsljspui/bitstream/1/11134/2/BSL_Smashing_the_avocado_debate_youth_unemployment_hotspots_Mar2019.pdf.

32. Australian Government National Water Grid Authority n.d., National Water Grid Authority, Australian Government, viewed 16/4/2022, https://www.nationalwatergrid.gov.au/.

33. Infrastructure Partnerships Australia n.d., *Pipeline forecast by expenditure*, Infrastructure Partnerships Australia, viewed 4/5/2022, https://infrastructure.org.au/chart-centre/.

Chapter 5

1. Yates, A. 2012, Government as an informed buyer: *How the public sector can most effectively procure engineering-intensive products and services*, Engineers Australia, viewed 18/4/2022, https://www.engineersaustralia.org.au/sites/default/files/resources/Public%20Affairs/2018/Government%20as%20an%20informed%20buyer%2C%202012.pdf.

2. Donaldson, D. 2017, Contracts and convicts: how perverse incentives created the death fleet, *The Mandarin*, 16 January, viewed 18/4/2022, https://www.themandarin.com.au/73989-contracts-and-convicts-how-perverse-incentives-created-the-death-fleet/.

3. Sturgess, G. 2015, Queensland must accept state ownership as history, *Financial Review*, 4 February, viewed 17/4/2022, https://www.afr.com/opinion/queensland-must-accept-state-ownership-as-history-20150204-135k0a.

4. Gittins, R. 2015, Searching for our salvation in privatisation, *Sydney Morning Herald*, 7 February, viewed 18/4/2022, https://www.smh.com.au/business/searching-for-our-salvation-in-privatisation-20150206-137njz.html.

5. Gittins, R. 2015, Take rational measures on electricity privatisation issue, *Sydney Morning Herald*, 28 March, viewed 18/4/2022, https://www.smh.com.au/business/take-rational-

measures-on-electricity-privatisation-issue-20150327-1m
92f3.html.

6. Remembering the past Australia n.d., *NSW Department of Public Works (Phillip Street) Sydney 1859 – 1895*, viewed 18/4/2022, https://remembering-the-past-australia.blogspot.com/2017/04/public-works-office-phillip-st-nsw-1896.html.

7. NSW Government 2021, *Procurement methods guidelines: NSW Construction Leadership Group*, Infrastructure NSW, viewed 18/4/2022, https://www.infrastructure.nsw.gov.au/media/3031/infr9595-procurement-guidelines-final-web-002.pdf.

8. Allen, G. 2001, *The Private Finance Initiative (PFI) Research Paper 01/117*, UK Parliament, 18 December, viewed 18/4/2022, https://researchbriefings.files.parliament.uk/documents/RP01-117/RP01-117.pdf.

9. PwC 2018, *Reimagining public private partnerships*, PwC, viewed 18/4/2022, https://fdocuments.in/document/reimagining-public-private-partnerships-pwc-pwc-reimagining-public-private.html?page=1.

10. O'Sullivan, M. 2018, Sydney's Northconnex toll road delayed by up to six months, *Sydney Morning Herald*, 5 October, viewed 18/4/2022, https://www.smh.com.au/national/nsw/sydney-s-northconnex-toll-road-delayed-by-up-to-six-months-20181005-p507wy.html?ref=rss&utm_medium=rss&utm_source=rss_feed.

11. ABC News 2021, *New West Gate Tunnel deal to cost Victorian taxpayers another $1.9 billion*, ABC, 17 December, viewed 18/4/2022, https://www.abc.net.au/news/2021-12-17/victorian-government-strikes-deal-on-melbourne-west-gate-tunnel/100707864.

12. Australian Constructors Association and Bis Oxford Economics 2020, *Sustaining the infrastructure industry: Challenges, solutions and case studies*, Australian Constructors Association, viewed 18/4/2022, https://www.constructors.com.au/wp-content/uploads/2020/09/ACA-IA-Response-Final-Version.pdf.

13. NSW Government 2001, *Working with government: Guidelines for privately financed projects*, NSW Government, viewed 18/4/2022, https://www.elvetia.org/mnec/Sdit/Docs/wwgguidelines.pdf.

14. NSW Government 2018, *NSW Government action plan: A ten point commitment to the construction sector*, NSW Government, viewed 18/4/2022, https://www.infrastructure.nsw.gov.au/media/1649/10-point-commitment-to-the-construction-industry-final-002.pdf; note, too, the subsequent publication of a *Progress Report: NSW Government 2021, A ten-point commitment to the construction sector*, NSW Government 2021, viewed 18/4/2022, https://www.insw.com/media/3268/progress-report-2021.pdf.

15. Steele, J. 2021, *Report: P3 megaprojects often lose money for contractors*, Construction Dive, 28 September, viewed 18/4/2022, https://www.constructiondive.com/news/report-p3-megaprojects-often-lose-money-for-contractors/606480/

16. Infrastructure NSW 2021, *Framework for establishing effective project procurement*, Infrastructure NSW, 3 June, viewed 18/4/2022, https://www.infrastructure.nsw.gov.au/media/2944/procurement-framework_3-june-21_final.pdf.

Chapter 6

1. Serco, 2021, *Serco continues to help make Melbourne one of the world's most liveable cities*, viewed 4/7/2022, https://www.serco.com/aspac/news/media-releases/2021/serco-continues-to-help-make-melbourne-one-of-the-worlds-most-liveable-cities

2. Chuter, A., 2020, UK government to retake control of its atomic weapons management from industry *Defense News*, viewed 20/4/2022, https://www.defensenews.com/global/europe/2020/11/02/uk-government-to-retake-control-of-its-atomic-weapons-management-from-industry/

3. Railway Technology 2015, *Serco agrees to sell its Great Southern Rail to Australia's Allegro Funds*, Railway Technology, 30 March, viewed 20/4/2022, https://www.railway-technology.com/news/newsserco-agrees-to-sell-its-great-southern-rail-to-australias-allegro-funds-4543939/

4. Cameron, J. 2005, *Franchising Melbourne's train and tram system*, Auditor General Victoria, September, viewed 21/4/2022, https://www.parliament.vic.gov.au/papers/govpub/VPARL2003-06No154.pdf.

5. Moore, T. 2008, Brisbane missed the bus on light rail: Greens, *Brisbane Times*, 13 March, viewed 21/4/2022, https://www.brisbanetimes.com.au/national/queensland/brisbane-missed-the-bus-on-light-rail-greens-20080313-ge9rgm.html; Lynch, L. 'Is it a bus, tram or train?': What is Brisbane Metro and do we need it? *Brisbane Times*, 16 February, viewed 21/4/2022, https://www.brisbanetimes.com.au/national/queensland/is-it-a-bus-tram-or-train-what-is-brisbane-metro-and-do-we-need-it-20190701-p522z8.html.

6. The report of an investigation on the possibility of travelising the Ecchujima freight line – outline October 11, 2000, Koto Ward Urban Service Department.

7. Rail World LLC 2019, *Rail World LLC*, viewed 21/4/2022, http://railworld-inc.com/RailWorldInc.htm.

8. Light Rail Transit Authority n.d., *LRTA history*, viewed 21/4/2022, https://www.lrta.gov.ph/lrta-history/.

9. Satre, G.L. 1998, The Metro Manila LRT System— A historical perspective, *Japan Railway & Transport Review*, viewed 21/4/2022, https://www.ejrcf.or.jp/jrtr/jrtr16/pdf/f33_satre.pdf.

10. Vanzi, S.J. 2000, Erap wants LRT Loop completed before 2004, *Philippine Headline News*, 6 August, viewed 21/4/2022, http://www.newsflash.org/2000/06/tl/tl001161.htm.

11. WikiPilipinas n.d., *Light Rail Transit Line 1 (LRT-1) Cavite Extension*, WikiPilipinas; viewed 21/4/2022, https://en.wikipilipinas.org/view/Light_Rail_Transit_Line_1_(LRT-1)_Cavite_Extension; Wikipedia n.d., *Light Rail Manila Corporation*, Wikipedia, viewed 21/4/2022, https://en.wikipedia.org/wiki/Light_Rail_Manila_Corporation; Light Rail Transit Authority 2012, *Light Rail Transit Line 1 Cavite Extension Project (Baclaran to Cavite)*, viewed 21/4/2022, https://ps-philgeps.gov.ph/home/images/BAC/ForeignAssitedProjects/09272017/6_Part%20

2_d_4.pdf; *LRMC secures P24-B loan for LRT extension*, ABS-CBN News 12 February 2016 https://news.abs-cbn.com/business/ 02/12/16/lrmc-secures-p24-b-loan-for-lrt-extension Viewed 4/5/2022; Barrow, K. 2017, Manila breaks ground on LRT 1 Cavite extension, *International Railway Journal,* 4 May, viewed 21/4/2022, https://www.railjournal.com/regions/asia/manila-breaks-ground-on-lrt-1-cavite-extension/; Metro Pacific Investments n.d., *Light rail*, Metro Pacific Investments, viewed 21/4/2022, https://www.mpic.com.ph/investor-relations/invest ments/light-rail.

12. Wikipedia n.d., *List of typhoons in the Philippines (2000–present)*, viewed 21/4/2022, https://en.wikipedia.org/wiki/List_of_typho ons_in_the_Philippines_(2000%E2%80%93present)#:~:text= The%20storm%20killed%2040%20people,only%20resulted%20 in%2026%20deaths.

13. Wikipedia n.d., *Rizal Day bombings*, viewed 21/4/2022, https:// en.wikipedia.org/wiki/Rizal_Day_bombings.

14. Rankin 2014, Serco shares crash after latest profits warning, *The Guardian*, 10 November 2014, viewed 20/4/2022, https://www .theguardian.com/business/2014/nov/10/serco-profits-warning-shares-crash; Farrell, S. 2015, Serco profit warning sends shares crashing, *The Guardian*, 7 December, viewed 20/4/2022, https:// www.theguardian.com/business/2015/dec/07/serco-profits-warning-sends-shares-crashing.

15. Transport RailCorp 2012, *RailCorp rolling stock public private partnership: Updated summary of contracts*, NSW Parliament, 2 March, viewed 22/4/2022, https://www.parliament.nsw.gov .au/tp/files/32205/Rolling_Stock_PPP_contracts_summary.pdf.

16. Ferguson, A. 2000, Transfield's Blood Feud, *Financial Review*, 8 December, viewed 22/4/2022, https://www.afr.com/ companies/transfields-blood-feud-20001208-kb721.

17. Grain Infrastructure Advisory Committee 2004, *Report on rail/ road options for grain logistics*, Grain Infrastructure Advisory Committee, viewed 22/4/2022, https://catalogue.nla.gov.au/ Record/3357675.

18. NSW Treasury 2008–09, *Mini Budget 2008–09*, NSW Government, viewed 22/4/2022, https://www.treasury.nsw.gov.au/sites/default/files/pdf/2008-2009_Budget_Papers_Mini-Budget.pdf.

19. ICAC 2014, *RailCorp and Department of Family & Community services – allegations of public officials corrupting soliciting funds (Operation Spector)*, ICAC, viewed 23/4/2022, https://www.icac.nsw.gov.au/investigations/past-investigations/2014/railcorp-and-department-of-family-community-services-operation-spector/railcorp-and-department-of-family-community-services-allegations-of-public-officials-corrupting-soliciting-funds-operation-spector.

Chapter 7

1. Macquarie Dictionary n.d., Context, Macquarie Dictionary, https://www.macquariedictionary.com.au/features/word/search/?search_word_type=Dictionary&word=context&fuzzy=on.

2. Radvansky, G.A., Tamplin, A.K., Krawietz, S.A. 2010, Walking through doorways causes forgetting: Environmental integration, Psychonomic Bulletin & Review, vol. 17, iss. 6, pp.900–4.

3. Robinson, O.J., Vytal, K., Cornwell,B.R., Grillon, C. 2013, The impact of anxiety upon cognition: Perspectives from human threat of shock studies, *Frontiers in Human Neuroscience*, vol 7, pp. 203.

4. Sinek, S. 2009, *How great leaders inspire action*, TED, viewed 27/4/2022, https://www.ted.com/talks/simon_sinek_how_great_leaders_inspire_action?language=en.

5. Sinek, S. 2011, *Start With Why: How great leaders inspire everyone to take action*, London, UK, Portfolio.

6. Clear, J. n.d., *The 3 stages of failure in life and work (and how to fix them)*, viewed 27/4/2022, https://jamesclear.com/3-stages-of-failure.

7. Porras, J.I., Collins, J. 1994, *Built to Last: Successful habits of visionary companies*, New York, USA, Harper Business.

8. Lencioni, P.M. 2002, Make your values mean something, *Harvard Business Review*, July, viewed 27/4/2022, https://hbr.org/2002/07/make-your-values-mean-something.

9. Panizza, F., Vostroknutov, A., Coricelli, G. 2021, How conformity can lead to polarised social behaviour, *PLOS Computational Biology*, 20 October 2021, viewed 27/4/2022, https://journals.plos.org/ploscompbiol/article?id=10.1371/journal.pcbi.1009530.

10. Communication Theory n.d., *The Johari Window Model*, Communication Theory, viewed 27/4/2022, https://www.communicationtheory.org/the-johari-window-model/.

11. Dalio, R. 2017, *Principles,* New York, USA, Simon & Schuster.

12. Erhard, W., Jensen, M. and Zaffron, S. 2009. Integrity: A Positive Model that Incorporates the Normative Phenomena of Morality, Ethics and Legality. *SSRN Electronic Journal.*

13. Burnett, D. 2016, *The Idiot Brain*, London, UK, Guardian Faber Publishing.

14. Kahneman, D. 2012, *Thinking, Fast and Slow*, New York, USA, Farrar, Straus and Giroux.

Chapter 8

1. Terrill, M., Emslie, O., Moran, G. 2020, *The rise of megaprojects: Counting the costs,* Grattan Institute, viewed 9/4/2022, https://grattan.edu.au/report/the-rise-of-megaprojects-counting-the-costs/.

2. Thomas, A. 1988, Does Leadership Make a Difference to Organizational Performance?. *Administrative Science Quarterly*, 33(3), p. 388.

3. Lieberson, S. and O'Connor, J. 1972, Leadership and Organizational Performance: A Study of Large Corporations. *American Sociological Review*, 37(2), p. 117.

4. Knies, E., Jacobsen, C. & Tummers, L.G. 2016, Leadership and organizational performance: State of the art and research agenda. In: Storey, J., Denis, J.L., Hartley, J. & 't Hart, P. (Eds.). *Routledge Companion to Leadership* (pp. 404-418). London: Routledge. https://www.researchgate.net/publication/304780869_Leadership_and_organizational_performance_State_of_the_art_and_research_agenda Viewed 2/5/2022

5. McKinsey & Company, 2017, The art of project leadership: Delivering the world's largest projects, viewed 1/5/2022, https://www.mckinsey.com/~/media/mckinsey/business%20functions/operations/our%20insights/the%20art%20of%20project%20leadership%20delivering%20the%20worlds%20largest%20projects/the-art-of-project-leadership.pdf

6. Kahneman, D. 2012, *Thinking, Fast and Slow,* New York, USA, Farrar, Straus and Giroux.

7. Refer to, for example Borgatta, E., Bales, R. and Couch, A. 1969. Some Findings Relevant to the Great Man Theory of Leadership. *Personality and social systems.*, pp. 391–396.

8. Sarah, Neil, 2015, What's in a Name? A brief history of some of Australia's construction Giants, *Construct Magazine,* ed. 3, viewed 2/5/2022, https://www.constructmagazine.com.au/wp-content/uploads/2018/10/Construct_Three_2015_WEB.pdf

9. Ferguson, A. 2000, Transfield's Blood Feud, *Financial Review,* 8 December, viewed 22/4/2022, https://www.afr.com/companies/transfields-blood-feud-20001208-kb721

10. Collins, J. 2001. *Good to great.* London: Random House Business.

11. Barolsky, J. 2019, Avoiding the Bermuda Triangle of law firm management, *Relationship Capital,* viewed 2/5/2022, https://relationshipcapital.com.au/2019/03/02/avoiding-the-bermuda-triangle-of-law-firm-management

12. Thompson, M. 2016, *Enough said,* St Martin's Press.

Part 3

1. Tzu S 2005, *The Art of War*, London, UK, Hodder & Stoughton.

Chapter 9

1. Murray, L., Alagich, R, 2006, *So, You Want to Be a Coach*, Rennicks Publications.
2. Porter, M.E. 1996, What is strategy?, *Harvard Business Review*, December, viewed 28/4/2022, https://www.uniba.it/docenti/somma-ernesto/whatisstrategy_porter_96.pdf.
3. Andrews, K.R. 1971, The concept of corporate strategy, in McKienan, editor, *Historical Evolution of Strategic Management Volumes I and II*, Homewood, IL., Dow Jones-Irwin.
4. Raeburn, A. 2022, *SWOT analysis: What it is and how to use it*, 8 April, viewed 28/4/2022, https://asana.com/resources/swot-analysis.
5. Porter, M. 1980, *Competitive Strategy: Techniques for analyzing industries and competitors*, New York, USA, Free Press.
6. Porter, M.E. 1979, How competitive forces shape strategy, *Harvard Business Review*, April, viewed 28/4/2022, https://hbr.org/1979/03/how-competitive-forces-shape-strategy.
7. Barney, J. 1991, Firm resources and sustained competitive advantage, *Journal of Management*, viewed 28/4/2022, http://lib.cufe.edu.cn/upload_files/other/4_20140522031841_Firm_resources_and_sustained_competitive_advantage.pdf.
8. Collis, D.J., Montgomery, C.A., Competing on resources: Strategy in the 1990s, *Harvard Business Review*, August, viewed 28/4/2022, https://hbr.org/1995/07/competing-on-resources-strategy-in-the-1990s.
9. Von Neumann, J., Moregenstern, O. 1944, *Theory of games and economic behavior*, New Jersey, USA, Princeton University Press.
10. N.d., Nash Equilibrium, *ScienceDirect*, viewed 29/4/2022, https://www.sciencedirect.com/topics/computer-science/nash-equilibrium.
11. Romer, K. 2022, How AI is teaching card sharks new tricks, *Financial Review*, 11 February, viewed 29/4/2022, https://www

.afr.com/life-and-luxury/arts-and-culture/how-ai-is-teaching-card-sharks-new-tricks-20220201-p59st9.

12. Bowling, M., Burch, N., Johanson, M., Tammelin, O. 2017, Heads-up limit hold'em poker is solved, *Communications of the ACM*, November, viewed 29/4/2022, https://poker.cs.ualberta.ca/publications/heads-up_limit_poker_is_solved.acm2017.pdf.

13. Ghemawat , P. 1986, Sustainable advantage, *Harvard Business Review*, September, viewed 29/4/2022, https://hbr.org/1986/09/sustainable-advantage

14. CFI n.d., *Market positioning*, CFI, viewed 29/4/2022, https://corporatefinanceinstitute.com/resources/knowledge/strategy/market-positioning/.

15. Adapted from Shirlaws positioning framework, August 2010.

16. Expert Program Management n.d., *STP marketing model*, EPM, viewed 29/4/2022, https://expertprogrammanagement.com/2019/11/stp-marketing-model/.

Chapter 10

1. Wikipedia n.d., *Batting average (cricket)*, Wikipedia, viewed 28/4/2022, https://en.wikipedia.org/wiki/Batting_average_(cricket).

2. Wikipedia n.d., *Par (score)*, Wikipedia, Viewed 28/4/2022, https://en.wikipedia.org/wiki/Par_(score).

3. Conn, C., McLean, R. 2018, *Bulletproof problem solving*, New Jersey, USA, Wiley.

Part 4

1. The Deming Institute n.d., *PDSA Cycle*, The Deming Institute, viewed 25/4/2022, https://deming.org/explore/pdsa/#:~:text=The%20PDSA%20Cycle%20(Plan%2DDo,was%20first%20introduced%20to%20Dr.

2. Magnier, M. 1999, Rebuilding Japan with the help of 2 Americans, *Los Angeles Times*, 25 October, viewed 25/4/2022, https://www.latimes.com/archives/la-xpm-1999-oct-25-ss-26184-story.html.

Chapter 11

1. Levitt, T. 1975, Marketing myopia, *Harvard Business Review*, viewed 25/4/2022, https://motamem.org/wp-content/uploads/2018/12/Marketing-Myopia-Theodore-Levitt.pdf.
2. Brittanica 2022, *John Stevens biography: American inventor and lawyer*, Brittanica, viewed 25/4/2022, https://www.britannica.com/biography/John-Stevens.
3. Barney, J.B. 1995, Looking inside for competitive advantage, *The Academy of Management Executive*, vol. 9, iss. 4, pp. 49–61.
4. Grant, R.M. 1991, The resource-based theory of competitive advantage: Implications for strategy formulation, *California Management Review*, vol. 33, iss. 3, pp. 114–35.
5. Stringleman, P. 2019, *Here's a new way to balance small improvements with big change*, Create, 1 January, viewed 25/4/2022, https://createdigital.org.au/balance-small-improvements-big-change/.
6. Agile Manifesto 2001, *Manifesto for agile software development*, viewed 25/4/2022, http://agilemanifesto.org/
7. McKinsey & Company 2010, *Building organizational capabilities: McKinsey Global Survey results*, McKinsey & Company, viewed 25/4/2022, https://www.mckinsey.com/business-functions/people-and-organizational-performance/our-insights/building-organizational-capabilities-mckinsey-global-survey-results.
8. Bower, J.L., Christensen, C.M. 1995, Disruptive technologies: Catching the wave, *Harvard Business Review*, February, viewed 25/4/2022, https://hbr.org/1995/01/disruptive-technologies-catching-the-wave.

Chapter 12

1. Grant, A. 2013, In the company of givers and takers, *Harvard Business Review*, April, viewed 26/4/2022, https://hbr.org/2013/04/in-the-company-of-givers-and-takers.

Chapter 13

1. Fellman, D., Ritakallio, L., Waris, O., Jylkkä, J. and Laine, M., 2020. Beginning of the Pandemic: COVID-19-Elicited Anxiety as a Predictor of Working Memory Performance. *Frontiers in Psychology*, 11.

2. See for example: Waber, B 2009, The Truth About Open Offices, Harvard Business Review, Viewed 30/4/2022, https://hbr.org/2019/11/the-truth-about-open-offices

3. Cain, S, *Quiet: The Power of Introverts in a World That Can't Stop Talking*, Penguin Group 2012

4. PWC 2022, *Reimagining the outcomes that matter: PwC's 25th Annual Global CEO Survey*, PWC, viewed 30/4/2022, https://www.pwc.com/gx/en/ceo-agenda/ceosurvey/2022.html.

5. Investopedia 2022, *Pareto Principle*, Investopedia, Viewed 30/4/2022, https://www.investopedia.com/terms/p/paretoprinciple.as

6. Dorst, K., 2011. The core of 'design thinking' and its application. *Design Studies*, 32(6), pp.521–532.

7. Conn, C. and McLean, R., 2019. *Bulletproof problem solving*. Wiley.

8. Monte Carlo simulations (or multiple probability simulations) are used to model the probability of different outcomes in a process that cannot easily be predicted due to the intervention of random variables. It is a technique used to understand the impact of risk and uncertainty in prediction and forecasting models. The technique can be used to tackle a range of problems in virtually every field such as finance, engineering, supply chain, and science.

9. Shell, G., 2006. *Bargaining for advantage*. Penguin.

10. Chowdhury, M., 2022. *The Science & Psychology Of Goal-Setting 101*. PositivePsychology.com, viewed 10 June 2022, https://positivepsychology.com/goal-setting-psychology.

11. Kahneman, D. and Egan, P., 2012. *Thinking, fast and slow*. Penguin.

12. Liu, W., Liu, L. and Zhang, J., 2015. How to dissolve fixed-pie bias in negotiation? Social antecedents and the mediating effect of mental-model adjustment. *Journal of Organizational Behavior*, 37(1), pp.85–107.

13. Clear, J., 2022. *This Coach Improved Every Tiny Thing by 1 Percent and Here's What Happened*, viewed 10 June 2022, https://jamesclear.com/marginal-gains.

Chapter 14

1. Smallwood, N. and Ulrich, D., 2022. Capitalizing on Capabilities, *Harvard Business Review*, viewed 10 June 2022, https://hbr.org/2004/06/capitalizing-on-capabilities
2. SBCA Industry News 2021, *Katerra Employees Weigh in on Why It Failed*, SBCA Industry News, viewed 30/4/2022.
3. Georgia Tech Library 2018, *From immigrant to entrepreneur and NBA owner – Vivek Ranadivé*, Youtube, 1 November, viewed 4/5/2022, https://www.youtube.com/watch?v=nHMCLzGcHu4
4. Baghai, M., Coley, S. and White, D., 2000. *The alchemy of growth*. Cambridge, Mass.: Perseus Books.
5. Reeves, M., Moose, S. and Venema, T., 2014. *BCG Classics Revisited: The Growth Share Matrix*, BCG Global, viewed 10/06/2022, https://www.bcg.com/publications/2014/growth-share-matrix-bcg-classics-revisited.
6. Adapted from Shirlaws valuation framework, July 2008.

Conclusion

1. Sinek, S 2019, *The Infinite Game*, Penguin Business
2. Open Door Coaching. 2022. *Trends in coaching - the 2020 ICF Global Coaching Study*, viewed 29/4/2022, https://opendoorcoaching.com.au/trends-in-coaching-unpacking-the-2020-icf-global-coaching-study.
3. Hyland, C 2013, *Connect Through Think Feel Know*, Panorama Press.
4. Wikipedia 2022, William Moulton Marston, viewed 29/4/2022, https://en.wikipedia.org/wiki/William_Moulton_Marston
5. Marston, W., 2014. *Emotions of normal people*. Routledge.
6. Jung, C., 1971. *Psychological Types*. Routledge.

Index

Printed and bound by CPI Group (UK) Ltd, Croydon, CR0 4YY
10/08/2022
03140840-0001